Webmaster's

Building Internet Database Servers with CGI

Jeff Rowe

New Riders Publishing, Indianapolis, IN

Webmaster's Building Internet Database Servers with CGI

By Jeff Rowe

Published by:
New Riders Publishing
201 West 103rd Street
Indianapolis, IN 46290 USA

Printed in the United States of America 1 2 3 4 5 6 7 8 9 0

```
Rowe, Jeff, 1960-
   Building Internet Database Servers with CGI /
   Jeff Rowe.
        p.  cm.
  Includes index.
  ISBN 1-56205-575-5
  1. World Wide Web servers. 2. Database management.
  I. Title.
TK5105.888.R68  1996
005.75--dc20                                  95-53880
                                                   CIP
```


Warning and Disclaimer

Every effort has been made to make this book as complete and as accurate as possible, but no warranty or fitness is implied.

The information is provided on an "as is" basis. The author(s) and New Riders Publishing shall have neither liability nor responsibility to any person or entity with respect to any loss or damages arising from the information contained in this book or from the use of the disks or programs that may accompany it.

Publisher Don Fowley
Publishing Manager Jim LeValley
Marketing Manager Mary Foote
Managing Editor Carla Hall

Product Development Specialist
Julie Fairweather

Acquisitions Editor
Ian Sheeler

Development Editors
Cliff Shubs
Suzanne Snyder

Project Editor
Cliff Shubs

Copy Editors
Chris Cleveland
Phil Worthington

Associate Marketing Manager
Tamara Apple

Acquisitions Coordinator
Tracy Turgeson

Publisher's Assistant
Karen Opal

Cover Designer
Karen Ruggles

Book Designer
Sandra Schroeder

Production Manager
Kelly Dobbs

Production Team Supervisor
Laurie Casey

Graphics Image Specialists
Sonja Hart, Clint Lahnen
Laura Robbins, Craig Small
Todd Wente

Production Analysts
Jason Hand
Bobbi Satterfield

Production Team
Heather Butler, Angela Calvert, David Garratt, Aleata Howard, Erika Millen, Erich J. Richter, Karen Walsh

Indexer
Brad Herriman

WDB Copyright Notice

Trademark Acknowledgments

- Mini SQL is included from the courtesy of Hughes Technologies Pty Limited, Australia.
- Mini SQL is not public domain software. Any use of this software by commercial organizations requires that a license be purchased from Hughes Technologies. Non-commercial and educational organizations may use the software free of charge. Further details of the usage policy, license, and commercial registration procedure can be found in the documentation included in the software distribution. For further information, Hughes Technologies can be contacted on the WWW at `http://hughes.com.au`.

About the Author

Jeff Rowe currently works for COSMO, Incorporated as a member of the Database Management Team at NASA's Langley Research Center. He combines software engineering, database administration, and World Wide Web publishing duties into a fun and challenging career. Jeff has developed software for MS-DOS, MS Windows, OS/2, and various flavors of Unix, as well as administered Sybase and Infomatrix databases. While at Langley, Mr. Rowe began exploring the possibilities of connecting databases to the Web. The results were a series of Web pages designed to give kindred seekers access to the information he had unearthed. Jeff has also made a career of following Air Force spouse, Captain Amy, from place to place around the country. He certainly never complains of boredom with his job(s).

Dedication

To Amy: Hopefully, the next 16 years with you will be as wonderful as the last 16 were. I love you.

Acknowledgments

Although I may have written the words that went into this book, there are many other people who have provided information, support, or some other influence on the contents of these pages.

My family: If my wife, Amy, and son, BJ, had not agreed to forget I existed for a few months, I would not have had the time to frantically write this book. I'll be back around soon, you two, so don't enjoy the peace and quiet TOO much.

My coworkers: I work with a great bunch, and they also happen to be some of the brightest people I've ever known. Thanks to John Davis, my Team Leader at NASA Langley, for all the bad puns and the knowledge you lent me to add to the book. Thanks to Joe Reisel, Kevin Marlowe, and Branson Matheson for your technical knowledge and suggestions for ideas and topics. You can't have any of the royalties, but you have my thanks. And, Branson, your paintballs are TOO THICK! OW!

My employer: COMSO, Incorporated is the neatest organization I've ever worked for. When your boss invites you to lunch and has a beer with her Chinese food, you know you've found a home. Thanks to Margaret Mix and my project manager, Bob Lynn, for support. Get well soon, Bob. I should also mention I'm subcontracted to Computer Sciences Corporation at Langley, and thanks go to the project manager, Chris Matthews, for her support while I was writing.

To Steve Dotson: Thanks, dude, for getting me my first Unix job. I hated it, but sure learned a lot about system administration. To Jeff Makusky: Thanks for getting me interested in Linux. Without Linux running on my PC at home, most of the examples in this book would not exist. To Andrea Whitlock: Thanks for keeping me on my toes. I've never met anyone who learns stuff as quickly as you, and the garbage I learned to keep up with you all contributed to the book. To Mary Fenno: Thanks for the support and inspiration while you were at NASA Langley.

To NRP: Jim LeValley discovered my Web pages and invited me to write this book. I don't know whether to thank him or shoot him. When it's over, I'll thank him. Cliff Shubs did most of the editing, so if you don't like something, it's his fault. Cliff, no matter how much you, Phil, and Chris tore up my prose, you were always right, and I hate you for it. You've done your job well. Julie "The Cheerleader" Fairweather was a great source of inspiration. Thanks, Julie, and take care of your new baby. Tracy Turgeson did a whole bunch of stuff, including putting together the CD for the book. Thanks Tracy, and I apologize for misspelling your name on all my FedEx packages. And lastly, Suzanne Snyder took over when Julie went on maternity leave. Thanks Suzanne.

My mother: I have to mention my mother, Sue Rowe, or she'll slug me. Thanks, Mom, for all the help from your Prayer Guerrillas and the phone support when I needed sympathy. Amy and BJ weren't sympathetic at all when I was using both computers and trying to watch football, too.

Contents at a Glance

Table of Contents

Database Servers and the World Wide Web

A new era is dawning in the world of information management. There are many subtle changes in the way we receive our information and the places from which we choose to get it, but the rising of a new era is always gradual and subtle. We are fortunate enough to witness the incredible explosion of information available to us, and each day brings a new aspect, another step to another way of living. As you read this, it is about 6 a.m., and people are just beginning to awaken to another day, one step further into the Information Age.

The Information Age

We know we are in the middle of the Information Age. Up until now, we have been producing information by the boatload, spitting out facts about everything imaginable. New trends, theories, and discoveries happen every day and are reported to a voracious public. Although some of us might suffer from information overload, the deluge shows no signs of abating.

Where has all of this information gone? Into files and databases that only the masters of an arcane magic called *data management* can retrieve. If you want to find something, you have to find *someone* first—someone who knows how to retrieve data from the mystic regions in which it is stored.

This is beginning to change. And you are here to witness the movement of information from the hands of the data wizards to the hands of those who use it.

Early Forms of Data Management

Databases have been around a long time. Archaeologists have found inventory lists that are thousands of years old written in an ancient language called cuneiform. Ancient scribes kept tallies of baskets of wheat, loaves of bread, and clay pots of wine. However, once the information was collected, the storage and retrieval methods left a lot to be desired. Caves can only hold so many clay tablets, and clay has an annoying tendency to break when dropped. Can you imagine a scribe trying to find one tablet in a pile, knowing it was in there somewhere?

Things improved as paper became available, and filing cabinets became the database of choice. Unfortunately, the scribes who recorded the information might have lousy handwriting, not be good spellers, or copy something wrong. When a piece of paper was inserted in the wrong place in a filing cabinet, it could be lost forever. And, again, storerooms and archives can only hold so many filing cabinets. The evolution of the database is shown in figure 1.1.

Then came the computer. In its original incarnation, the computer was notoriously unreliable, hard to operate, and required vast amounts of money, space, and power to run. Luckily, computers improved over the next few decades until powerful mainframes that only required part of a room were popping up in banks, government offices, and universities all over the world. They were still expensive, but for those who used them, they were priceless.

It has only been in the last few years that the rise of cheap electronic information storage and retrieval has made data warehousing the hottest topic in the business world.

Figure 1.1
The evolution of the database.

Data Warehousing

What is *data warehousing*? First of all, it is a redefinition of what type of data goes into a database. Some organizations put everything they have into a database. Others store only carefully selected items. A data warehouse is a cross section of the state of your business at any point in time. A new cross section should be added to the database at a regular interval that makes sense for your business. If you do millions of dollars worth of business daily, maybe you should add another time slice to the database every day. If business is slow, maybe you should add data every month. The basic concept of the data warehouse is shown in figure 1.2.

Data warehousing also forces you to think about how you use your data to make your business better. What does your data tell you about your business? What can data gathered over time tell you about your business now? Who needs your data? Are you storing the information you need? Lastly, how do you get the information out? Grab a handful of data wizards and feed them questions until they manage to extract what you want?

Note

Data warehousing is a system in which your data is put into a database in recognizable form on a regular basis, and a process is developed for anyone authorized or interested in getting meaningful data in a reasonable amount of time.

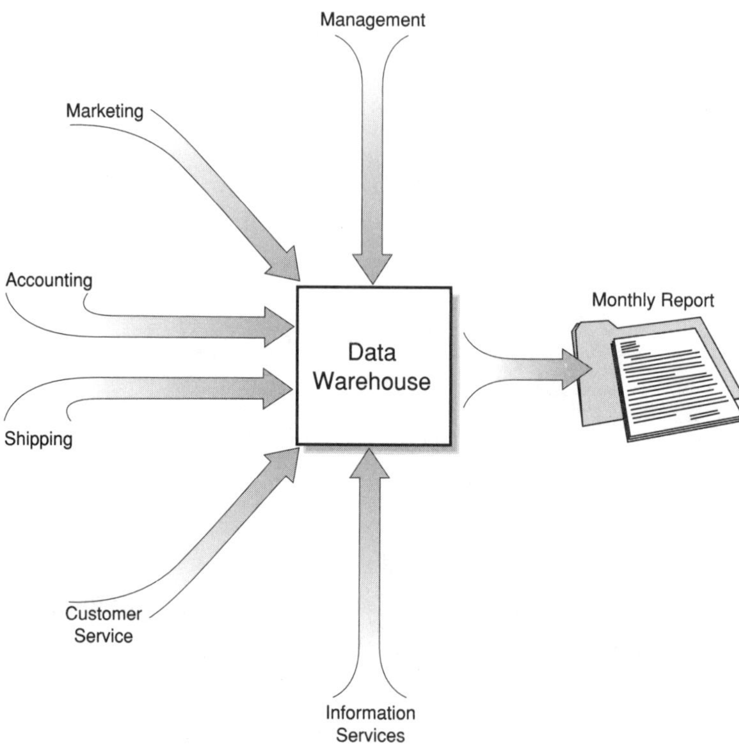

Figure 1.2
The concept of data warehousing.

Why is data warehousing a new idea? For decades, organizations, businesses, and groups of all sizes have been collecting data. Inventories, employee information, and membership lists are just a few of the items that are being amassed. As businesses and organizations grow, the data they keep grows right along with them until the hardware becomes inadequate to support the databases, the databases themselves are unable to contain the data, or just running a simple query causes the lights in the building to dim and everything computer-related to come to a grinding halt because all available computer power is given to process data.

This problem is often worsened by inadequate database design. Though small amounts of data present no problem, at some point, the data reaches critical mass. The data is scattered across multiple database tables with little thought given to data integrity, speed of access, or efficient information retrieval. A single query can run for hours hunting through old, outdated data, searching millions of lines in hundreds of tables, and matching up foreign key relationships that shouldn't exist.

Advances in Database Management Systems

People are smarter today about what should go into a database, how it should be stored, and how to get information out. Data is being stored in databases of a size unimaginable just a few years ago—measured in gigabytes of data. This feat is unparalleled in human history.

Note

A byte is a single character. A megabyte is a million characters. A gigabyte is a billion characters. Some organizations are now talking about collecting and storing petabyte databases—one quadrillion characters!

What does one do with all this data? More importantly, how does one go about getting meaningful data out of a huge database in a reasonable amount of time? Once you have the knowledge of humanity stored on a machine, it does you no good to be unable to do anything with it.

You need to make the data available to people who can use it. The easier your database is to use, the more people will use it. You need a network of machines, all connected together and with access to your database. What if the people who need the information are scattered across the city, state, or world?

You could construct your own worldwide network, but very few organizations have the money required to do this. Even a data pipeline from one state to another is a major project. Luckily for you, such a network already exists—the Internet. Just hook your database to the Internet and voilá! You have just made your database available to the entire planet. By taking a few basic precautions, you can protect your machines and your data, and those whom you allow to use the data can do so. A book about computer security, such as New Riders' *Actually Useful Internet Security Techniques*, would be a good place to learn more about these issues.

Even people sitting at home or in a hotel room can call over a telephone line and get what they need. Communications speeds keep going up and are now fast enough to enable you to get some real work done. You literally have instant information at your fingertips.

What is making this possible?

- Cheap storage
- Advances in computer technology
- Internet access
- Advances in database technology

The combination of these factors makes information storage easier, more affordable, and available to more of the people who need it.

Cheap Storage

Data has to be stored somewhere. Until about two years ago, hard drive space had been prohibitively expensive. Recent advances in technology and manufacturing have brought prices down to usable levels. Three years ago, the huge hard drives required to store large databases were the most expensive. A 1-gigabyte high-performance hard drive was around $3,000. Today, you can buy one for around $500. For the price of 1 GB three years ago, you can have 6 GB of storage. As hard drives increase in size, the cost per megabyte continues to drop. An 8-GB drive can cost half as much per MB as a 1-GB drive.

Even so, really large storage requirements in the hundreds of gigabytes are still very expensive. If the data is not constantly needed, or if the purpose is to archive information, optical drives have 1-GB cartridges for $100, and mass storage tape drive systems are even cheaper. Optical and tape storage have a much larger capacity than hard drives because you can simply add more tape or optical cartridges. However, the increase in storage capacity comes at the expense of speed.

Note

Large storage requirements can be met by optical jukeboxes that contain multiple optical platters. They operate very much like the jukeboxes that play CDs in a bar, with the exception that several platters can be read at once. Platters are contained within the case and are swapped into and out of the readers as needed.

There are truly huge storage systems that contain thousands of tape cartridges and are managed by robot arms that constantly search the storage shelves, grab the right cartridge, and insert it into a reader. While data is being pulled from the tape, the robot arm pulls any unneeded tape from another reader and dashes off to put it away and grab another. Requests are handled by a high-powered computer that keeps track of cartridge locations and the amount of data stored on each one. These storage systems theoretically have no upper limit on storage capacity.

Advances in Computer Technology

Another very important contribution to the Information Age is the ever-increasing power of today's computers. New technology puts more transistors on a computer chip, which increases the computing power of a single CPU. This also allows a single chip to have more than one CPU etched on it, allowing a computer to process more than one instruction at a time. The chip components are smaller, reducing the time electrical impulses spend traveling between components, and also reducing the amount of power required to run the chip. Database activities that once brought a computer to its knees can be accomplished in a few minutes.

Even with more powerful computer brains, database servers can still be processor hogs. Equally important is the amount of memory a computer has. Traditionally, RAM chips have been even more expensive than hard drives, but increasing the RAM a database server has to work with is the best thing you can do to increase server performance. Memory prices have fallen along with hard drive prices and where multi-gigabyte hard drives contain the data, it isn't unusual to find a gigabyte of RAM on a database server.

It also is not unusual for a business to have multiple database servers with each server running on its own computer. To facilitate fast communications between servers, the traditional ethernet connections are being replaced with fiber-optic networks. Fiber optics can carry many times the data ethernet is capable of, and at speeds that will be able to handle the fastest computers for some time to come.

Internet Access

Now that you have enough storage for your data, and powerful computers to serve it, how do users get to it? Local area networks (LANs) or wide area networks (WANs) are sufficient for many organizations, but what about businesses with people scattered all over a country or even the world?

More than that, what if you are a company in the business of providing information to as many people as possible? That is where the Internet comes in.

For many years the Internet was forbidden to companies trying to make a buck. However, since the National Science Foundation (NSF) decided it was unable to pay for the main Internet backbone, the cost was transferred to the companies that specialize in communications: the long-distance telephone companies. We all know long-distance companies are hardly going to provide the Internet for free, so, as using the Internet became more expensive, commercial ventures arose that charged usage fees to get onto the Internet. This opened the door for commercial usage of the Internet, but it also provided an incentive for more people to get connected.

Suddenly computer users with a modem or a university e-mail account found themselves on this vast communications network that seemed to have no limits. Smart businesses recognized the possibilities and connected themselves to the Internet in large numbers. This enabled them to communicate all over the world for a fraction of the cost of using the telephone or fax machine, and to spread their corporate resources much farther.

As soon as users got onto the "Net," they wanted to know what was available to them. Databases that contain nothing but program listings are constantly busy. And now that the World Wide Web (WWW) has exploded across the Internet, everyone can surf the Web with nothing but the click of a mouse.

Wouldn't it be great to put information on a powerful machine, with plenty of storage and a fast connection to the Internet? From hundreds of miles away, corporate vice presidents can keep up with what is going on back at the office by checking their e-mail. Salesmen can download the price list released just this morning by using a modem, a hotel phone jack, and a local access number for their Internet provider. Branch offices feel more in touch with the parent company by being in constant contact with key personnel at the home office.

Additionally, each location can keep its own copy of the database, or merely keep the information important to their local office. A central office can make routine sweeps to collect new data and incorporate it into the main data warehouse.

As any military commander knows: Quick, accurate information is a weapon. This is no less true in the business world.

Advances in Database Technology

More powerful computers, cheap storage, and fast communications are all well and good, but if database software does not change to take advantage of the new technology, what is the point? Luckily, database software has been progressing right along with hardware technology.

One of the biggest challenges is learning how to get information out of a database. You can have the best data in the world, but if you can't get it out, you've wasted your time and money. A powerful query language called the *Structured Query Language* (SQL, pronounced *sequel*) is becoming the standard by which data is selected from a database. SQL enables users to construct precise, complex query statements to pick through the database and return the data that matches the query constraints.

Using Query Optimizers

Though SQL is a great tool, a complex query could tie up all available database resources while all the data is sifted, compared, discarded, collected, and finally returned. One of the biggest advances in database technology is a new breed of query optimizers. A *query optimizer* is a program that analyzes the SQL statement and decides the most efficient manner in which to collect the requested data. The optimizer holds important information about the following:

- The structure of the database
- Where on the hard drives the data is kept
- Which fields have been indexed
- What referential constraints exist between tables
- What kind of hardware is available to perform the query

A query might be performed in pieces, getting all the data that matches part of the query constraints, then weeding out the data that doesn't match the rest of the constraints. Or, data might be gathered in bursts, selecting a group of data that matches all of the constraints, but only getting a portion at a time. As each new piece arrives, it is merged into the whole.

If the database is running on a multi-CPU computer, the optimizer might assign parts of the query to five CPUs while the sixth performs the data collation, and the remaining two CPUs process another user's request. If there are four SCSI controllers in the machine, the optimizer can make the most efficient use of each controller by scheduling the order in which data is retrieved from the hard drives.

If the optimizer is extremely sophisticated, each separate process can be an independent thread. This means all the processes are on their own. Nothing that happens to one thread can affect another. If one thread is stopped waiting for data, others continue gathering data. Once threads start returning data, another thread can begin to piece it together, just like an automobile assembly line assembles car parts. An example of a sophisticated database engine is shown in figure 1.3.

Figure 1.3
A multithreaded database engine.

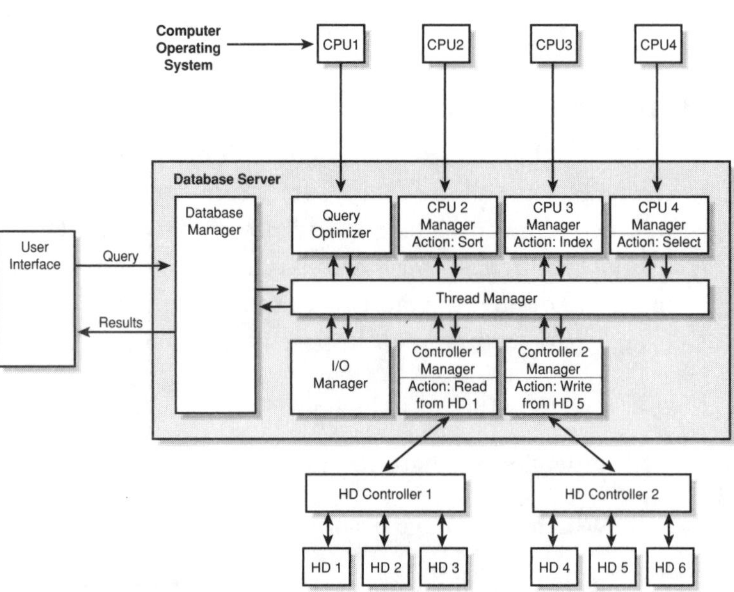

Database Interface Options

All of this power and sophistication is nice to have, but how do you give commands to the database for processing? Most databases come with different tools for exactly that purpose. If you have direct access to the database server, you can use a command-line utility that enables you to type SQL statements and submit them to the database. The results are returned to your screen. This doesn't work very well if your returned data is more than a few lines long because it scrolls off the screen and cannot be seen. Perhaps you can save the output to a file, then use a text editor to page through the data, but that is only a little better. Users today are getting used to polished, graphically based applications that make use of a windowing environment and a mouse. Why can't you do this for a database?

You can. Most databases come with an *application programming interface* (API) that provides programmers with function calls to talk to the database. Programmers can construct an interface into which users enter data, then the data is fed into the database using the provided function calls. If adding the data succeeds or fails, a code is returned to indicate exactly what happened.

The intricacy of the tools available for constructing database front ends is becoming very impressive. Some databases work with builder tools that enable programmers to construct a forms-based database interface very quickly. Text boxes, buttons, scroll bars, pull-down menus, select lists, and so forth are shown on a tool palette, and the programmer selects one, places it on the form, and writes the instructions that tell the item what to do if it is pressed, moved, or selected using a mouse.

Storing Data

One of the things that makes database servers so attractive to use today is how much "smarter" data managers have become about how to store the data in the database. In the past, as was mentioned previously, human data wizards were the only interface between a company and its laboriously collected data. The wizards were the only ones who understood how the data was stored and how to get it out. Why?

- *SQL is a tough language to master.* On the surface, SQL database queries make sense, but when you start adding pieces to narrow a database search or exclude unwanted items, add nested subqueries, group items by characteristics, sort the data, or include aggregate functions, "sense" can go out the window. SQL is meant to manipulate data, not to be read as a coherent sentence. It works very well if the person using it knows what she is doing, but it is not guaranteed to have obvious meaning to the casual observer.

- *The complicated nature of database construction.* Data should not be put into a database as a free-form collection of fragments. Sometimes it is, which presents obvious problems. Considerable thought has been devoted to the ideal method of storing data. Redundancy is to be avoided in order to take less space, but some repeated data is necessary to make retrieving data quicker. The result is an often arbitrary structure that does not lend itself to easy comprehension by someone who was not part of the design or construction process.

Database design is not an exact science, but we know more now than we ever have before, simply by virtue of experience. By applying this knowledge and by trying new ideas in database construction, data warehousing is becoming a viable means of keeping track of inventories, employee records, marketing trends, or even meta-data, which is data that describes other data.

With the recent introduction of database design tools that help guide the user through the design process, databases are becoming less mysterious and more useful. Information can be represented graphically in a way that makes retrieving it a matter of clicking on a list of items to query. Although this method is less than perfect, further advances in "smart software" will continue to bring database management into the mainstream by making databases easier to use. Smart software may be able to create an optimal database structure based on a general outline provided by a programmer, or "learn" what information a database user is trying to find and make suggestions on how to find it.

When this happens, data will no longer be static, waiting for data wizards to make it meaningful; it will truly be useful information because it will be easier for everyone to find the data they need. Databases will become warehouses full of "living" data that changes as the world changes. And data wizards will give way to the people who really need the information. As a beginning, databases of all kinds are popping up all over the World Wide Web, providing access to information in a way never seen before.

Why Use the Web to Access Data?

Consider this scenario: You have just started a small business. You keep all of your business records, inventory, payroll, and business contacts in a single database on your only PC—the same PC the secretary uses for sending letters, logging calls, and taking orders.

After a few months, business is good, and the database is getting big. You decide to buy another PC and split the database between two machines. Only now there are more people who use the database and they don't understand computers as well as you do. You find a college kid to whip up a simple Visual Basic front end for both databases and everything runs smoothly. For a year or two.

Suddenly you find yourself with 10 PCs, each with its own special database, and the things are running slowly because they are fat with information. Maybe you upgrade to Windows NT and SQL Server and, with a little tweaking, your Visual Basic applications still work.

Two more years down the road, your SQL Server isn't big enough. You decide to go with a big database on a powerful Unix server. You get the system set up and the data transported into your new, big database. Then you realize that none of your Visual Basic applications work with your new database, and new software will cost you big bucks and take several months to develop. What do you do? And when your database has to be modified or extended, how do you upgrade your custom applications?

This scenario could repeat itself many times over the next few years, resulting in expensive, time-consuming database front end development. What you need is a standard language that works the same on any machine, no matter where you move your database, and no matter what machine you try to access the database from.

The World Wide Web could be your solution whether you want to access your data from anywhere in the world or just on a local network. It is estimated there are five times more local Web servers than ones that are connected to the Internet. So what makes the Web so wonderful to use?

- Writing applications in a standard language—HTML
- Graphical user interface (GUI)
- Cross-platform support
- Network support

All of these features give the user powerful tools to access data with a minimum of expense and effort, and by using tools that are the same no matter what database, operating system, or computer hardware is used.

Writing Applications in a Standard Language—HTML

With the *HyperText Markup Language* (HTML), you can write applications that are accessible from almost any type of computer. Programmers have a single language to learn, the components needed to create applications using HTML are commonly available at no cost, and any changes can be made quickly and easily. Examples of functional HTML programming are presented later in the book to give you an idea of how it works, and how easy it is to use.

HTML requires no expensive compiler, can be created and read with any simple text editor, and doesn't take long to learn. Most importantly, any changes made to the HTML standard will only add functionality, not eliminate it. Applications written in an older version will work just as well under the new version as they did under the old.

Before you jump for joy, however, there are some limitations to consider. HTML is not a "real" programming language. It can't execute instructions that respond to user input or perform calculations. HTML is good for creating quick, graphically based applications that require simple functionality.

For more complicated applications, HTML contains a gateway to other programs. The *Common Gateway Interface* (CGI) enables you to call external programs from within an HTML program and get back the results. If HTML won't allow you to do something, chances are you can write a CGI program to do it. Examples of CGI programming are covered later in the book to show you how to pass information from HTML through CGI to your database programs.

Graphical User Interface (GUI)

For most users, a graphical user interface is necessary for database access. Databases can be complicated beasts that confound even experienced users from time to time. A GUI can make things easier for the user, and also can prevent data entry errors, or at least limit them.

Users like using a GUI because they can see what they are doing. Using a mouse to select items from a list or pick an action to perform is far easier than mastering the intricacies of a database query language, and is much more productive. Users can enter plain text into text fields presented by the GUI and let database programs create the complicated queries for them, using the information provided by the user.

HTML applications are run by a graphical front end called a Web browser. The *browser* reads the HTML code and converts it into a graphically based application run with a mouse. Data can be entered into fields, selected from lists, or selected by pressing a button. A simple press of a button then sends the data to be processed.

There are browsers available for virtually every kind of computer. HTML programs written on one type of machine can be run by a browser on another. The Netscape browser is the choice of about 70 percent of browser users, but browsers by Mosaic (the first browser) and Lynx (a text-only browser), among others, give the user a choice of which browser to use based on the features they want. After a browser type is chosen, users learn a single GUI and can run all HTML applications from the same browser. The browser is driven with mouse clicks, and the programming complexity is handled transparently, hidden from the user.

By using a browser, you have no custom-written GUI to write or support. There are enough different kinds of browsers to meet your needs, and new versions appear constantly. Instead of investing a mountain of time and money in developing a new GUI, you spend a short time writing the functional code, and the browser handles all of the front end functions, such as reacting to menu selections, the moving or resizing of windows, or changing the shape of the mouse cursor depending on its location.

Not only that, but the machine load is spread across many machines. Instead of many copies of a program running on a machine for each user, the user's local machine runs the browser, and the remote database machine runs the database server and the database access program. This requires less "horsepower" on the server machine and gets more use from the user's machines.

By keeping the database access programs on the database server, you have a single copy of the programs. There are no version control problems that cause different machines to run different versions of a program.

Also, you can control access to your database if the programs are on the same machine as the database server. HTML programs are sent to the browsers by servers designed to transport HTML programs. The server can grant or refuse access to individual machines or users based on how you configure it.

Cross-Platform Support

One of the nicest features of HTML browsers is that they are available for many different kinds of computers. You can have your database server and HTML programs on a Unix machine and use a PC or Macintosh to access the database. You don't have to replace your existing machines, which saves you lots of time, money, and aggravation.

To get this cross-platform support, you don't have to develop applications for multiple machines yourself, as you would if you had a custom-designed front end. Just download a browser from an ftp site for each type of machine you have on your network. And to upgrade your browsers, you just download new versions as they are developed.

Network Support

Something else to consider when designing custom database applications is how to access your database from a remote machine. Buying a database server is only part of the cost of accessing your data if you have to buy expensive database networking software. There often is a per-machine license fee that can add up in a hurry.

HTML browsers and servers have built-in networking capabilities. They are designed to send and receive information across the Internet or a local network, from one kind of machine to another, eliminating the need for proprietary vendor programs. There are no per-client license fees, and you don't have to worry about whether the database networking software supports your computers. This eliminates the need for your application programmers to learn networking or intermachine communications, which can save large amounts of development time and frustration. It also enables you to use your existing computers to access your database without having to worry if they can "talk" to another computer. Now they can.

Put all of these features together and you have what you need to make cheap, flexible database access software that requires a minimum of effort on your part. In the next chapter, you are shown some of the tools that can be used to access a database using the World Wide Web. Once you understand what tools are available, you are shown how to use them in subsequent chapters.

Tools for Accessing Data via the Web

To connect a database to the WWW, you must be familiar with some basic tools. After you learn how to use HTML tags, links, and forms to create HTML documents, called pages, *you can take the next step of passing information back and forth between a Web browser and your database by using elements of your Web pages.*

This chapter covers the three most basic tools of the World Wide Web:

- *HyperText Markup Language (HTML)*
- *Using a Web browser*
- *An introduction to Web servers*

HyperText Markup Language (HTML)

HTML contains three basic elements, each of which has been used separately for some time. By putting the characteristics of these elements together, however, something new and far more useful for computer programming has been created. The three elements of HTML are indicated in its name:

- **Hypertext** is just a fancy name for a link. If you see hypertext, it's telling you, "I am a link to some other information. Click on me, and I'll show you more." If you have ever used any form of online help facility, you have probably used hypertext links. Think, for example, of an online library card catalog. After you look up a particular book, it often has a "See also" heading at the bottom of the page, and a list of other related books and authors. By clicking on one of those hypertext links, you can jump to another book synopsis. If it isn't what you're looking for, you can go back to the original book listing and try another link.
- **Markup** is just what it says—a system of symbols written on or in a document that allows the processor, whether human or machine, to recognize how to display and format the document. Before the days of electronic publishing, writers, editors, and typesetters used a common markup language to indicate deletions, insertions, the start of new paragraphs, transposing letters, and so on. Although a submitted document might be a real mess because of all the additional writing on it, the final product was just as it should have been after all the marked changes were made.
- A **language** is a bunch of symbols or sounds that allow things to communicate. If I speak French and you speak German, we can't communicate very well. If we both know Spanish as a second language, however, we have a common means of communication and can exchange ideas.

Put the three together, and you get a hypertext markup language—you get a common set of symbols to format documents, links to other Web pages, and working communication between Web browsers around the world. A well written HTML document looks almost exactly the same on any type of Web browser.

Some Web browsers recognize non-standard extensions to HTML that enables you to do more with a document than the recognized standard allows, but Web browsers have a solution to the symbols they don't recognize; they ignore them. Any time a browser encounters an unfamiliar symbol, whether because it's new or the author misspelled something, it simply ignores everything the tag refers to and picks up processing at the next recognizable symbol.

Using HTML

HTML documents are composed of nothing but text. Some of the text are instructions to the Web browser to do something special with the associated plain text. These instructions are called *tags*. Tags are delineated by using angle brackets, what some call "greater than" (>) and "less than" (<) symbols. A < begins the tag and a > ends it. Most tags are used in pairs, to turn a formatting feature on and off around a block of text. The ending tag is the same as the starting tag except with a slash (/) in front of the tag identifier. The following are a small subset of the many tags available in HTML.

HTML Tags

A complete discussion of HTML tags is beyond the scope of this book, but you can create a fully functional Web page with just the following ones:

> **<HTML>...</HTML>.** The html tag is the first and last tag in an HTML document. It tells the Web browser to display the document as hypertext instead of plain text.
>
> **<HEAD>...</HEAD>.** The head tag identifies the beginning section of the HTML document. Among other things, the document title goes in the document head.
>
> **<TITLE>...</TITLE>.** The title tag contains the title that appears in the title bar of the Web browser.
>
> **<BODY>...</BODY>.** The body tag surrounds the largest portion of a Web page. It contains everything that a user sees when he or she accesses your Web page.

<Hn>...</Hn>. Header tags create various sizes of text headers. Replace the *n* with a number between one and six. The lower the number the bigger the header.

<HR>. The horizontal rule tag draws a horizontal line across the Web page, making it easier for a user to read.

**
.** The break tag causes a line break. Several of them together create blank lines, which makes a Web page easier to read.

<P>. The paragraph tag is a good way to separate blocks of text to make them more readable.

The following is an example of an HTML document that uses the preceding tags.

```
<HTML>
  <HEAD>
    <TITLE>
      This is a Sample Web Page
    </TITLE>
  </HEAD>
  <BODY>
    <H1>
      This is a Top-Level Header
    </H1>
    <HR>
    <BR>
    <BR>
    <H2>
      This is a Secondary-Level Header
    </H2>
    <P> With just a few HTML tags, you can create some very
        functional Web pages.
    <P> Once you get the hang of basic HTML, you can add
        more and more functionality to your Web pages by
        using additional tags.
    <P> One thing to notice: when this document is displayed
        by a Web browser, the extra blank spaces between
        words on different lines will not be displayed.
        HTML only recognizes a single space and ignores any
        following spaces until another character is found.
  </BODY>
</HTML>
```

When displayed by the Netscape Web browser, this HTML document looks like figure 2.1.

Figure 2.1
A simple Web page created with HTML tags.

Links

One of the really neat things about hypertext links is that a single HTML document can contain links to any other Web page on any Web server in the world. Just by clicking on the link, a user can jump from page to page without having to worry about where they are located. This is one of the powerful attractions of the WWW, and is also the main reason it's called a Web.

Linking to Documents

A link in an HTML document is called an *anchor*, and it contains the instructions on where to find a document. The link can refer to a Web page that resides on the same server as the document that contains the link, or on another computer somewhere else. You can also use links to create a table of contents for a Web page. Clicking on one of the links will take you to the corresponding place in the document, as shown in the following examples.

To create a link to a document in the same directory, you can use an anchor, such as the following:

```
<A HREF="document2.html"> Click here </A>
```

The text `Click here` appears underlined on the page to identify it as a hyperlink. Clicking on the text causes the Web browser to go look for document2.html and display it.

To link to a document on another computer, you have to tell the Web browser which machine to contact and where the Web page is located.

```
<A HREF="http://site.domain.com/~username/document3.html">
Click here </A>
```

In this case, HREF refers to a Uniform Resource Locator (URL), which is discussed later in this chapter. The URL tells the Web browser to contact the machine named site.domain.com and look in username's directory for document3.html.

Constructing a Table of Contents

For a table of contents (TOC), just name the anchor and refer to it as if you were referring to another document. If you had the following headers in your document…

```
<H3> <A NAME="horse"> Horse Section </A> </H3>

<H3> <A NAME="moose"> Moose Section </A> </H3>
```

…you could create a table of contents for the document as follows:

```
<A HREF="#horse"> Go to the Horse Section </A>

<A HREF="#moose"> Go to the Moose Section </A>
```

You can jump directly to a specific section of a document by clicking on one of these links.

A TOC can refer to other HTML documents as well. If the previous anchors were in document2.html, you could refer to one of the sections from another html document in this way:

```
<A HREF="document2.html#horse"> Read About Horses </A>
```

By using these few simple commands, you can construct Web pages and link them to other pages you create or pages that are on another computer anywhere in the world.

HTML Forms

One of the most powerful and useful of all HTML features is the form. *Forms* enable you to enter information into a Web page and have the information passed to another page, or to an external program for processing using the Common Gateway Interface (CGI), which is discussed more fully in the next chapter. This is especially useful for getting data to put into a database or for detailing a query for searching a database.

A form can consist of text boxes, check boxes, radio buttons, pull-down menus, pick lists, and so on. After a user enters or selects the pertinent information, pressing a button submits all of the fields on the form, along with their values, to whatever program is indicated in the form using the Common Gateway Interface. You can think of CGI as a pipeline that enables you to pass information out of a Web page to an external program, which can be written in virtually any programming language. The external program acts on the information and uses the CGI pipeline to return the results for display in the Web page.

The information entered by the user is passed to the CGI program as name/value pairs. Each element of an HTML form, such as a text field or a list of values, is given an identifying name, and the data associated with it is its value. When information is entered in a text field or a value is selected from a list, that information becomes associated with the name of the HTML element used to capture it. When the form is submitted to the CGI program, the names and values are passed as pairs, name=value, with an ampersand (&) between the pairs. It may sound confusing, but the following example should make it clearer.

The following sample HTML code sets up an HTML form, which is used to pass user comments to a CGI program:

```
<HTML>
  <HEAD>
    <TITLE>
      User Comment Form
    </TITLE>
  </HEAD>
  <BODY>
    <H1>
      User Comment form.
    </H1>
    <P>
      If you have anything to say about our company, whether
      good or bad, please take a moment to share your views
      with us. We appreciate your input.
```

```
      </P>
      <FORM ACTION="/cgi-bin/user_comments.cgi" METHOD="POST">
        <P>
        Enter your name and phone number where we can contact
        you. If you prefer contact by e-mail, enter your e-mail
        address.
        <P>
        Name     :<INPUT TYPE="text" NAME="name" SIZE=32><BR>
        <BR>
        Phone    :<INPUT TYPE="text" NAME="phone" SIZE=13><BR>
        <BR>
        E-mail   :<INPUT TYPE="text" NAME="email" SIZE=32><BR>
        <BR>
        Comments :<BR>
        <TEXTAREA NAME="comments" COLS=55 ROWS=5>
Replace this text with your comments.
        </TEXTAREA>
        <BR>
        <BR>
        <INPUT TYPE="submit" VALUE="Submit Comments">
        <INPUT TYPE="reset">
      </FORM>
    </BODY>
  </HTML>
```

When displayed by a Web browser, the form appears as shown in figure 2.2.

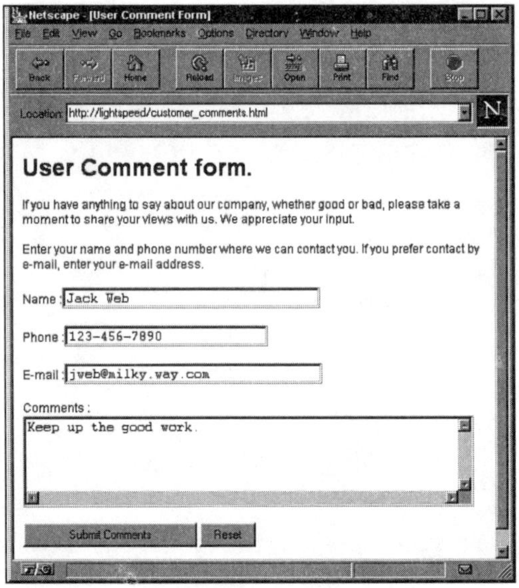

Figure 2.2
An HTML form for entering comments.

Assuming Mr. Web has entered the data shown in the form and wants to submit it, when the Submit Data button is pressed, the information is passed as name/value pairs to the CGI program /cgi-bin/user_comments.cgi and will look like this (the small arrow indicates all the text really appears on one line):

```
name=Jack+Web&phone=123-456-7890&email=jweb@milky.way.com
➥&comments=Keep+up+the+good+work.%0D%0A
```

Before the name value pairs are passed to the CGI program, they are encoded to protect them from being altered or misunderstood as they cross the network. It would be an unfortunate coincidence if an unusual character happened to be a command that instructed a network router to send the information to a computer halfway across the world. To prevent this from happening, spaces are changed to a + by the Web browser to make sure the spaces arrive intact. Special characters are passed as hexadecimal characters, indicated by a percent sign (%). In this string, `.%0D%0A` is a carriage return and line feed.

After the user_comments.cgi program receives the previous string, it breaks it into pairs, replaces the plus signs with spaces, replaces the hexadecimal characters with the ASCII equivalent (if possible, and ignores them if not), then processes the pairs. There are many other field types that can be used in a form, and all of their values can be passed in the same way.

After the CGI program processes the input into its original form, it can reformat it for insertion into a database or include it in an e-mail message to the customer service department. CGI programs can do anything you write them to do, just as if they were ordinary programs.

Using a Web Browser

The tool used to travel around the World Wide Web (often called Web surfing) is called a Web browser. The *browser* provides the graphical user interface (GUI, pronounced *gooey*) that enables users to see Web pages and to access other pages with the click of a mouse button. There are several different kinds of browsers available, and they all provide at least a common minimum set of functions.

A Web browser loads pages and displays them. A page can have formatted or unformatted text, images, sounds, and videos included in it. Web browsers automatically recognize some types of these items and can process them. Other formats of images, videos, and sounds can be included, but a Web browser cannot display or hear them unless the user has external software installed.

It is usually a bad idea to use non-standard images if a Web page is being produced for general Web access. However, if pages are only used within a company or organization, and all machines are assured of having the extra software, this is a good way to access non-standard documents without having to print them for general distribution.

A Web browser is half of what it takes to go out and find Web pages. The other half is a Web server, which is discussed later in this chapter. The two work together to pass information back and forth across a network using their built-in networking protocol called the *HyperText Transfer Protocol*, also discussed later in the chapter.

Uniform Resource Locators

To access HTML documents, Web browsers have to know where to look. They get this information from a Uniform Resource Locator (URL). The URL contains the pieces of information a Web browser requires to locate a page on the Web. Look at the URL to a Web home page. A *home page* is the primary Web page that serves as a starting point to any other pages a user might have. The following line is the address of a specific home page on the domain.com server:

```
http://somesite.domain.com/~username/index.html
```

The `http` tells the browser to use the hypertext transfer protocol to get the Web page. This means the Web browser is accessing a Web site, instead of one of the other types of sites it could be accessing, such as ftp, gopher, or WAIS, which are recognized by the Web browser and tell it what to do to connect to a remote site. If the first part of the URL were `ftp`, which stands for *file transfer protocol*, that would tell the Web browser to request a connection to an ftp site and log in anonymously in order to download files.

The `somesite.domain.com` is the name of the computer the Web browser will connect to. A computer name consists of a unique machine name (`somesite`) and a domain name (`domain.com`), which uniquely identifies a machine connected to the Internet. Once a Web browser has the machine name, the browser knows exactly where to look for the Web page.

The `~username` tells the Web browser where to start looking on the machine it is contacting. The tilde (~) indicates this is the home directory of a user. Depending on how the Web server receiving the connection request is configured on somesite.domain.com, the Web server may expand the home directory name to add other path information. Users on this machine might, for example, be required to create a directory under their home directory as a place to put their Web pages. A common directory name is public_html, the directory name would be appended to the username, and the Web server would begin looking in ~username/public_html.

The `index.html` tells the Web browser the name of the file to ask for, and the `html` extension of the filename indicates this is an HTML document. With many Web servers, index.html is the name of the default file to look for. Even if the URL looked like the following, the Web server would send back the file index.html if it existed in the ~beowulf/public_html directory.

```
http://cscsun1.larc.nasa.gov/~beowulf/
```

Once the Web browser knows where a Web page is located on the Internet, it issues a request to the Web server on the remote computer. The Web server accepts or denies the request according to its own configuration. If the request is accepted, and the requested file exists, the Web server sends the requested page to the Web browser. The Web browser gets the page, processes the HTML tags, looks for instructions to get any included images, and issues other requests as necessary (see fig. 2.3).

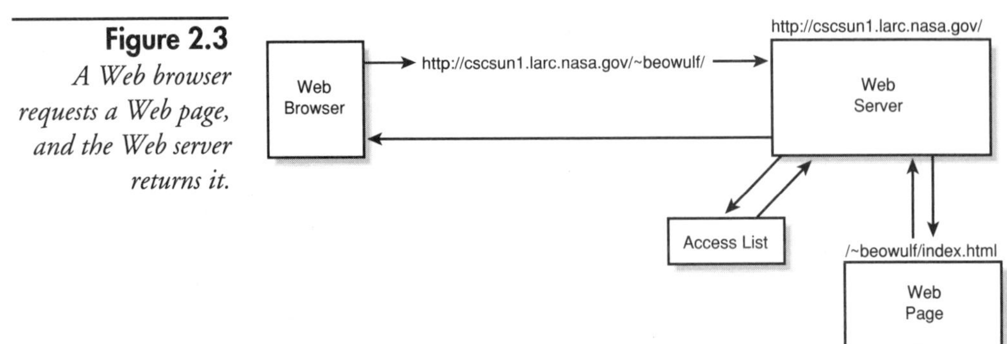

Figure 2.3
A Web browser requests a Web page, and the Web server returns it.

An Introduction to Web Servers

A Web server is a program that listens for connections from a Web browser, gets the information about the calling machine, searches the server configuration files to see if it has any instructions about accepting or denying requests from the machine that is calling, and acts accordingly. If the connection is accepted, the server looks at the URL sent to it by the browser and tries to find the file or program requested.

HyperText Transfer Protocol (HTTP)

Transferring HTML documents across the Internet is accomplished using HTTP. HTTP is a method of transmitting data in hypertext format that ensures the encoded data will arrive intact at the Web browser, regardless of how badly the data is treated by the network. Web servers are designed to transmit hypertext as efficiently as possible. Web servers are so closely identified with HTTP that they are often called HTTP servers.

Setting Up a Web Server

The HTTP server has a minimal set of built-in security functions designed to regulate access to directories and the files in them. Any attempt to access a file in a protected directory causes the HTTP server to issue a username and password verification demand—the Web browser displays a window for the user to enter a username and password. If the information matches the username and encrypted password for the protected directory, the access is granted. If not, access is denied.

This password protection is good for any file in the protected directory, and any subdirectories and files underneath it. If a Web browser issues a request for a document that resides anywhere in the protected directory tree, access will depend on providing the correct username and password.

One of the most popular HTTP servers is the NCSA server, which is fast, dependable, and free. It runs on almost any Unix platform and can be set up quickly. One of the features of the NCSA HTTP server is the built-in access control. If you want to protect access to your database programs, this is a good way to do it. You can find more information about NCSA security issues at this address:

`http://hoohoo.ncsa.uiuc.edu/security.`

Access Control

To set up access control using an NCSA server, choose the directory you want to protect. For this example, you will choose the directory /home/jsmith/public_html/html where you will create a file called .htaccess. The period beginning the name is very important. It is part of the name the HTTP server looks for. A period beginning a filename also tells a Unix machine to hide the file from the casual user.

In the .htaccess file, type the following:

```
AuthUserFile /home/jsmith/public_html/.htpasswd
AuthGroupFile /dev/null
AuthName Access
AuthType Basic

<LIMIT GET>
require user beowulf
</LIMIT>
```

`AuthUserFile` is the directory where you want the password file to reside. Don't pick the same directory as the one you want to protect.

`AuthGroupFile` is used to control group access. You don't have a group, so you use the /dev/null device, which in Unix means, "It doesn't exist."

`AuthName` is what will appear in the title bar of the window asking the user for a username and password.

`AuthType` is the type of access you want to grant. Basic access gives the user access to most Web applications on your system.

The `<LIMIT>` tag tells the http server to limit access to the current directory and who is allowed access.

The NCSA server comes with a program called htpasswd. It is probably somewhere in the directory tree where you installed your server program. Htpasswd is used to create the .htpasswd file and add usernames and passwords to it. The following command creates the .htpasswd file and adds the username "beowulf" to it:

```
htpasswd -c /home/jsmith/public_html/.htpasswd beowulf
```

You are asked for a password twice, and the encrypted password is put into the .htpasswd file as the password for beowulf.

Keep in mind this username has nothing to do with any of the usernames owned by other users on your local system. Users do not need an account on your local computer system to access the protected directory. All they need to know is the username and password you specified above.

If you want to create a usergroup and grant access to a group of usernames, change the following in the .htaccess file you just created:

```
AuthGroupFile /home/jsmith/public_html/.htgroups
<LIMIT GET>
require group goodnames
</LIMIT>
```

Then create the file /home/jsmith/public_html/.htgroups. In it, put the groupname and the usernames that you want to belong to the group:

```
goodnames: beowulf grendel hrothgar wiglaf
```

Next, use the htpasswd program to give each username a password. You can create multiple groups and control access to several directories with a single .htpasswd and .htgroups file. Just put a .htaccess file in each directory you want to protect and dictate which group or username should have access to it using the method outlined previously.

Secure Servers

You might need to protect access to more than just files or programs. You also might need to protect everything that goes on between the HTTP server and the Web browser that connects to it. In this case, you would need a secure Web server. A secure Web server uses a complicated encryption scheme to encode everything passed back and forth between the Web server and the user's Web browser.

When a user connects to your secure Web site using a Web browser that has encryption capabilities, RSA encryption (invented in 1977 by Ron Rivest, Adi Shamir, and Leonard Adleman, thus the "RSA") is used to encode everything sent back and forth between the browser and server. If you transfer information that you or the user do not want anyone else to see, the encryption prevents anyone who can intercept the data from being able to read it.

Web sites that might need this kind of security include online stores that request users' credit card information, online stock brokers that transfer financial information to users, or adult Web sites that transfer sensitive material to shy users.

Even if a data thief has the knowledge and opportunity to intercept data flowing in and out of a secure Web site, the data will be worthless because of the data encryption.

Naturally, a secure Web server costs more than a regular Web server because of the extra complexity and technology involved. If you really must protect the data you send or receive across the Internet, however, data encryption is the best way to do so, and a secure Web server does it for you transparently.

Now that you are familiar with HTML, Web browsers, and Web servers, the only tool left to explain is the Common Gateway Interface. The next chapter shows you how to pass information through CGI in various ways and gives you an idea of how CGI programs can be used to process information.

CHAPTER 3

Common Gateway Interface

One of the most powerful aspects of HTML is the Common Gateway Interface *(CGI). HTML contains tags that enable users to put professional-looking documents together in a very short time, but it would be great if HTML had some tags that would let users run programs using a Web browser and process the results into an HTML document for display. Does it? The answer is no—and yes. Instead of trying to make their own programming language when there are already so many good ones out there, the designers of the HTML standard did something even better by designing the Common Gateway Interface.*

To help you understand how to use CGI to access a database from the World Wide Web the following CGI topics are discussed:

- The process behind CGI
- Setting up a Web server for CGI access
- Passing data through CGI
- Examples of using CGI
- Security issues

The HTML designers built a gateway into the HTML standard that allows HTML programmers to call a program written in any language they want to use. This is called the *Common Gateway Interface.* A *gateway* is a connection to the external operating system. CGI gives programmers a way for HTML Web pages to call external programs and get back the results.

The Process Behind CGI

The action of running a CGI program from a Web browser is a simple one for the user, which is one of the attractions of using the Common Gateway Interface. From the programmer's perspective, however, the CGI process is a little more complicated. Several things must occur for a CGI program to execute successfully:

1. The user calls a CGI program by clicking on a link or by pushing a button.
2. The Web browser contacts the Web server asking for permission to run the CGI program.
3. The Web server checks the configuration and access files to make sure the requester is allowed access to the CGI program.
4. The Web server checks to make sure the CGI program exists.
5. If it exists, the CGI program is executed.

6. Any output produced by the CGI program is returned to the Web browser.
7. The Web browser displays the CGI output.

Information can be passed from the Web browser to the CGI program in a variety of ways, and the program can return the results with embedded HTML tags, as plain text, or as an image. The Web browser interprets the returned results just like it does any other document. With just a mouse click, this provides an extremely powerful tool for running virtually any program and allows programmers to access any external database that provides a programming interface. And instead of having to design a front-end application that is tied to a specific database, the front end can remain the same no matter what type of database is used underneath.

Setting Up a Web Server for CGI Access

For CGI programs to work on your system, your Web server must be configured to allow CGI access. CGI access is viewed as a possible security risk by some system administrators, and they deny all users the ability to use it. On other systems, CGI access is granted on a user-by-user basis, and only CGI programs written by authorized users can be run by the server.

The NCSA Web server was used as an example in Chapter 2 and is used again here. The NCSA Web server is a popular server on Unix platforms, and also comes with source code for curious programmers to poke around in. The NCSA Web server is ideal for examples such as these.

To set up your NCSA server to recognize CGI scripts, you need to add the following line to the srm.conf file in the HTTP configuration directory:

```
ScriptAlias /cgi-bin/ /serverpath/httpd/cgi-bin/
```

Where `serverpath` is the directory where your HTTP server software resides. This line tells the HTTP server to recognize programs in the /cgi-bin directory off the main HTTP server directory. If you want to allow CGI programs to be somewhere other than the just-named main CGI directory, add the other directories in the same manner by using the ScriptAlias directive.

If you want to open your system so anyone can run CGI programs from anywhere on the system, add the following line:

```
AddType application/x-httpd-cgi .cgi
```

This line allows the HTTP server to recognize files with the "cgi" extension as CGI programs, regardless of where the files are located. It also allows CGI programs written by any user on your system to be run by the server.

If you want to keep control of who runs CGI programs on your server, you can either create an HTTP user and only allow select people to use the HTTP account, or require users to submit CGI scripts for review before they are placed in the system /cgi-bin directory.

Passing Data through CGI

CGI is a two-way gateway. Data can be passed to the CGI program to be processed. CGI programs can also pass information back to the Web browser to be displayed. CGI programs give programmers a way to make HTML pages interactive. Information entered by the user can affect the behavior of the CGI program, and the results returned by the program are a direct result of user input.

A Web browser loads an HTML document and displays it. In some cases a CGI program is executed as the page is loaded, and the results are displayed as part of the Web page. In other cases, the user presses a button or clicks on a link to activate a CGI program, and the results are displayed as part of another Web page.

CGI programs don't have to be used as traditional programs. For example, a counter on a Web page that indicates how many visitors have accessed the page is a CGI program. Often, counters are CGI programs that return numbers as a GIF graphical image, which is not something you would expect a traditional program to do.

The count of Web visitors is kept in a file, and when the Web page is accessed, the count is read from the file. The count is incremented and written back to the file, and the CGI program parses the count digit by digit and selects a GIF image for each digit. The GIF images are passed back to the Web browser as the result of the CGI program, and the user sees the count as an image imbedded in the Web page. All that is required is a header that identifies the result returned by the counter program as a GIF. The Web browser knows how to process GIF images. This is just one way to use CGI.

Getting Data Back from a CGI Program

In most cases, the programmer wants to return some sort of information back to the Web browser for display. This is simple enough to do, but it requires the CGI program to return a header as the first line of output. The header tells the Web browser how to display the output of the CGI program.

The information passed back is almost always some sort of text, whether plain text or HTML. Plain text is displayed exactly as you would think: plainly. HTML is displayed the same way as any other HTML document. If the program produces HTML text, the header must look like this:

```
Content-type: text/html
```

The header must also be followed by a blank line as a signal to the browser that the header section is over and whatever follows should be processed as HTML.

For output to be displayed as plain text, the header should look like this:

```
Content-type: text/plain
```

Again, the header must be followed by a blank line. Anything after the text/plain header will be treated as ordinary text by the browser.

For the counter example presented before, the header for returning GIF images looks like the following:

```
Content-type: image/gif
```

Once again, do not forget the trailing blank line.

These headers are part of the *Multipupose Internet Mail Extensions* (MIME) standard. MIME was originally developed to enable e-mail messages to include other types of media other than plain text. The Web also makes use of the MIME standard to determine how to handle multimedia.

If your Web browser recognizes the media types present in a Web page, it displays text, images, and video clips, plays audio files, or starts up an external application to display a spreadsheet or word processing document.

If your browser does not understand the header type, it displays an error message asking you how you want to handle the incoming data. You have the option of ignoring the unrecognized data, trying to use some other program to process the data, or telling the Web browser where the program resides that can process the data correctly. After you tell your Web browser how to handle a data type, it stores the information and will call the matching program itself when it receives data of that type in the future.

Examples of Using CGI

The following four methods are used to pass information from a Web browser to a CGI program. How the data is passed depends on how the CGI program is called in the HTML document.

- Passing parameters on the command line
- Passing environment variables to CGI programs
- Passing data to CGI programs via standard input
- Using extra path information

Each method is named for the manner in which it sends data to the CGI program. The method used determines how the CGI program must read the information and the type of processing that must be done to the information before it can be used by the program. Each of the preceding methods are detailed with examples in the following sections.

Common Languages for CGI Programming

There are many languages available for writing CGI programs. No single language meets the needs of every program, but if you think of programming languages as a set of tools, you can select the proper tool for the task at hand. The following are the three main languages used for CGI programming:

- If the CGI program is to be used primarily to perform system commands, a Unix shell script can handle the chore.
- An executable program written in a language such as C is a good choice if program execution speed or the security of the source code is a big issue.
- If ease of use or a rich feature set is what you desire, Perl would best suit your needs.

Each programming tool has many things to offer, and it depends on the job to be done as to which tool is used. All of these languages are used to create sample CGI programs in the following sections.

Passing Parameters on the Command Line

This method to pass parameters uses the command line in the same way as invoking a program from the command-line prompt on your computer does. If you invoke a text editor by entering **edit do_something.cgi** or **vi do_something.cgi**, those are examples of command lines. The first word on the command line is the name of the program being invoked, and the following parameters are read by the program itself as it starts up. A text editor expects to get the name of the file to edit from the command line, in addition to any other parameters that detail how the editor should act.

A CGI program can read command-line parameters in the same way as a text editor. If you have existing programs that work by reading command-line parameters, this method enables you to use the programs you have instead of writing new ones. If your programs are commercial products or are part of your computer's operating system, you do not have the option of rewriting them, and the command line method is the only one open to you without writing your own programs.

The HTML language provides a simple command line method called *ISINDEX*. Using the ISINDEX method is the only way to send command-line parameters to a CGI program. <ISINDEX> is an HTML tag that should be placed inside the <HEAD> section of your HTML document. It tells the Web browser to create on your Web page a field that enables you to enter keywords to search for.

The CGI program for this example will be written as a Unix shell script. Shell scripting is an easy way to write CGI programs, but there are a few things you should know about Unix shells first.

Writing Unix Shell Scripts

The first example is written in the Unix Bourne shell. Any shell, such as C-shell, Korn shell, bash, tsch, and so forth, can be used. Each type of shell has its particular strengths, and choosing one depends on which one the programmer is comfortable working in.

One advantage to the Bourne shell, however, is that you can be quite sure it will be present on any Unix box you write programs on. Other shells might exist as well, but using Bourne ensures maximum portability for your Unix shell programs. For this reason, any shell script written for this book was written using the Bourne shell.

Using a Unix shell script gives the programmer access to all the system commands that deal with file and process management, such as grep, ps, and mail. Not everyone needs a full-blown database to meet their needs of putting information on the Internet. Sometimes, just searching a collection of files for pertinent information is good enough.

Using ISINDEX and the Bourne Shell

Using the ISINDEX method can be confusing. You create an HTML page that contains a text entry field for the user to enter data. The user then presses a button to send the data to a CGI program. This sounds simple, but when using the ISINDEX method, the HTML document and the CGI program are both contained in the same code.

There's a reason for this: When a Web page uses the ISINDEX method, there is no way to tell the ISINDEX method where to send the command-line parameters. The parameters are sent to the only program the ISINDEX method knows about, which happens to be itself. Confused? The following example will help.

In this example, a small library has files containing book information stored on a computer somewhere, and they want to provide users with a way to search for a book title or author name. Using the ISINDEX method is an easy way to ask the user for keywords to search for. You can create a CGI program called "search_library.cgi" that uses the ISINDEX method. A keyword search field is displayed when you first access the program, and you can enter a title or author to search for.

The keywords are passed to the CGI program, which uses the Unix *grep* command to search the book files for matching lines. The output of the grep command is any line in the library book file that contains one of the given keywords. The output of the /cgi-bin/ search_library.cgi program is returned as an HTML document for the Web browser to display.

As you look over the following Bourne shell program, search_library.cgi, pay close attention to the comments in the program. There are three important points to note:

- A single CGI program displays the keyword search page as well as the results of the keyword search. This is the only way to make use of the ISINDEX method using CGI.
- The CGI program decides which page to display based on the number of command-line parameters passed to it.
- The CGI program outputs a header and HTML tags that a Web browser accepts as if it were reading an ordinary HTML document. This makes it easy to generate on-the-fly HTML pages that can react to user input and tailor the output based on what the user does. (The small arrow indicates the line normally fits on a single line.)

```
#!/bin/sh
#
# search_library.cgi - searches files for matching keywords using
# ISINDEX.
#
#################################################################################
# The following two lines are VERY important.  They identify the
# ouput of this script as HTML to the Web server and browser, and
# then send a blank line which indicates the end of the header
# section.  The blank line is necessary.
#################################################################################
echo "Content-type: text/html"
echo
```

```
############################################################################
# Here we check the number of command-line arguments by using
# '$#'.  If '$#' is 0, display the ISINDEX page.  If '$#' is
# greater than 0, process the keywords that have been passed to
# the program.
############################################################################
if [ $# -eq 0 ]
then

  echo "<TITLE>Welcome to the Lightspeed Library</TITLE>"
  echo "<HEAD>"

  ##################################################
  # This is the <ISINDEX> tag.  Simple, isn't it?
  ##################################################
  echo "<ISINDEX>"
  echo "</HEAD>"

  echo "<BODY>"
  echo "<H1>Welcome to the Lightspeed Library</H1>"
  echo "Enter the names of books or authors you want to search for
  ➥in the field"
  echo " above. Separate multiple keywords with spaces."
  echo "</BODY>"

else
  echo "<HEAD>"
  echo "<TITLE>Lightspeed Library Query Results</TITLE>"
  echo "</HEAD>"
  echo "</HEAD>"

  echo "<BODY>"

  echo "The following matches were found as the results of your
  ➥query for: <BR>"

  ############################################################
  # The next section prints the keywords in a nice format.
  ############################################################
  i=0
  for keyword in "$@"
  do
    i='expr $i + 1'
    if [ $# -eq $i ]
    then
      if [ $# -ne 1 ]
      then
```

```
        echo "and $keyword."
      else
        echo "$keyword."
      fi
    else
      if [ $# -eq 2 ]
      then
        echo -e "$keyword \c"
      else
        echo -e "$keyword, \c"
      fi
    fi
  done

  echo "<BR>"
  echo "<PRE>"

 ##################################################################
  # This for-loop processes the command-line parameters one at a
  # time, and displays the results.  The search conducted by the
  # 'grep' command is case-insensitive, as indicated by the '-i'
  # flag.  The library files are stored in the 'library' directory
  # located under the directory where this script is stored.
 ##################################################################
  for keyword in "$@"
  do
    i='expr $i + 1'
    grep -i $keyword library/*
  done

  echo "</PRE>"
  echo "</BODY>"
fi
```

Notice that search_library.cgi contains no URL information or any other way for the ISINDEX page to know where to send the command-line data. When you first call search_library.cgi, the keyword search Web page is shown in figure 3.1.

Note that the URL for the preceding Web page is a CGI program, instead of an HTML document. When a user submits keywords to search for, the URL changes by having the keyword information appended to the URL, as shown in figure 3.2.

If the user specifies the keywords "melville," "hawthorne," and "hobbes" in the query field, then submits the request, the search result displays the library book information (see fig. 3.2).

Figure 3.1
An ISINDEX form to search library files.

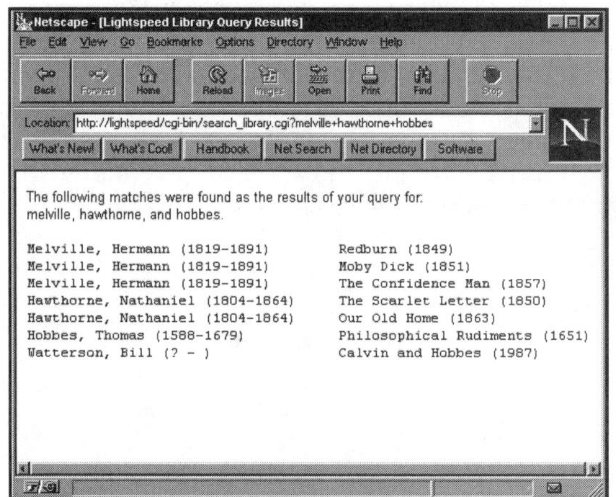

Figure 3.2
Results of library search.

Notice that the URL displayed by the Web browser plainly shows exactly how the query data is appended to the URL. A question mark is appended, and the keywords entered in the ISINDEX field follow the question mark, separated by plus signs, then the new URL is sent to the Web server. The server breaks the keywords off of the URL, replaces the plus signs with spaces, and calls the CGI program, passing the arguments to the program as command-line parameters. The CGI program reads the parameters and searches the library files for matching information. Any data returned is passed back to the Web browser and displayed as an HTML document.

This is just a simple example of using the ISINDEX method in a Bourne shell script, but it illustrates some important points:

- The ISINDEX method requires a CGI program to do two different things based on the number of command-line parameters that are passed to the program.
- A CGI program can output HTML tags that a Web browser treats as a normal HTML document.
- A Bourne shell script gives you access to any Unix command available to the shell from your Web documents by using CGI.

If all you need is a way to search text files for keywords and return the information found, this example shows you how to do exactly that.

Passing Environment Variables to CGI Programs

Another way to pass information to a CGI program is by using environment variables. When you log on to a Unix-based computer, you are in your own copy of the command shell. Your copy is distinct from the shell given to any other user on the system. Your copy of the shell is called your environment. You can customize your environment to suit yourself.

The same thing happens when you start up a DOS-based PC. There are no other users on your machine, but you still have an operating environment similar to the Unix shell that can be customized as you like.

Within the environment are variables called *environment variables.* These variables stay with you from the time your command shell starts to the time you log off the machine. If you set the value of an environment variable, that value stays with your environment until you change it or log off.

Environment variables can be set by programs when they are installed on your computer, or by you when you need to use one. Some programs look in your environment to see what the values of certain variables are. If the variable does not exist in your environment, the program may use a default value, or it may fail, giving you an error message that you must set the value of an environment variable before the program can execute.

As an example of environment variables, a variable used in both the Unix and PC command shells is the PATH variable. The *PATH* variable contains the standard locations for programs on your computer. When you try to run a program, the operating system gets the value of your PATH variable and looks in every directory specified in your path for the program you are trying to run. As soon as it finds a program with the correct name, it stops looking and executes the program.

If the operating system does not find the program, it fails, usually with an error message such as `Command not found`. This means the operating system looked in all of the directories in your path and did not find the name of the program you entered. If you want to run a program without having to find it yourself every time, you can add the program directory to your path, then the program will run the next time you try it.

A Web server makes use of environment variables in a similar manner. A Web server does not run in your copy of the command shell, but it gets a copy to itself. The Web server sets the values of several environment variables every time it calls a CGI program. The CGI program can access the contents of these variables if it needs them and use them within the program.

Here is a list of the environment variables passed by the Web server:

AUTH_TYPE	ANNOTATION_SERVER
CONTENT_LENGTH	CONTENT_TYPE
GATEWAY_INTERFACE	HTTP_ACCEPT
HTTP_REFERER	HTTP_USER_AGENT
PATH_INFO	PATH_TRANSLATED
QUERY_STRING	REMOTE_ADDR
REMOTE_HOST	REQUEST_METHOD
REMOTE_USER	SCRIPT_NAME
SERVER_NAME	SERVER_PORT
SERVER_PROTOCOL	SERVER_SOFTWARE

Some of these can be more useful than others. For example, if you want to know what kind of Web browser a visitor is using to view your Web pages, check the value of HTTP_USER_AGENT. The value in this variable can be used to display information to the user in different formats depending on the capabilities of the browser they are using.

To see where a visitor is coming from, look at REMOTE_HOST for the hostname and REMOTE_ADDR for the IP address. If you want to see the last page a visitor accessed before coming to your Web site, look at HTTP_REFERER.

Using Environment Variables with C Programs

The C programming language was used to create two examples of using the values of environment variables. C or C++ can be a very useful language for writing CGI programs. When combined with a Web browser as the GUI, executable programs provide the fastest way to access a database via the Web.

The C programming language is useful because, in many cases, database vendors provide an application programming interface (API) for accessing the database via C programs. The API is usually a library of function calls a programmer can use to create database access programs.

Because there has been no discussion of databases or database interfaces to this point in the book, using a database API is shown in Chapter 5, "Database Interfaces." As a prelude to learning how to use an API, however, the second C example in this section shows you how to set up a secure method of restricting database access by using the access security built into the NCSA Web server. When you are shown how to use a database API in Chapter 5, you can combine the secure method illustrated here with the API example to provide access to your database.

Example 1: Printing Environment Variables

The following C program, show_env.c, prints out the values of the environment variables set by the HTTP server.

```
/*
 * show_env.c - Prints environment variables set when called from
 *              an http server.
 */
```

```
#include <stdio.h>
#include <stdlib.h>

int main()
{

  /*
   * Must have this to tell the http server and browser to print
   * plain text,instead of trying to interpret the output as HTML.
   */
  fprintf(stdout, "Context-type: text/plain\n\n");

  fprintf(stdout, "The environment variables set by the http
  ➥server:\n\n");

  /*
   * Print the values of all the available environment variables.
   * Some of these will be NULL depending on how the CGI program is
   * called.
   */
  fprintf(stdout, "AUTH_TYPE: %s\n", getenv("AUTH_TYPE"));
  fprintf(stdout, "ANNOTATION_SERVER: %s\n",
  ➥getenv("ANNOTATION_SERVER"));
  fprintf(stdout, "CONTENT_LENGTH: %s\n",
  ➥getenv("CONTENT_LENGTH"));
  fprintf(stdout, "CONTENT_TYPE: %s\n", getenv("CONTENT_TYPE"));
  fprintf(stdout, "GATEWAY_INTERFACE: %s\n",
  ➥getenv("GATEWAY_INTERFACE"));
  fprintf(stdout, "HTTP_ACCEPT: %s\n", getenv("HTTP_ACCEPT"));
  fprintf(stdout, "HTTP_REFERER: %s\n", getenv("HTTP_REFERER"));
  fprintf(stdout, "HTTP_USER_AGENT: %s\n",
  ➥getenv("HTTP_USER_AGENT"));
  fprintf(stdout, "PATH_INFO: %s\n", getenv("PATH_INFO"));
  fprintf(stdout, "PATH_TRANSLATED: %s\n",
  ➥getenv("PATH_TRANSLATED"));
  fprintf(stdout, "QUERY_STRING: %s\n", getenv("QUERY_STRING"));
  fprintf(stdout, "REMOTE_ADDR: %s\n", getenv("REMOTE_ADDR"));
  fprintf(stdout, "REMOTE_HOST: %s\n", getenv("REMOTE_HOST"));
  fprintf(stdout, "REQUEST_METHOD: %s\n",
  ➥getenv("REQUEST_METHOD"));
  fprintf(stdout, "REMOTE_USER: %s\n", getenv("REMOTE_USER"));
  fprintf(stdout, "SCRIPT_NAME: %s\n", getenv("SCRIPT_NAME"));
  fprintf(stdout, "SERVER_NAME: %s\n", getenv("SERVER_NAME"));
```

```
    fprintf(stdout, "SERVER_PORT: %s\n", getenv("SERVER_PORT"));
    fprintf(stdout, "SERVER_PROTOCOL: %s\n",
    ➥getenv("SERVER_PROTOCOL"));
    fprintf(stdout, "SERVER_SOFTWARE: %s\n",
    ➥getenv("SERVER_SOFTWARE"));

}
```

The source code for show_env.c is compiled into the program show_env.cgi. When accessed by a Web browser, show_env.cgi produces the output displayed in figure 3.3.

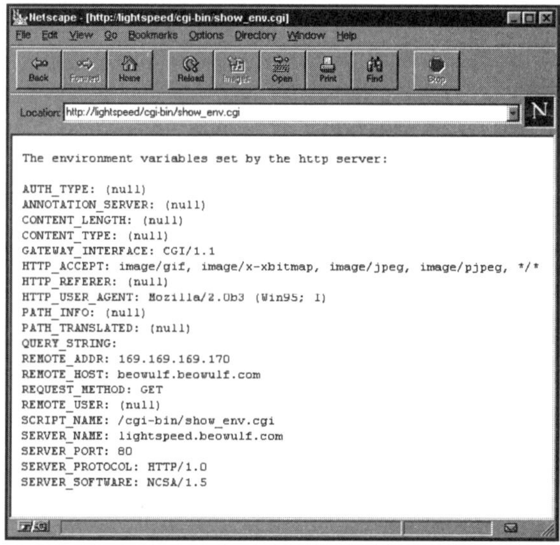

Figure 3.3
The environment variables set by an HTTP server when calling a CGI program.

By looking at the values returned by the show_env.cgi program, the following assumptions may be made:

- The HTTP_REFERER variable is empty, so the CGI program was called directly by a Web browser, and not by clicking on a link in another Web page.

- The HTTP_USER_AGENT variable refers to the Mozilla Web browser. For the uninitiated, *Mozilla* was the original name of the Netscape Web browser, and the Netscape programmers still refer to it by that name. Mozilla version 2.0b3 (Win95; I) was used to access the cgi program, which is version 2, beta 3 of the Windows 95 Netscape

Web browser. Other Web browsers display similar information to help you identify them.

- REMOTE_ADDR, SERVER_NAME, and REMOTE_HOST show the made-up names and IP address of the computers used to create the examples for this book.
- The SERVER_SOFTWARE variable shows the NCSA Web server version 1.5 was used to return information from the CGI program to the Web browser.

As mentioned previously, some of the Web server environment variables are more useful than others, but all of them can be accessed by a CGI program. A more substantial example of using environment variables is presented in the next section.

Example 2: Using Environment Variables to Restrict Database Access

For this example, the environment variable SCRIPT_NAME is of particular interest. SCRIPT_NAME contains the name of the CGI program that is called by the HTTP server. On the surface, this sounds fairly useless, but consider the following scenario.

You have a CGI program on a Unix system that is used to access your online database from the Web. You want to provide general users with query access only, but your database administrators (DBA) also need insert, update, delete, create, and so forth. Much of the code in the program would have to be duplicated if you used several different versions to grant or restrict database access, and you would have to maintain and upgrade all versions. Then you would have to come up with some sort of access control process, probably involving usernames and passwords.

Instead of doing this, let the HTTP server handle the access control for you as described in Chapter 2, "Tools for Accessing Data via the Web." There is no need for breaking your database access program into several pieces, and then having to provide maintenance to all of them. Here is an easy way to provide the proper level of access to whomever needs it. The C source code for the database access program do_database.c is shown here:

```
/*
 * do_database.c - Prints environment variables set when called
 *                 from an http server.  Grants pseudo database
 *                 access based on the contents of the
 *                 QUERY_STRING environment variable.
 */

#include <stdio.h>
#include <stdlib.h>

/*
 * Define the levels of access available.
 */
#define QUERY_ONLY 1
#define INSERT_UPDATE 2
#define DELETE 3
#define DB_ADMIN 4
#define NO_ACCESS 5

int main()
{
  int access_level = 0;
  char script_name[128];

  /*
   * Must have this to tell the http server and browser to print
   * plain text, instead of trying to interpret the output as
   * HTML.
   */
  fprintf(stdout, "Context-type: text/plain\n\n");

/*
   * Save a copy of the SCRIPT_NAME environment variable.
   */
  strcpy( script_name, getenv("SCRIPT_NAME") );

  fprintf(stdout, "\n\nIf I were a database program, I would grant
  ➥you:\n");

  /*
   * Determine the level of access a user gets based on the name
   * of the program called.
   */
  access_level = set_access_level( script_name );

  switch (access_level) {
```

```
    case QUERY_ONLY:
       fprintf(stdout, "query only access.\n");
    break;
    case INSERT_UPDATE:
       fprintf(stdout, "query, insert, and update access.\n");
    break;
    case DELETE:
       fprintf(stdout, "query, insert, update, and delete
       ➥access.\n");
    break;
    case DB_ADMIN:
       fprintf(stdout, "total access.\n");
break;
    case NO_ACCESS:
       fprintf(stdout, "NO ACCESS!!.\n");
    break;
  }
}

/*
 * Determine a user's access level.
 */
int set_access_level( char *script_name )
{
  if ( strcmp(script_name, "/cgi-bin/dbusers/query/
  ➥query_only.cgi") == 0 ) {
    return QUERY_ONLY;
  }

  if ( strcmp(script_name, "/cgi-bin/dbusers/update/
  ➥insert_update.cgi") == 0 ) {
    return INSERT_UPDATE;
  }

  if ( strcmp(script_name, "/cgi-bin/dbusers/delete/delete.cgi")
  ➥== 0 ) {
    return DELETE;
  }

  if ( strcmp(script_name, "/cgi-bin/dbusers/dbadmin/dbadmin.cgi")
  ➥== 0 ) {
    return DB_ADMIN;
  }

 /*
   * If they aren't legal, turn off all access.
   */
  return NO_ACCESS;
}
```

Do_database.c is complied into the program do_database.cgi and placed into the /cgi-bin/dbusers/bin directory. To implement the user access scheme, create a directory on your system for each class of user who needs a different level of database access, such as query_only, insert_update, delete, and full_access. Create a .htpasswd file in each directory and create a different user or user group and password for access to each directory. Put the executable program in the bin directory. The final structure of the /cgi-bin/dbusers directory looks like this:

```
drwxr-xr-x   2 http         1024 Jan 15 16:27 bin/
drwxr-xr-x   2 http         1024 Jan 15 18:58 delete/
drwxr-xr-x   2 http         1024 Jan 15 18:58 full_access/
drwxr-xr-x   2 http         1024 Jan 15 18:57 insert_update/
drwxr-xr-x   2 http         1024 Jan 15 18:53 query_only/
```

In each directory, create a symbolic link to the executable program. A *symbolic link* is a Unix feature that enables you to refer to a file by another name without having to make a duplicate of the original file. Any number of links can be created to a single file. Make sure you give each link a different name. The files and symbolic links in each directory look like the following:

```
bin:
total 11
-rwxr-xr-x   1 http    13083 Jan 15 16:27 do_database.cgi*

delete:
total 1
-rw-r--r--   1 http      162 Jan 15 19:10 .htaccess
lrwxrwxrwx   1 http       22 Jan 15 18:58 delete.cgi -> ../bin/
➥do_database.cgi*

full_access:
total 1
-rw-r--r--   1 http      167 Jan 15 19:10 .htaccess
lrwxrwxrwx   1 http       22 Jan 15 18:58 full_access.cgi -> ../
➥bin/do_database.cgi*

insert_update:
total 1
-rw-r--r--   1 http      169 Jan 15 19:10 .htaccess
lrwxrwxrwx   1 http       22 Jan 15 18:57 insert_update.cgi -> ../
➥bin/do_database.cgi*
```

```
query_only:
total 1
-rw-r--r--   1 http      166 Jan 15 19:09 .htaccess
lrwxrwxrwx   1 http       22 Jan 15 18:53 query_only.cgi -> ../
➥bin/do_database.cgi*
```

This system has good benefits: a single program to maintain; access control provided for you by the HTTP server; and, inside your database access program, you use the SCRIPT_NAME environment variable to determine which symbolic link was used to call the program. The program name in SCRIPT_NAME tells you which version of the CGI program is needed, and what access to grant to the user calling the program. Flags in your CGI program can disable portions of the program depending on the access level of the user.

A brief outline of the process follows:

1. Assume your database access program, do_database.cgi, is in the directory /cgi-bin/dbusers/bin.
2. Create these directories:
   /cgi-bin/dbusers/query_only
   /cgi-bin/dbusers/insert_update
   /cgi-bin/dbusers/delete
   /cgi-bin/dbusers/full_access.
3. Create the respective usernames dbuser, dbupdate, dbdelete, and dbadmin, and give them passwords using the htpasswd program.
4. In the directories you created, create symbolic links like this:

   In /cgi-bin/dbusers/query_only, type this:

   ln -s ../bin/do_database.cgi query_only.cgi.

   In /cgi-bin/dbusers/insert_delete.cgi, type the following:

   ln -s ../bin/do_database.cgi insert_update.cgi.

In /cgi-bin/dbusers/delete, type this line:

```
ln -s ../bin/do_database.cgi delete.cgi.
```

And in /cgi-bin/dbusers/dbadmin, type this:

```
ln -s ../bin/do_database.cgi full_access.cgi.
```

5. You can tell a file is a symbolic link by using the `ls -l` command. A link shows up like the following:

```
dbadmin.cgi -> /../bin/do_database.cgi
```

6. Inside do_database.cgi, check SCRIPT_NAME to see which program name was called. If you are using an executable C program, use the following command to copy the value of SCRIPT_NAME into the string script_name:

```
strcpy(script_name, getenv(SCRIPT_NAME));
```

Depending on the value of `script_name`, you can set a variable, such as access_level, to an appropriate value. If a user tries to access a protected function and does not have the correct access level, your program can ignore the attempt or react accordingly.

If the database access program is on a machine where symbolic links are not an option, you can copy the program into each directory under the appropriate name and the program doesn't have to change. At least this way there is only one version of the program to maintain. However, this is at the expense of using more hard disk space for the extra copies of the program.

After the preceding scenario is implemented, and a Web browser calls /cgi-bin/dbusers/delete/delete.cgi, the Web browser requires a username and password as indicated in figure 3.4.

When you enter the correct username and password, you will see the results shown in figure 3.5.

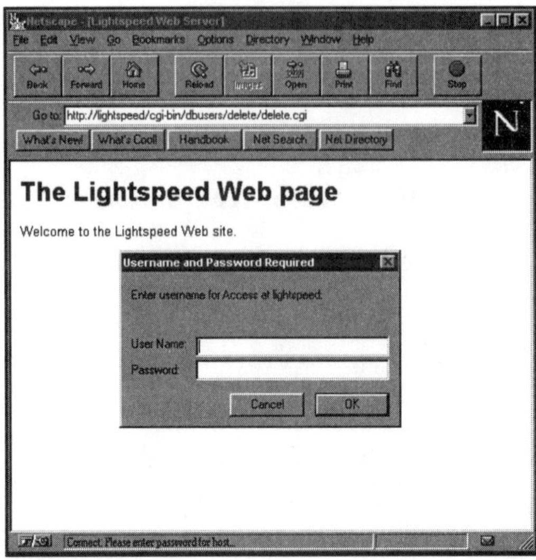

Figure 3.4 *Username and password request form.*

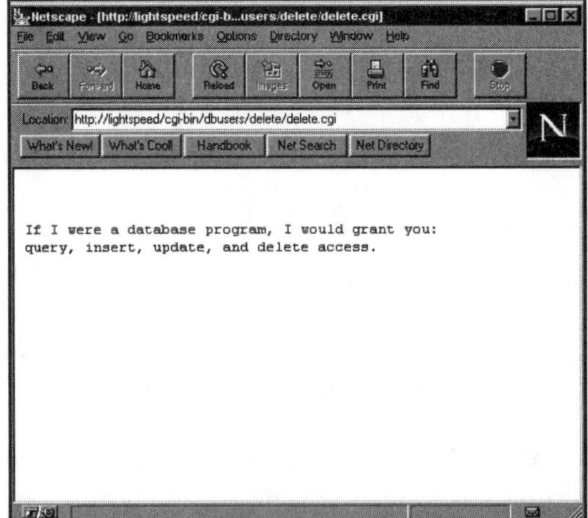

Figure 3.5 *Environment variables and access level granted.*

Now imagine there is a crafty hacker visiting your Web site, and she wants more access to your database. Even if she can determine the master program is /cgi-bin/dbusers/bin/do_database.cgi, and even though there is no password protection on that directory, trying to access the master program produces an error message and denies her access (see fig. 3.6).

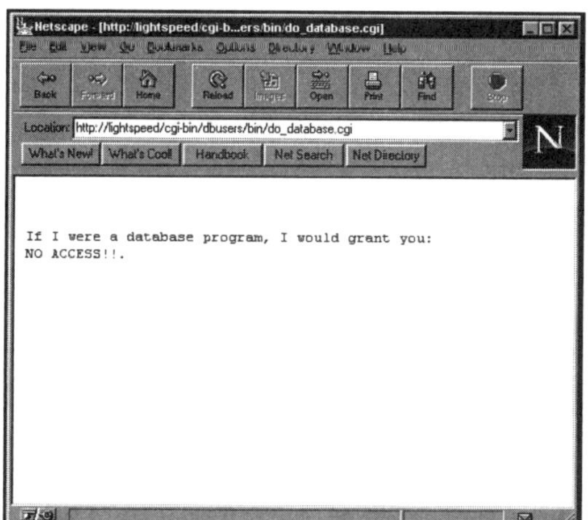

Figure 3.6
No access is granted.

If she accesses the program without going through the proper directory and giving the correct username and password, she simply cannot access the database—assuming the program is written correctly.

Passing Data to CGI Programs via Standard Input

If a programmer wants to use HTML forms to provide users with text fields, checkboxes, picklists, text-entry boxes, and other interactive features that HTML provides, then passing information via standard input is the way forms send information to the HTTP server, and hence to the CGI program.

Standard input is a common method for passing information to any program. Usually, standard input is the terminal you are using to run the program. If a program requires you to enter information, such as a software setup program asking you what directory in which to install the software, the information is passed from your terminal to the program via standard input.

If a program produces output as it runs, the output comes to your terminal screen via *standard output.* If the program produces error messages, they are sent to your terminal screen using *standard error.* Standard input, output, and error are data channels provided by the operating system to connect an input/output (I/O) device such as your terminal to a running program.

An I/O device does not need to be a piece of hardware, however. Any piece of computer hardware or software capable of sending input to a program and receiving output from it will work just fine. An HTTP server fits this description. The HTTP server can take data entered by the user and send it to a

CGI program via standard input, then get back the results via standard output.

Unlike when the ISINDEX method is used, the HTTP server does not process the arguments for you before passing them to the CGI program. Arguments arrive at the program encoded the way the Web browser sent them, and it is up to the program to decode them into the proper format.

Writing CGI Programs in Perl

An easy way to decode the input passed from HTML forms is to use Perl. Perl is quickly becoming the de facto standard for CGI programming, especially on Unix-based platforms. Perl combines most, if not all, of the capabilities of the various Unix shells, as well as sed and awk, and adds a host of other features besides.

To avoid reinventing the wheel, most Perl programmers use Steven Brenner's (`S.E.Brenner@bioc.cam.ac.uk`) cgi-bin.pl library of Perl routines to process information sent to a CGI program. The following is a source code listing of the ReadParse() function which will be used in the Perl example for this section.

```
#!/usr/local/bin/Perl -- -*- C -*-

# Perl Routines to Manipulate CGI input
# S.E.Brenner@bioc.cam.ac.uk
# $Header: /people/seb1005/http/cgi-bin/RCS/cgi-lib.pl,v 1.2 1994/
# 01/10 15:05:40
#
# Copyright 1993 Steven E. Brenner
# Unpublished work.
# Permission granted to use and modify this library so long as the
# copyright above is maintained, modifications are documented, and
# credit is given for any use of the library.

# ReadParse
# Reads in GET or POST data, converts it to unescaped text, and
# puts one key=value in each member of the list "@in"
# Also creates key/value pairs in %in, using '\0' to separate
# multiple selections

# If a variable-glob parameter (e.g., *cgi_input) is passed to
# ReadParse, information is stored there, rather than in $in, @in,
# and %in.
```

```
sub ReadParse {
  if (@_) {
    local (*in) = @_;
  }

  local ($i, $loc, $key, $val);

  # Read in text
  if ($ENV{'REQUEST_METHOD'} eq "GET") {
    $in = $ENV{'QUERY_STRING'};
  } elsif ($ENV{'REQUEST_METHOD'} eq "POST") {
    for ($i = 0; $i < $ENV{'CONTENT_LENGTH'}; $i++) {
      $in .= getc;
    }
  }

  @in = split(/&/,$in);

  foreach $i (0 .. $#in) {
    # Convert plus's to spaces
    $in[$i] =~ s/\+/ /g;

    # Convert %XX from hex numbers to alphanumeric
    $in[$i] =~ s/%(..)/pack("c",hex($1))/ge;

    # Split into key and value.
    $loc = index($in[$i],"=");
    $key = substr($in[$i],0,$loc);
    $val = substr($in[$i],$loc+1);
    $in{$key} .= '\0' if (defined($in{$key})); # \0 is the multiple
   ➥separator
    $in{$key} .= $val;
  }

  return 1; # just for fun
}
```

ReadParse first determines which method of communication the Web browser is requesting. The *GET* method is used by ISINDEX and when arguments are passed in the QUERY_STRING environment variable. When HTML forms are used to send information to standard input, the method is *POST*.

If the method is GET, ReadParse just reads the QUERY_STRING environment variable. If the method is POST, the CONTENT_LENGTH environment variable contains the length of the data passed to standard input. Using that length, ReadParse reads data from standard input one character at a time.

If the information was passed from an HTML form, the name/value pairs will have the & characters between them. ReadParse removes them. Spaces are encoded as + symbols, and special characters are encoded as their hexadecimal equivalents. ReadParse restores the spaces and converts the hex characters back into ASCII.

After the data is completely decoded, ReadParse does something especially nice by putting the name/value pairs into an associative array called "%in." Associative arrays are a feature of Perl that work with name/value pairs especially well, as explained in the following section.

Associative Arrays

A regular array is a data structure that contains a list of data elements, and each element is referred to by an index number, such as name[1] or address(7). Perl's *associative arrays* take that concept one step further by associating a key value with an array element. If you have a list of names and addresses, you can put them both into an associative array with the name as the key value and then find the address by referring to the name, as in the following line:

```
$address{"john"}.
```

This works very well with name\value pairs because the name of an HTML form element can be used as the key with which to find the value of the element. In the next section, Perl and associative arrays are used in an example to process the data entered in an HTML form.

Using Standard Input with Perl Programs

The HTML form used in this example is the customer comment form first seen in Chapter 2 and reproduced in figure 3.7.

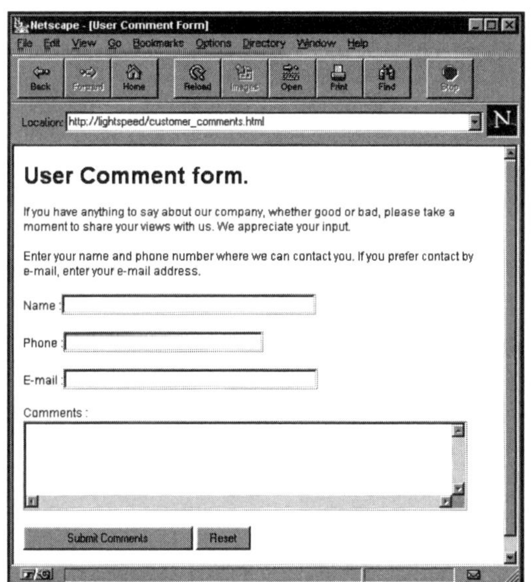

Figure 3.7
A customer comments form.

In this case, when the Submit Comments button is pressed, the Perl script /cgi-bin/user_comments.cgi is called. The source code for user_comments.cgi is shown here:

```
#!/usr/bin/Perl
#
# user_comments.cgi - a Perl script that takes comments from an
#                     HTML form and composes a mail message for
#                     posting to the Webmaster, and a response for
#                     display to the user sending the comments.
##################################################################

# Use Steven Brenner's library of Perl functions.
#----------------------
require "cgi-lib.pl";

# Print the standard html header.
#---------------
print &PrintHeader();

# Read the information from standard input and put it in an asso-
# ciative array.
#------------------------------------
&ReadParse();
```

```
# Make sure the customer really had something to say.
#-------------------------
if ( !$in{"name"} ¦¦ !$in{"email"} && !$in{"phone"} ) {
  print "<HEAD><TITLE>Customer comments</TITLE></HEAD>";
  print "<BODY><H1>Insufficient Customer Information</
  ➥H1><HR><BR>";
  print "Please enter your personal information before submitting
  ➥comments.";
  print "<br>Comments require a name and either your phone or
  ➥email address.";
  exit 1;
}

# Compose the mail message and mail it.
#-------------------
$message = "Webmaster,\n\n";
$message .= "A valued customer";
$message .= ", $in{\"name\"}," if $in{"name"};
$message .= " ($in{\"phone\"})" if $in{"phone"};
$message .= "\nwhose e-mail address is $in{\"email\"}," if
➥$in{"email"};
$message .= "\nhad the following comments about our
➥organization:\n\n";
$message .= $in{"comments"} if $in{"comments"};

# Create a semi-unique file name for the mail message so
#  mutliple users don't clobber each other's mail messages.
#-------------------------
$unique = time + rand;
$mail_file = "/tmp/tempfile.".$unique;

open(DUMMY, ">$mail_file");
print DUMMY $message;
close(DUMMY);

system("/bin/mail -s \"Customer comment\" http < $mail_file");

unlink($mail_file);

# Compose the response to display.
#---------------
$response = "Thank you";
if ( $in{"name"} ) {
  $response .=  ", $in{\"name\"}.";
} else {
  ", valued customer.";
}
```

```
$response .=  "<br>The following message has been mailed to our
➥Webmaster.";
$response .=  "We value your input and we promise your comments
➥will get";
$response .=  " our undivided attention.";

# Print the response and show the customer the composed e-mail.
#-------------------------------
print "<HEAD><TITLE>Customer comments</TITLE></HEAD>";
print "<BODY><H1>Thank you for your comments</H1><HR><BR>";
print "$response";
print "<br><br>-- Message Follows: --<br>";
print "<pre>";
print "$message";
print "</pre>";
print "-- End of Message --";
```

User_comment.cgi uses the ReadParse function to process the data, composes a response to the message based on which fields the user filled, mails the comments to the Webmaster, and returns the response as HTML for the Web browser to display. The response is displayed by the Web browser (see fig. 3.8).

Unfortunately, there is no program to decide whether user comments are particularly meaningful.

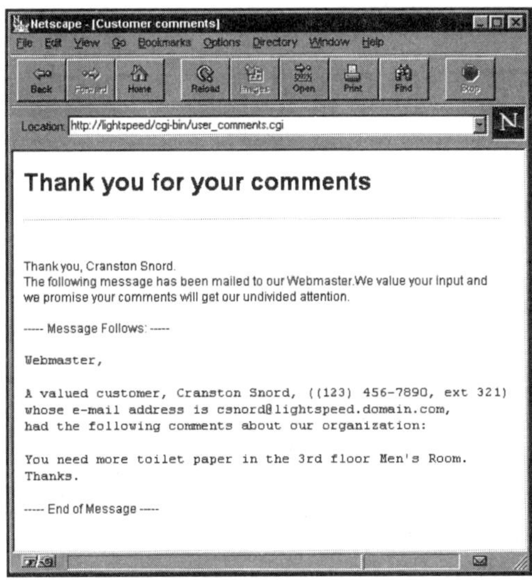

Figure 3.8
Response to customer comment.

Using Extra Path Information

The final method of passing information to CGI programs only works because the HTTP server recognizes /cgi-bin (or whatever it is called in your server configuration) as a special directory that holds programs. If you call a CGI program with the following URL, for example:

```
http://name.site.com/cgi-bin/do_something.cgi/extra_path_info?3
```

The HTTP server knows do_something.cgi is the program to call because cgi-bin is in the URL, and it passes extra_path_info to do_something.cgi using the environment variable PATH_INFO.

Everything after the ?—the 3 in this case—gets put into the QUERY_STRING environment variable. Using this method, your CGI program can read PATH_INFO to find a particular configuration file, for example, or use the information in the QUERY_STRING variable as configuration parameters that dictate how your program behaves.

The pathname specified in extra_path_info can be any length and can contain any complete directory path available on your system, not just those recognized by the HTTP server. This gives you a way of accessing files outside of the HTTP directory structure. Consider the following URL:

```
http://name.site.com/cgi-bin/run_me.cgi/home/beowulf/
config?cgi.conf,http.conf
```

This address sends the path /home/beowulf/config to the CGI program run_me.cgi in the PATH_INFO environment variable, and puts cgi.conf,http.conf in the QUERY_STRING variable. If run_me.cgi needs to open a configuration file for some runtime information, it now knows what directory to find it in and has a list of the filenames to open.

The information following the ? can be anything. Any number of arguments can be passed in the QUERY_STRING variable, as long as they follow the ?. If that method of passing information sounds familiar, it is. When a CGI program uses the ISINDEX method, the command-line arguments are appended to the URL. That appended information is also put into the QUERY_STRING environment variable.

Where the HTTP server decodes those arguments before passing them to the CGI program, however, the QUERY_STRING variable contains the raw information. This might not sound useful, but if you want to append information to a URL without using the ISINDEX method, that information is readily available in the QUERY_STRING environment variable. You can decode it yourself or not, depending on what you want to do with it.

Security Issues

As you begin to write CGI programs for fun and profit, proceed with caution. As mentioned earlier, some system administrators view CGI programs as potential security holes in their system. Although this is an unkind characterization, there is some validity to the sentiment.

Many HTTP servers are set up by the system administrator and are run under an innocuous username so that if a hacker does gain illicit entrance to the system, he or she can't do much damage because the HTTP username has limited system access. However, if you are running an HTTP server under your username, keep in mind that the HTTP server has all the system privileges you do.

Although hackers might not be able to damage the system using your user privileges, they can certainly damage your files, send mail in your name, or make a general nuisance of themselves until the system administrator shuts down *your* HTTP server or even revokes *your* account. So be cautious. There are some basic precautions you can take:

- Don't write any CGI programs that allow visitors to pass commands directly to the operating system to be executed. This is a disaster waiting to happen.
- Put an index.html file in all directories available to the HTTP server. This prevents curious eyes from listing the contents of your directories and trying to download your programs to examine them for weaknesses.
- If you use .htaccess files, be aware that passwords are transferred across the network in uuencoded format. Passwords are not in plain text, but anyone with the technical equipment and knowledge can grab and uudecode them.

- It is a good idea to browse your server logs fairly often to see whether you notice any suspicious access attempts. Check the error_log and access_log files regularly.

Don't be afraid to be paranoid. But don't be afraid to use CGI programs. With a few basic precautions and a little common sense, you can keep your system safe from unfriendly visitors.

Through wise use of CGI programs, you can greatly enhance the usefulness of your Web pages. CGI programs are what you need if you intend to hook a database to a Web front end. In Chapter 9, "Alternatives to Databases," you will see how CGI programs can access a database using an interface that is written for a specific database. For now, the next chapter, "Choosing a Database," guides you through some of the factors you should consider when selecting a database to use as your Internet database server.

Choosing a Database

Choosing a database for your personal or corporate use can be a bad experience if you don't know what you need. By doing a little exploration into your data needs up front, you can save yourself a lot of confusion later on. A database purchase can be a major expense. The more you know about the data you intend to store and who will access it, the better prepared you will be to make an informed decision.

When choosing a database that is appropriate for your needs, as illustrated in figure 4.1, consider the following factors:

- *Expense*
- *Database features*
- *Hardware support*
- *How much data?*

- User load
- Network support
- Available interfaces
- Third-party support
- Level of server administration
- User manuals

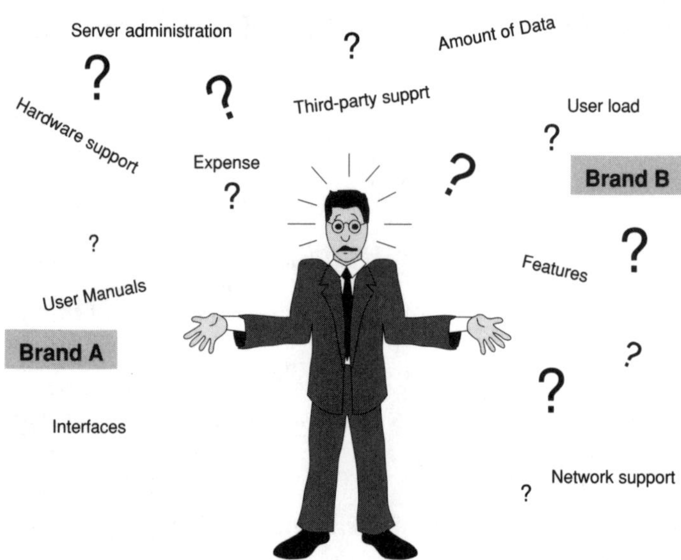

Figure 4.1
Choosing a database.

Databases have strengths and weaknesses, and the better informed you are about why you need a database, what kind of data will go in it, what kind of people will use it, and who will maintain it, the easier your decision will be.

Considering Expense

Big commercial databases are expensive. It would not be uncommon to pay $100,000 for a database, associated software, user licenses for 200 or so users, and a long-term maintenance agreement. If your needs are more modest, you can probably hold the price tag below $10,000.

Before you decide that is too much to pay, consider how important your data is to you or your company. If you depend on vital customer information in a database, you want to make sure it doesn't disappear because something went wrong with your server. If you just need a place to keep your golf scores, though, there are low-cost alternatives that don't require the mammoth investment in hardware and software required for a big database.

As you decide how much to spend, you should know exactly what you will get for your money. Choices range from big commercial databases to light-weight free databases. This chapter covers some of the features offered by all types of databases.

Commercial Databases

Powerful, multi-user database servers running on expensive Unix computers cost a lot for a reason. A database is not just a piece of software. The reputation of a database vendor is on the line with every client they gain. If one customer has a bad experience with a database, that kind of news gets around. A database server is as "hardened" as a piece of software can be. Thousands of man-hours (or woman-hours) are spent designing, implementing, and testing the software.

Small, single-user PC databases cost little for a reason. They are not intended to support 50 people simultaneously or hold terrabytes of data. Many people do not need the large feature set or tremendous processing capabilities of a big database. As your needs grow, however, can your database grow with them?

One of the big database buzzwords these days is *scalability.* As your database needs to change scale, can your database change with you or will you have to throw out what you have and start over with something different?

What Do You Get for Your Money?

As you evaluate the possibilities, ask yourself: Exactly what do I get for the money I spend on a database? As the price goes up, so does the list of things a database will do (see fig. 4.2). At some point, the database does what you want, but can you afford it?

Figure 4.2
Balancing database features versus cost.

Brand A	Brand B	Brand C
Ho-Hum $	Ho-Hum $	Ho-Hum $
	WOW $$	**WOW** $$
		Sexy $$$
Total $	Total $$$	Total $$$$$$

The trick is to find a database and hardware platform that support everything you want to do without stretching your finances to the breaking point. Consider three things as you decide:

- How much technical support is included in the deal?
- How often is the software upgraded?
- Does the deal include professional support such as the installation of software?

Technical Support

One of the biggest issues is technical support. How good is it? How long does it take to get in touch with technical support personnel? And how responsive is the vendor to solving problems?

If you have a small PC database, technical support might only be provided at additional expense. Software companies sell software at ever-lower prices in order to gain customers, but to do that something else must be sacrificed. In many cases, what goes is free technical support. If you want it, be sure it is included in the purchase price or pay the additional fee when you buy the software.

Almost all commercial products, regardless of their size or level of sophistication, have some form of online help available. Web pages with frequently asked questions (FAQs) and answers are common. Another good source of information is the online forums provided by services such as CompuServe, Prodigy, or America Online. Technical support personnel often monitor the forums and answer questions or help solve problems.

Another excellent source of information is the Usenet newsgroups on the Internet. Users of the most common databases exchange their problems and experiences with each other in a freeform way. Posting a question to a newsgroup puts your news article in front of literally millions of people who might have a solution.

A quick search on the keyword "database" brings up the following list of newsgroups:

- comp.databases
- comp.databases.gupta
- comp.databases.ibm-db2
- comp.databases.informix
- comp.databases.ingres
- comp.databases.ms-access
- comp.databases.ms-sqlserver
- comp.databases.oracle
- comp.databases.paradox
- comp.databases.pick
- comp.databases.progess
- comp.databases.rdb
- comp.databases.sybase
- comp.databases.xbase.fox
- comp.sys.mac.databases

Undoubtedly, there are others. Many of the databases listed above have user groups, mailing lists, or other forms of support. Commercial databases are used by millions of people, so the support base is enormous.

Web pages, online forums, and newsgroups are excellent ways of learning more about database vendors and the products and services they offer. After you wade through the marketing hype and filter out the articles trumpeting the virtues of a particular database, there is a lot of useful information to be found. The truth is that most big commercial databases are very similar at their core. They all offer the same basic functionality. The differences between vendors show up in the database extensions offered by a particular database, and the level of services provided by the vendor.

For example, database vendors have various levels of technical support. Finding the right support for your needs can be much easier by scrolling through a Web page. Different vendors offer similar plans, but there are unique aspects to each vendor that can appeal to a customer looking for just the right approach.

For big database vendors, the basic level of technical support entitles you access to online support forums, some sort of knowledge-base CD, and seven-day, 24-hour telephone support. Higher levels of support can include preferred treatment for your telephone support questions, a personal account manager for your company, and on-site support for critical problems, as shown in figure 4.3. Make sure you get the right level of support that includes what you are looking for. The following companies have varying levels of included support, for example:

- The Informix Web site (`http://www.informix.com`) has a link to their TechInfo Center, but it is only available for technical support packages above the basic level.
- The basic level of Sybase support (`http://www.sybase.com`) requires you to designate a single person to contact Sybase technical support. Multiple-person contacts require a more expensive support package.
- Oracle offers pay-per-incident support (`http://www.oracle.com`) on some of their products for those who rarely need technical help.

- Microsoft's Web site (`http://www.microsoft.com`) offers a searchable knowledge base to help you look for answers to common problems with their Access, FoxPro, or SQL Server databases.

Figure 4.3
There are different levels of technical support.

The level of support you get depends on how much you pay. If your database is a critical element of your business, having knowledgeable technicians available to diagnose the problem and talk your database administration people through the solution is a priceless commodity.

Software Upgrades

If your problem turns out to be a bug in the database software, database patches and fixes are available from the database vendor by request. Most vendors put out periodic general maintenance packs that fix reported problems or add minor enhancements. If you have a premium technical support agreement, the vendor may contact you to report problems and recommend a preventative solution.

Note

A *patch* is something the vendor provides as a software "jury rig" you install over your previous version of software. A patch is a negative thing to the vendor because it implies the database software isn't perfect, and they have to admit that fact to their clients.

A *fix* can involve a change to a configuration file, or some other form of workaround that involves changes to something other than the database software, such as changing an element of the operating system.

If you happen to experience a problem that has not been reported before, and it turns out to be a bug in the database software, the vendor will direct the database software engineers to find a solution to the problem. A software patch will be sent to you. If the patch fixes the problem, it could become the basis for a maintenance upgrade for other customers.

Another useful upgrade is one that changes or improves the database documentation. This might be in the form of loose pages to put into the documentation notebook, or a CD-ROM. Some database vendors release a CD of updates and useful information on a regular basis. This CD subscription is usually included in all levels of technical support.

Not all upgrades are a result of problems. If you buy a version of the database software that meets your needs at the time but fails to provide all the features you need later, the database vendor offers competitive upgrade prices that enable you to move to a higher level of database server for a reduced price. This gives you an upgrade path that can cost far less than starting over completely.

Professional Services

One of the most compelling reasons so many customers buy a database from a big commercial database company is the range of professional services offered by the vendor.

Installing and setting up the database software is one of the services offered. Database technicians configure your hardware platform for maximum compatibility with the database engine and install the software for you. Once the database is running, they tune the server for maximum performance. All of this eliminates a lot of headaches later on. Improper installation and hardware conflicts are the cause behind most technical support calls.

If you have an older database version or a server from another vendor, most database companies have support personnel to assist you with upgrading to a newer database engine or migrating your data and applications from another database engine to theirs. This can involve a little or a lot of work, but the support team can limit the amount of time and effort spent converting from one database to another.

If you need it, database companies can provide people to design a complete system for you from the ground up, and this can involve tasks such as designing and constructing your database, creating applications for database access, and training your people to use the new database and applications. This full-featured service can be quite expensive, but if you have no development personnel of your own, or need a new system in a hurry, having the database vendor do it for you might be the way to go.

Database Training

An often overlooked aspect of buying a new database is training the people who will be using and maintaining it. Formal database administration training is vital to the smooth and efficient running of the database. Vendors offer several different classes to teach many subjects, including:

- **SQL**, which is the query language used to put data into the database and retrieve selected data from the database. Understanding SQL involves not only learning the language itself, but also learning how to construct a database so that SQL can manipulate the data efficiently.
- **Database administration**, which involves everything from installing the database software correctly to configuring the database engine so it will run under a particular operating system, or so it will use special hardware. Keeping the data in good condition is an important administrative duty, so no unwanted or incomplete data remains in the database, and user queries run more efficiently.
- **Database performance tuning**, which can involve tinkering with the database configuration to squeeze a little better performance out of it, or

completely restructuring the database to eliminate a design flaw that dooms the database to poor performance.

- **Database application development**, which gives you a working knowledge of the development tools offered by a database vendor and the best ways to apply them.

Having properly trained people in your organization can make the difference when a crisis arises, or when you need something done quickly.

Using Shareware or Freeware

The philosophy behind freeware or shareware database software (often called *independent software*) is exactly the opposite of the big commercial products. People or small companies that cannot afford a commercial database but who have technical experience and are capable of taking care of problems themselves often find independent software to be exactly what they need.

What Do You Get for Little or No Money?

The biggest draw, of course, is the small or nonexistent fee required for using independent software. The shareware concept gives you a fully functional version of software for a trial period. If you choose to keep it, you pay a small fee directly to the author of the software.

Free software is released into the public domain for no fee at all. Just because it is free does not mean you can do what you want with it, though. Most free software is released under terms of the GNU public license that grants everyone permission to use it, but it still remains under copyright. You can use the software, alter it to suit your needs, and redistribute it for no fee, but you must leave the copyright notice intact in the source code.

GNU, or *Gnu's Not Unix*, represents all that is good about the Internet—freely available software for the Internet community that runs on any Unix machine and performs many useful functions that would cost you a bundle if you had to pay for it. In that spirit, using independent software has the following benefits:

- Source code
- Quick fixes by the author
- Freedom from proprietary software
- Internet community support

These features are described more fully in the following sections.

Source Code

One of the biggest attractions of independent software is the source code that comes with it. You download the source code as a distribution package from an ftp site and compile it to run on your particular machine. Some software configuration programs have become very adept at detecting what kind of machine you are using and adapting the source code to use some of the available features on your version of computer and operating system, and avoiding others that might cause problems.

Some software might have different features for you to choose from, and the configuration program will ask whether you want to use each feature. You can customize the software to meet your needs and recompile it later if you change your mind. Try to imagine getting a commercial database vendor to do that for you.

If a feature you want is missing from the software, you can change the source code to add what you need, assuming you have the necessary skills. In many cases, independent software is no less sophisticated than its commercial counterparts. Adding changes and seeing what happens can be an excellent learning opportunity, but it can often be frustrating as well.

Quick Fixes by the Author

In some cases, independent software is no longer supported by the author, but many software packages are actively supported. An author might write the software in his free time, or as part of a research grant. Either way, many software authors welcome comments and suggestions on ways to improve the code or add features. If you are unable to add a feature yourself, maybe the author would be willing to do it for you.

One of the ways an author will test his software is to make a copy of a new version (usually called a *beta* version) available for download. Users can download a copy of the software and use it for a time, reporting bugs or problems to the author. This kind of direct response between a software author and users can result in very quick turnaround from an unstable beta version to a stable release version.

If you can't afford to take a chance with untested software, however, your best choice is to use the last stable version of the software until the new version is thoroughly tested.

Freedom from Proprietary Software

In many cases, using software provided by a database vendor locks you into using only their products, and if what they offer does not meet your needs, you simply have to wait until it does or until you can afford to buy another database that does what you want. The term for this is *proprietary* software because it is not based on an open, standardized set of functions, but contains code that only programmers working for the database vendor ever see.

A very real benefit of using independent database software is the freedom it gives you to select what software to use with your database, and you can even use more than one database package. Where some applications need a full-featured database, others only need a minimal set of features. The cost involved in using independent software is not an impediment to using multiple databases because the cost per database is so much smaller than for the commercial databases.

If you choose one database, changing your mind is not so painful an experience either. Discovering that a database does not do everything you need can cause all sorts of bad things to happen. Choosing the wrong commercial database can cost you large amounts of time and money, and might even cost you your job. Changing to a different independent database software package might cost you some time, but if your investment is small, the consequences are not so dire.

It is also hard to enforce a proprietary database standard when the source code comes with the product. Computer professionals are not afraid to take existing code and change it so the original author would not recognize it, all for the sake of making the software do what is needed.

All of this takes time, however. Reading the source code and learning how it works are not trivial matters. Do you really want the responsibility of debugging someone else's code? Also, do you have the people to dedicate to supporting independent software?

You may be saving money at the start by not making a large investment, but over time you could end up paying more than you expect. Or you could get lucky and never have a problem. It depends on how you plan to use the database software and the skills of the people who will be supporting it.

Internet Community Support

Where customers of database vendors get most of their support from the database company, users of independent software get most of their support from the Internet community.

The biggest tool for support is e-mail. Somewhere in the source code will be an e-mail address, whether for the author or for some kind of mailing list. The author will generally respond to politely worded mail, with helpful hints or the address of some other person who can help.

Mailing lists are a useful process as well. By sending a message to a special address and including the word **subscribe** in the body of the message, you can subscribe to a mailing list that supports a particular independent software product.

By posting mail to the list, all of the subscribers on the mailing list receive your mail. Because all of the subscribers use or are interested in the same product, there is a good chance one of them can help you with your question.

As others post to the mailing list, you can see the types of problems people are having with a particular product, how the product is being used, its strengths and limitations, and who the experts are who can be trusted to answer questions truthfully and accurately.

Usenet newsgroups are a good place to get help or advice, too, but you might have to hunt for the right one to get the help you are looking for. Some independent software does not have a newsgroup devoted to it, so you may have to scour other newsgroups that are closely related.

Evaluating Database Features

The features offered by a database engine determine whether or not the database meets your needs. Even if the characteristics you need are offered by a vendor, they may only be available by paying extra or by purchasing a more advanced version of the database.

Most vendors offer more than one level of database. Versions intended for less powerful platforms such as a PC usually offer fewer features or features with less functionality. When looking at database literature or talking to a sales representative, be sure what you are reading or being told applies to the version of the database you plan to evaluate.

Understanding Database Features

The following features are just some of the issues to consider when appraising a database. Some are available in the base model of a database and some require an enhanced version. Feature sets vary from vendor to vendor and from version to version.

Some of the features we will look at are

- Database concurrency control
- Transaction support
- Data types support
- Custom data type definitions
- ANSI compliance
- Views
- Data constraints

By knowing which features you need, you can save yourself some money by not buying more database than you need. Neat features are nice, but if you don't need them there is no reason to pay the premium they require.

Database Concurrency Control

In a multi-user environment, a database must have a way to ensure data integrity when multiple users try to access the same data concurrently. That is, the data must be accurate and complete at all times. If a database is running on a powerful multi-processing platform, database operations are started and stopped as the operating system devotes the central processing unit (CPU) to each process in turn.

Under a multi-tasking environment, many different processes seem to be running at the same time, but in reality, each process is run only for a few milliseconds at a time before giving way to another process. A computer CPU can only run one process at a time, so switching between processes enables many users to work on one machine while making it seem like each user has his own computer. The operating system decides what priority to give to processes and when to give them CPU time based on complex scheduling algorithms.

In this environment, it is unavoidable that one database process will be interrupted before it finishes and another process is allowed to run. It too might be interrupted before finishing and yet another database process allowed to run, before the CPU gets back to running the original process. This is unavoidable and is one of the primary reasons some form of database locking is so important. A *lock* prevents other database processes from accessing a piece of data until the first process is finished altering the data.

If all of these concurrent database processes are working with different data, there is no problem. If they are working with data that overlaps, however, and the database has no form of data locking, severe problems can arise. Consider the following example.

A Database Locking Example

A toy manufacturer has a database containing information about all the toys they make. Among the information included is the toy type, the age range it appeals to, and the price. Three different processes, begun by different users, affect a large portion of the database (see fig. 4.4).

1. Process number one is an SQL update statement intended to lower the price on puzzles that are produced for children age three and under. The

first process runs long enough to lower a hundred prices before the operating system interrupts it and starts the second process.

2. The second process is an SQL insert statement adding a new product line of puzzles based on popular cartoon characters. The second process adds 20 new puzzles to the database before the operating system stops it and starts process three.

3. Process three is an SQL update statement launched to change the target age on cartoon puzzles from three to six to ages four to eight. The third process changes the age range on 20 puzzles that have had their price changed, 10 of the new puzzles, and 30 other puzzles before giving way to another process.

Figure 4.4
Database alterations without locking.

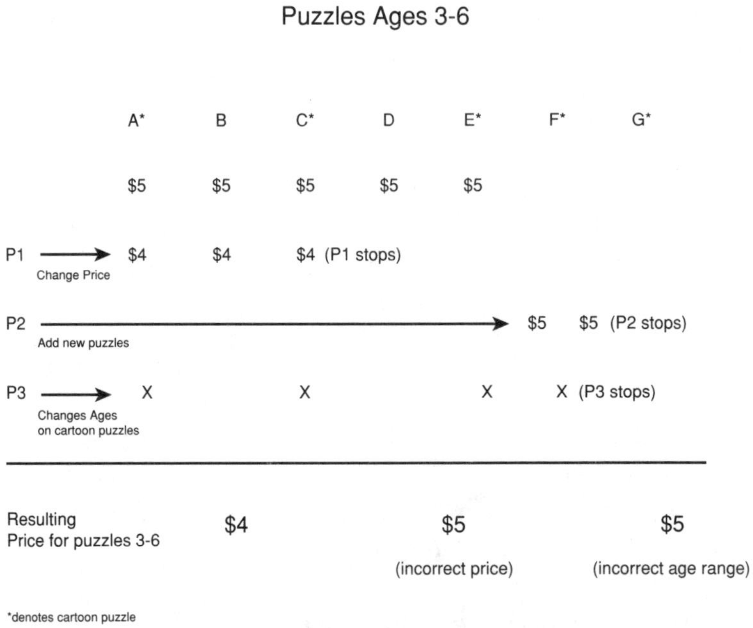

Even if no more processing is done, the database is ruined, due to the lack of a database locking mechanism. Some puzzles have the wrong prices, others have the wrong age group, and the new puzzles could end up with different age groups and prices, depending on when they were inserted into the database and whether the other processes changed their values or not.

Note

To prevent this kind of data corruption from happening, a database uses a *lock* to protect the data. A simple database query does not need to keep other users from accessing the same data, but must prevent other processes from changing or deleting the data until the query has finished retrieving the complete record. This kind of lock is called a *shared* lock because the data can be shared between processes that do not try to alter it, as shown in figure 4.5.

When data is being updated or deleted, however, it is vital to place an *exclusive* lock on the record so that no other database operation can access the record until the first operation is complete. If some other database operation tries to access the locked data, as illustrated in figure 4.6, it either waits until the first operation is complete or returns with an error.

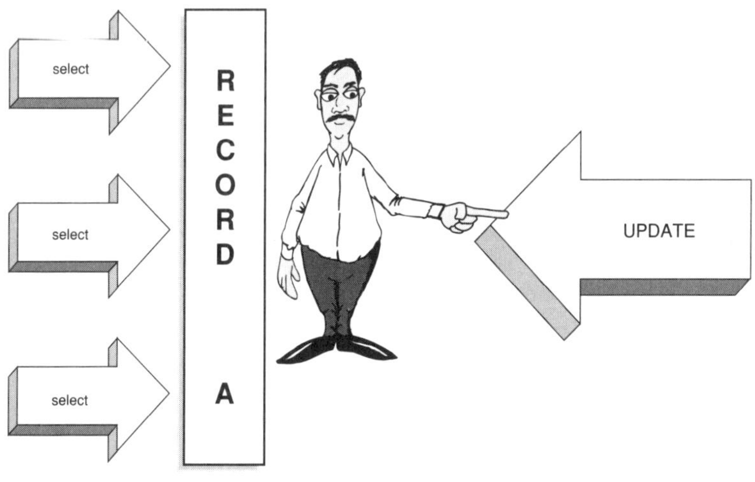

Figure 4.5
A shared database lock.

Figure 4.6
An exclusive database lock.

Database Locking Levels

Locking a record for the duration of a transaction prevents a user from retrieving partially updated data and eliminates the possibility of another transaction updating the data at the same time, which could result in a record with pieces of mismatched information.

A lock guarantees the database will reflect the true state of all database records at all times. This is essential to ensure the integrity of all the data in the database, but if several processes are trying to manipulate the same data, they all can end up waiting a long time for another process to complete.

Different locking strategies can be employed to reduce conflicts between database operations and therefore increase database performance. Some of those methods are

- Table-level locking
- Page-level locking
- Record-level locking

A database *table* contains a collection of related database information. If a database process wants to access a record in a table, some databases lock the entire table, so no other process can access any of the data in the table until the first process is finished. This *table-level* locking (see fig. 4.7) is a very inefficient way to manage data because it locks data that does not need to be protected and forces other database processes to wait until the table is unlocked before they can accomplish what they need to do. This can cause a big performance hit for a database.

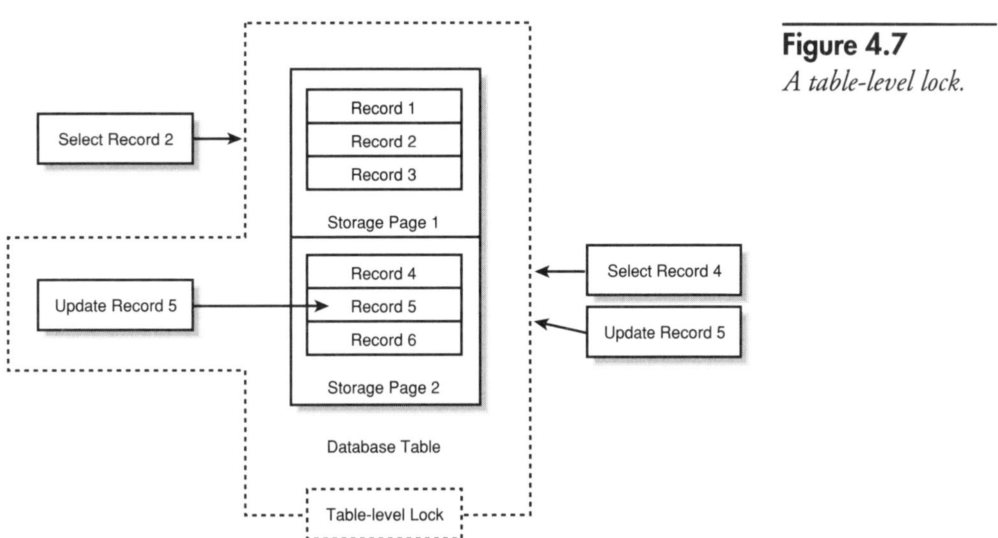

Figure 4.7
A table-level lock.

A more efficient method makes use of the way databases physically store information on the hard disk. Databases store information in units called *pages.* A page can contain multiple records or only part of a record, depending on the size of the information contained in each record. If a database contains many small records, a page will store several records. Some database engines lock the entire page if a single record stored on that page is being changed. Any other process that wants to access a different record on that page is held up, waiting for the first operation to finish. This *page-level* locking can cause a database to slow down (see fig. 4.8).

A different approach is to lock only the single record being changed. That way, other records on the same page are free for other processes to access them, and only processes attempting to access the locked record are held idle. This *record-level* locking lets the database run more processes in less time and increases database performance (see fig. 4.9).

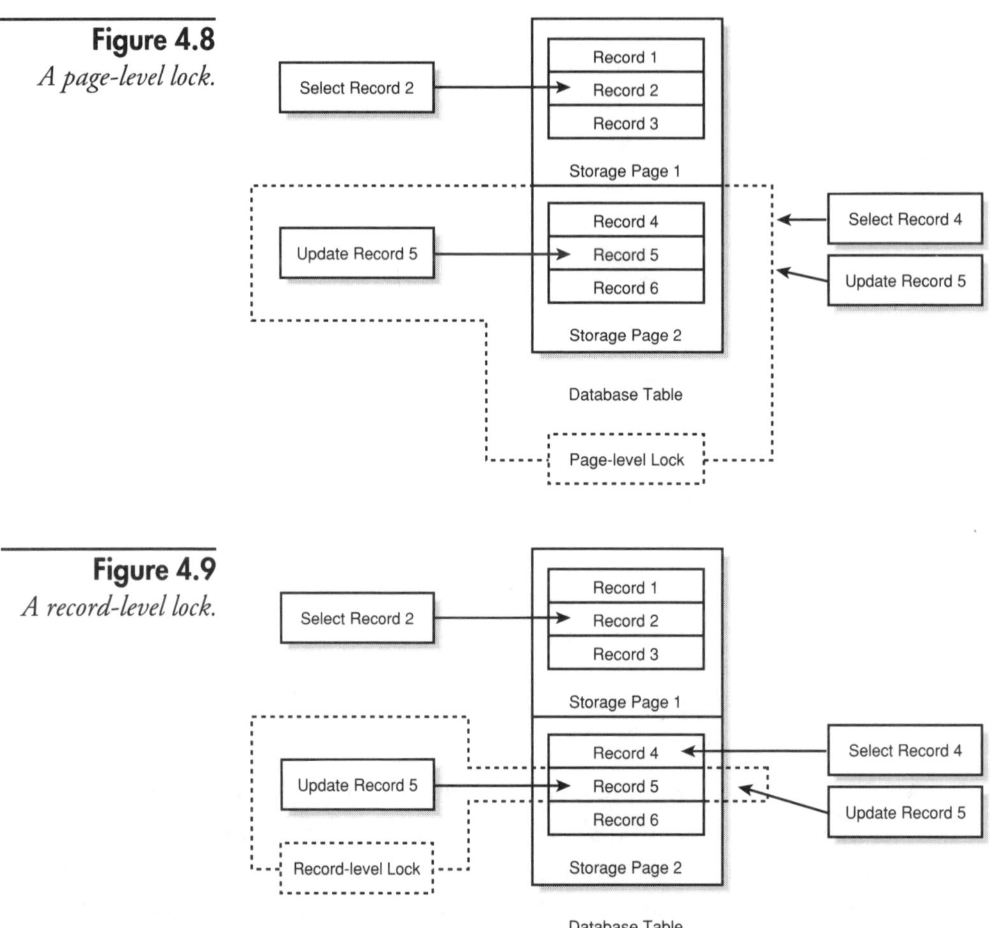

Figure 4.8
A page-level lock.

Figure 4.9
A record-level lock.

If performance is an important issue to you when choosing a database, be sure the database engine uses a finer-grained locking strategy such as record-level locking. This assures you faster performance in a multi-user environment or if you have a lot of automated processes updating the database at the same time.

Transaction Support

Database operations can often update information in many parts of the database at once. Updates need to be performed in a certain order, and if any piece of the operation fails, anything done up to that point is undone so that the database is restored to its original condition. A half-completed database operation can leave data in an unusable state. Although a lock can be placed on a single record by the database engine, if a database operation affects multiple records spread all over the database, traditional locks cannot protect all of the data at once. Another mechanism is needed to protect large amounts of data, even if multiple operations are performed one after the other.

The mechanism used is called a *transaction.* If a transaction is begun and fails before it completes, the changes up to that point are *rolled back* so the data is unchanged. Some databases support *implied* transactions in that every database operation is treated as a transaction that can be rolled back.

Other databases also support *user-defined* transactions so a user can specify where to begin a transaction and where to end it. If a transaction begins and has a problem at any point before the end, all changes are rolled back. This enables a user to execute multiple database commands and change data anywhere in a database with the same protection offered by traditional types of locking.

Consider, for example, the toy database mentioned in the section "A Database Locking Example." The three transactions to perform on the toy database are the following:

1. Add a new line of puzzles using cartoon characters.
2. Change the target age on cartoon puzzles from 3–6 to 4–8.
3. Lower the price on puzzles targeted at age 3 and under.

The three transactions should be performed in the order listed, as demonstrated in figure 4.10. If 2 is done before 1, the new puzzles will have the wrong target age on them. If 3 is done before 2, some cartoon puzzles will be sold at the wrong price. However, just performing the three actions in the right order does not protect against the failure of one of the actions.

If a single one of the listed actions fails, but the other two complete, the toy database will be incomplete and contain inaccurate data. By identifying all three actions as a single transaction, however, all three actions must process through completely *and* in the proper order. If one fails, any changes made by preceding actions will be rolled back so the accuracy of the database is protected.

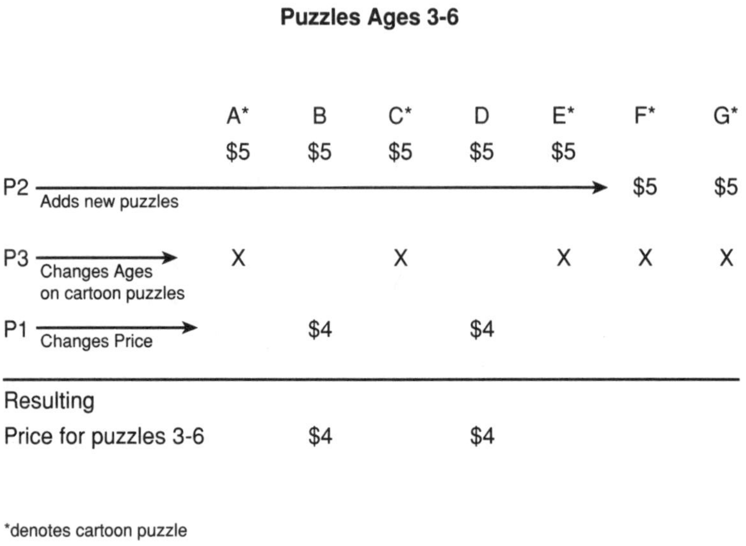

Figure 4.10
A user-defined transaction.

If you plan to execute database transactions as large jobs that will change a significant portion of the database, or if you will perform multiple database commands where one operation depends on the results of the preceding command, be sure the database supports user-defined transactions. This preserves the integrity of your database and provides you with a safe way to restore data to its original state if something unforeseen goes wrong.

Data Types Support

Not all of the information in a database is of the same type. There are character strings of various lengths, integers, floating point numbers of arbitrary accuracy, and many other types of data, as detailed in the following list.

- **Varchar.** There are several variations of the character data type. One modified form is *varchar,* which is a variable-length character string. Some databases require you to designate the length of a character string when you define the database, meaning you have to make the string definition as big as the largest string you will store in the database. If most of the character strings are short and only a few are of the maximum length, this can waste storage space in the database. A varchar data type enables you to store strings of varying length so only the minimal amount of database space is used.

- **Text Field.** Another form of the character data type is a *text field.* This data type is used for large collections of characters such as descriptions or comments. Text fields store characters in blocks instead of individual characters. Some databases enable you to use variable-length text fields, and others require you to define a maximum size.
- **Integer, Smallint, and Tinyint.** The integer data type has several variations as well. A typical integer occupies four bytes of database storage. A byte is the amount of storage needed to store a single character. Numerical data is stored differently than character data, but a byte is the minimum amount of space that can be allocated.

  If you have integer data whose value will not exceed the range from –32,767 to +32,768, it might be beneficial for a database to support the *smallint* data type, which is stored in two bytes. This would reduce the storage requirements for numerical data. If your numbers do not exceed 255, some databases support the tinyint data type, which is stored in a single byte.
- **Real and Float.** The *real* data type is similar to the *float* data type, but real numbers are stored in four bytes, while floating point numbers are stored in eight bytes. The amount of storage dictates the precision of a numerical data, including the number of decimal places and the size of the exponent.
- **Money, Date, Datetime, and Binary/Image.** Other data types include *money*, which is used to store monetary values; *date*, which stores month, day, and year values; and *datetime*, which includes time values along with the date information.

  Another useful data type is the *binary* or *image* data type, which is often referred to as a *Binary Large Object* (BLOB). If you have data that is of binary type such as gif images or sound files, this is a way to store them in a database in their native format.

Each data type has limitations on the values it can store, the precision of the data, the format of the data, or the size of the information it can contain. Some of these values are determined by the architecture of the computer the database runs on. Others are limits imposed by the database engine itself. If you have special data requirements, look carefully at the data types supported by a database as you perform your evaluations.

Custom Data Type Definitions

The data types provided by a database are sufficient for the large majority of database applications. In the rare case that no conventional type can do what you want, there is always the BLOB type that can take almost any kind of data, even though BLOB data usually requires special processing before storing and after retrieving.

If none of these data storage types can handle your special data, some databases provide a mechanism to define your own. This might involve combining several conventional types into a combination type, or actually defining a new type of data complete with rules of use and operators that will process the data for you like any other kind of data.

The design of custom data type definitions is an area where object-oriented databases offer many benefits. An *object* can be any part of a database or any combination of pieces that appear to the user as a seamless database component. Defining an object can greatly simplify dealing with multiple pieces of a database. The data object handles a lot of the operations that would normally be the programmer's responsibility when using an ordinary database.

If you have special data types or special data processing needs, you might want to consider evaluating an object-oriented database or a relational database that supports objects. The object paradigm is the newest frontier in database technology and offers many exiting opportunities that are not possible with traditional databases.

ANSI Compliance

The *American National Standards Institute* (ANSI) is involved in an ongoing attempt to define a standard SQL database language. ANSI itself does not create the standard but provides an organization for those interested to define the standard themselves. A critical idea behind ANSI standards is the partics interested in using the standard are the ones who have the input into defining the standard.

Many database vendors are involved in trying to establish a single standard version of the SQL language. In theory, the purpose is to make sure a database application designed for one database can be ported to another with minimum effort because the SQL statements used for one database should be exactly the same for any other.

In practice, this turns out not to be the case. Many features of SQL are shared by all databases, but some vendors have defined their own proprietary *extensions* to SQL that are not portable. This is not necessarily a bad thing because the extensions are often the most useful part of the SQL language offered by a database.

The ANSI SQL standard defines the command set to be included, the command parameters that determine what a command can do, and how each command should work. If a database offers a feature not covered by the standard, extensions have to be developed to use the added features. This allows database vendors to be innovative and develop new services for their database engines, but it prevents them from being fully ANSI-compliant.

Some forms of transaction, for example, are not part of the ANSI standard. Implied transactions are standard SQL, but the kind of transaction that allows a programmer to combine several SQL commands into a single transaction is not. Some data types supported by many databases are not part of the ANSI SQL standard. Varchar, BLOB, and datetime data types are not part of the standard.

Many government agencies, as well as some private organizations, require any database work done for them to be done under the ANSI standard. There are several levels of ANSI compliance, and not all databases adhere to the same level. Some database engines give you the option to create an ANSI-compliant database or not, as you wish.

If part of your database strategy involves multiple databases or requires strict adherence to the ANSI SQL standard, be sure to determine to what extent the database engine adheres and deviates from the standard before making your choice.

Views

Not all users want or need to see all the data contained in a database. The information stored in the database might cover a variety of different functional aspects, and users might only be interested in using a portion of the data.

A *view* is an alternative way of looking at data in a database. You can use a view to limit the data a person is able to see, or to present the data in a different way depending on the user's purpose in looking at the data. Views can also keep you from having to maintain several different databases by keeping all of your data in one place and defining different views to display it.

A view is transparent to the user. As far as the person looking at the data is concerned, what they see is the complete database. If they enter new information or update existing data, the only parts of the database they have access to are those defined by the view.

As an example, consider a hospital database that contains information about patients, doctor and nurse schedules, a medical supply inventory, and so on. One view would be designed for the head nurse to see all of the schedule information so she can make sure the patients have adequate care. Physicians would use another view to keep track of patients and the medications they have been given. The hospital pharmacy would need a view to keep track of the amount of medication they have in stock. The three views are shown in figure 4.11.

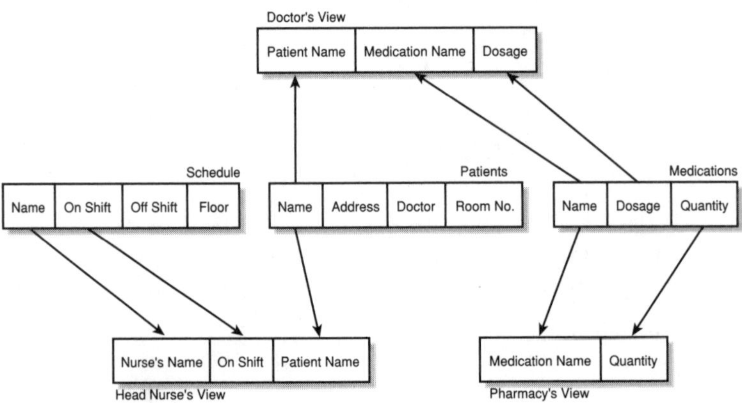

Figure 4.11
Three views from the same set of database tables.

All of the information would be stored in a single database because parts of it need to be available to different groups of people, but by using views to screen out superfluous information, the users get the data they need and aren't bothered with information they don't care about.

If your database will be used by diverse groups of people who are interested in different pieces of the database, or if you want to restrict the information available to any group, look for the ability to use views in the database you choose.

Data Constraints

There are many different ways to constrain data. You can specify a *domain* of values the data must belong to, such as orange, apple, or peach. Or you can create a *range* of values the data must be contained in, such as from 50 to 100. The value of the specified data must adhere to these constraints, or the database will not allow the data to be inserted. Any attempt to do so will cause an error.

Another type of constraint can be enforced when the value of one data element depends on another data element. It is called a *referential* constraint because one element refers to the value of another. As an example, consider a payroll database that contains employee information used to calculate salary, income tax, annual vacation accrued, and so on.

In order to pay an employee, the worker must have a Social Security number (SSN). A constraint can be enforced that requires a paycheck to have an associated SSN before it can be entered into the database. Another constraint can be enforced that requires the associated SSN to pre-exist in the database, or the entire paycheck information will be rejected. This can prevent data-entry errors and bogus SSNs from being entered into the database.

If the accuracy of your data is of vital importance, or you need to prevent the occurrence of simple typographical mistakes over the course of thousands of transactions, data constraints should be a feature of the database you eventually use.

When comparing the features of one database to another, and trying to decide which properties best suit your database needs, keep in mind that the previously mentioned features are only a small set of what might be available. Weigh the benefits of one set of features against another, together with the corresponding price tags. By careful evaluation, you can receive the best value for your money and obtain a database that will serve your needs for many years to come.

Choosing a Computer Platform to Host Your Database

Choosing database features is one way to determine how powerful a database you get for your money, but the computer the database runs on is a big factor in how well your database performs. Databases from the same vendor that are designed to run on different computer hardware cannot offer the same functionality from platform to platform because of the inherent limitations of each type of computer architecture and the operating system which is running on it.

Although the brand name may be the same on different database versions from the same vendor, the underlying database engine is not. When trying to decide the level of hardware support you require to meet your database needs, always remember that the more powerful the computer platform, the more powerful the database server will be as well.

Choosing an Operating System

For personal computers, the operating system is the single most important factor in determining the possible power of a database running on a PC. From the severe limitations of plain DOS, up through Windows 3.x, Windows 95, OS/2, and Windows NT, the capabilities of the operating system increases, and so the power of a database will be able to increase as well.

There are also several versions of Unix for the PC platform whether commercial, such as SCO Unix, or free, such as Linux and FreeBSD. Each of these increases the capabilities of the PC architecture, but the products available for these operating systems are limited.

The Macintosh platform is comparable in power to a PC running Windows 95 or OS/2, but again, the products available are limited.

Powerful Unix machines running SunOS, Solaris, HP-UX, AIX, IRIX, or another flavor of Unix are the platforms of choice for large databases running with a full set of features. Naturally, the capabilities of the platform cost more than a PC or Macintosh, but for running full-featured database engines on a large network, there is no other choice at present.

It is possible to run a database on a Unix platform and use cheaper machines such as PCs to access the data. Most database vendors offer client software that runs on other platforms and gives you access to your data from many different machines and operating systems. This can be an inexpensive way to provide multi-user access to a full-featured Unix database.

Using Multi-CPU Computers

The use of multiple CPUs in a single computer—a feature that was limited to Unix platforms until recently—can dramatically increase database performance. Multiple CPUs enable a computer to execute several processes at once, which increases the performance of all the programs running on the computer (see fig. 4.12). Most of the large commercial database engines have support for multiple CPU support. Informix, for example, has designed its top-end database servers to be as scaleable as the hardware on which they run.

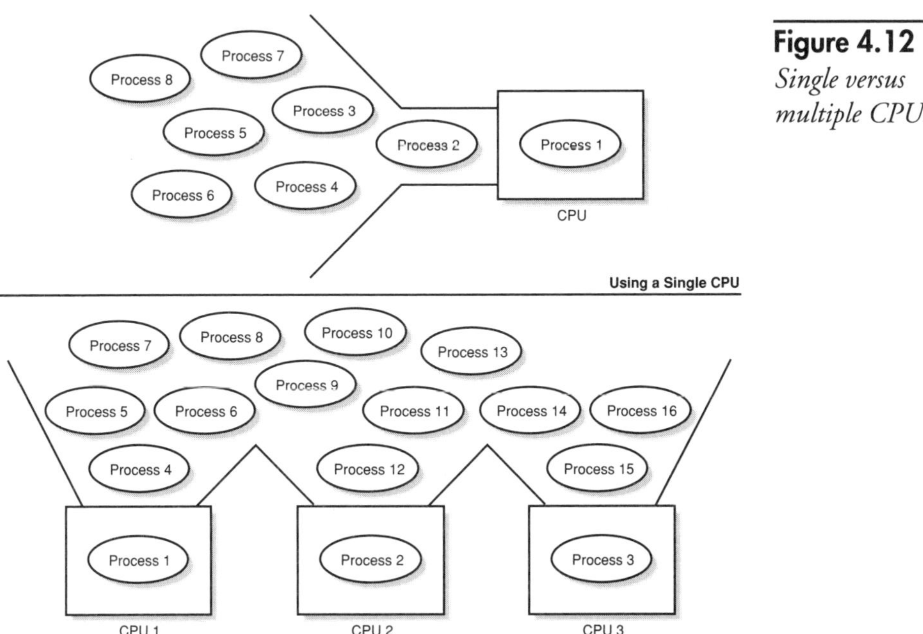

Figure 4.12
Single versus multiple CPUs.

As you add CPUs, Informix enables you to define more "virtual processors" inside the database engine and assign them to a CPU. In this way you can have a data indexing CPU, a query CPU, and a CPU dedicated to other database tasks such as sorts, scans, and joins. If you have a computer with 64 processors, you can designate multiple CPUs to each task. Processing multiple database transactions at the same time is as fast as it gets.

Personal computers have begun to move into the multi-CPU arena with machines running Intel's Pentium CPU, and are further closing the performance gap between PCs and Unix machines with the arrival of the Intel Pentium Pro processor. A multi-CPU personal computer offers an attractive price to performance ratio for a high-performance database server.

New database technologies that take advantage of every advance in computer hardware provide you with the ultimate in performance and can handle enormous amounts of data. If your needs are more modest, find a database that does what you want, but always keep an eye to the future and how your database needs might grow.

Determining Your Data Storage Needs

Another thing to consider when choosing a database is not only *what kind* of data you plan to store, but also *how much* data you plan to store. Even a modest database engine can handle upwards of two gigabytes of data, but if your data ranges into the billions of records, storage space becomes a big issue.

Some things to consider when deciding the type and amount of data you have to store are

- Native hard drive controllers
- SCSI controllers
- Data mirroring
- Optical storage

For PC-based databases, the native hard drive controller present on most PC motherboards will only control at most four hard drives. Even at three gigabytes of storage per hard drive, this is an inescapable upper limit on data storage space because when your hard drives fill up, you cannot just add more.

A different type of controller is the *Small Computer Systems Interface*, more commonly referred to as a SCSI (pronounced *scuzzy*) controller. A SCSI controller is the standard on Unix and Macintosh machines and can be installed in most PCs. SCSI controllers can handle up to seven devices each, and multiple controllers can be used at one time. As long as your computer hardware has the capacity to hold another controller, this gives you a lot of storage potential.

Extra hard drives can also be used to *mirror* data on more than one drive. If the database engine supports data mirroring, the data can be written to two different hard drives for safety. If one hard drive fails, the database switches automatically to the other (see fig. 4.13). When the original drive is returned to service, the database will update the data on the new or repaired hard drive to match the mirrored drive. When the new drive is completely updated, the database switches back to the original and continues to mirror the data on the alternate drive.

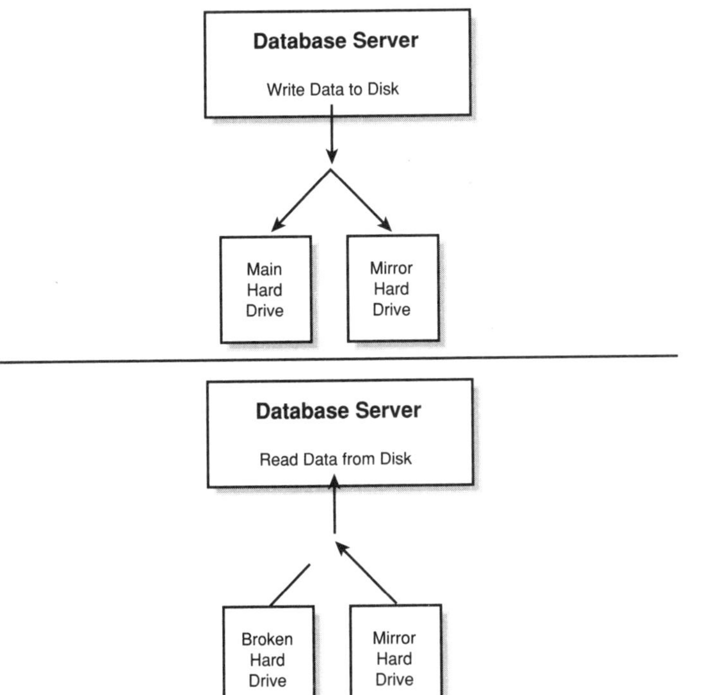

Figure 4.13
Data mirroring.

For truly enormous amounts of data, hard drives are far too expensive to use if you need terrabytes of storage. In this case, optical storage would be a good mass storage system. Optical disks can be removed when full, and, being virtually indestructible, make excellent archive agents.

When choosing a database, it is easy to focus all of your attention on the database engine itself. Although the database itself deserves careful evaluation, don't forget other essentials such as having enough storage space to contain all of your data, and enough extra space to perform database tasks that require temporary space.

Machine Capacity

When planning for a database, the computer hardware on which the database server will run is an item deserving careful consideration. It has been mentioned before that a database can only do as much as the hardware will allow. Some hardware items that deserve special consideration follow:

- The computer CPU
- Computer memory
- Input and output bandwidth
- Network capacity

The computer CPU is what does all of the database transaction processing, and the more powerful it is, the better your database will perform. If you have multiple CPUs and your database supports that type of architecture, you will be satisfied with the database performance. If you are using your grandmother's old 80286 PC, however, and you start to process two million rows of data, you might as well settle in with a good book and have your mail held until you emerge from hibernation because you won't be seen for a while.

Powerful computers cost more, but that is because they do more work in a shorter time. Today's computers work at astonishing speeds, and cven a modest CPU can do wonderful things. If you are investing in a good database, don't scrimp on the hardware.

The single most beneficial thing you can do for a database engine is provide it with more computer memory, or RAM. Databases are notorious memory hogs. If a database does not have enough memory to complete a transaction, it begins to use the hard disk. As fast as new hard drives are, they are no match for the speeds at which computer memory can run. By significantly increasing the amount of RAM a database has to work with, the performance will increase astronomically.

Computer Input and Output Devices

An often overlooked item is the input and output (I/O) hardware the computer uses to read data from and write data to the hard drives. Input and output is the slowest thing a computer does. If the CPU and RAM have to stop and wait to get something from the hard drive, the best CPU and all the RAM in the world cannot make the computer run any faster.

One way to improve I/O performance is by *load balancing* the hard drive controllers. Pieces of a database can be placed on separate hard drives, and the hard drives can be managed by separate controllers, if the computer has multiple hard drive controllers. By accessing the most heavily used parts of the database with separate hard drive controllers the I/O speed of a computer can be increased enormously.

Another possible performance bottleneck related to I/O speed is the capacity of the network the database server machine runs on. Getting the data to and from the database can slow to a crawl on a heavily loaded network.

There are a couple of ways to work around this, however:

- One solution is to put more than one network card in the database server machine if the operating system can handle multiple network connections. This spreads the data transfers across several networks instead of hammering on a single one, reducing the time users spend waiting for a response from the database.

- Another solution to a network bottleneck is to install fiber-optic cable and high-speed network cards. Fiber optics can process data at many times the speed of ordinary ethernet networks. This will take care of your network transport needs for a long time to come. Figure 4.14 compares networking methods.

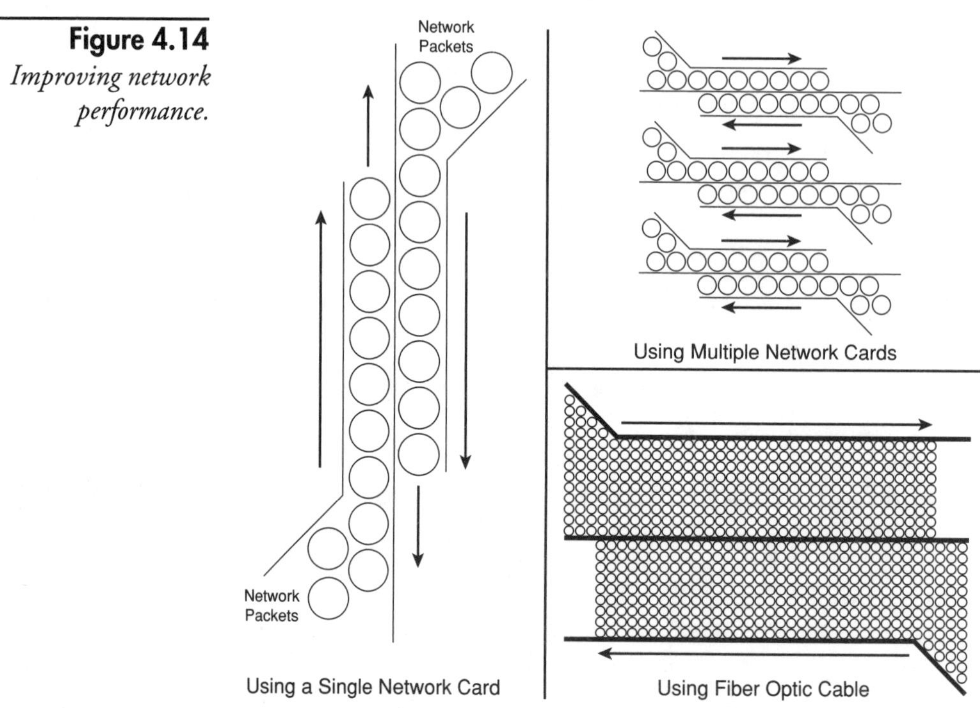

Figure 4.14
Improving network performance.

The computer hardware your database runs on will determine the sophistication of the database engine you can run, and the speed at which transactions are processed. Proper hardware configuration and ample capacity for your data and for database operations will determine how successful your overall database strategy is. Do not save a few dollars now and regret it later.

Determining the Database Load

As you decide on the computer and the database to use, there is another issue to consider—the number of users who will require access to the database. More users require more powerful hardware to handle the increased user load, but that is not the only consideration.

Big commercial database servers might be able to support a large number of users, but only if you buy the right to have a lot of simultaneous users connected to the database. A basic database server might be configured for eight users, and anyone who attempts to connect to the database after eight connections are established will be denied access until a connection is freed. For more users to connect to the database, you have to purchase more user licenses.

If your users make one connection to the database and stay connected all day, there is no way around buying more user licenses. However, if your database applications are designed to connect to the database, get or update data, and disconnect, the number of simultaneous users drops considerably. Using a Web browser as a database front end falls into the latter category.

A few user licenses will support far more people if the connections are of short duration. A connection may be denied occasionally, but trying again will succeed.

The database load caused by a large number of simultaneous users is only one issue. Another is the number of hours a day the database will be in use. While users are accessing data, it is a bad idea to run big batch jobs that change huge amounts of data and run for several hours. When a four-hour job starts, the lights dim, the building shakes, and any user unfortunate enough to be logged into the database can take a nap until the database is available again.

There are some database maintenance activities that are best done outside of business hours, such as backing up the database to tape, or running reports for the marketing department that determine the demographics for every customer from Virginia. Activities such as these are very processing intensive, and can soak up most of the database resources.

When you estimate the user load that will be placed on your database, determine whether the access will be constant or intermittent, and be sure to plan light usage hours for database maintenance. No database can run at full speed forever.

Interfaces Available for a Database

Just putting information into a database is not good enough. You must have a useful way to search the information and get back what you want. A command-line database interface provided by the vendor is adequate for typing in simple SQL commands and getting back a few rows of results, but for more complicated programming and formatting the output, a command-line interface simply will not suffice. See Chapter 5, "Database Interfaces," for more information.

If you plan to develop a front end to the database, a graphical user interface (GUI) will provide the easiest interface to work with, and the database users will thank you. Regardless of the type of front end used, the database server must have some kind of programming interface to access the database from an external program.

One type of programming interface is the *application programmer interface* (API). In short, an API is a collection of functions a programmer can use to make a database do things. The API provides a way to open connections to the database, send and receive data, and perform almost any other database operation. An API enables a front end application to interact with a database server at an intimate level that provides better performance.

Another method of writing a database front end program is to use a fourth-generation language (4GL) that provides extensions to an existing programming language such as C, Fortran, or Cobol. The extensions include commands that manage the database connections, enable you to construct SQL commands, and process data returned from the database, all without requiring you to learn how to use an API. The 4GL code is translated into whatever programming language you use, and then a regular compiler creates the executable program.

Some vendors have either developed their own set of builder tools or acquired a company that produces builder tools for their database. Builder tools are exactly what they sound like: tools to make building database applications easier. They are graphically oriented and are far easier to use than an API or a 4GL. They also cost more. Builder tools can cut application development by half or more when used by experienced programmers. In some cases, the builder tools can create applications that can be easily ported to other computer platforms and operating systems, allowing you to access the database from several types of computers.

Whatever method you choose to develop your database interface, it is important for the target database to provide you with some way to interact with it at a sophisticated level. Simple transactions can accomplish a lot, but more complex processing requires a more complex interface. Choose one that will leverage your existing programming language and give you an easier way to use your database.

Choosing Third-Party Support

No matter how good a database is, the vendor cannot develop all the software everyone will need for the database. There is a thriving market for third-party add-on and customization tools for any commercial database engine, and for many shareware ones.

If you have the resources to hire contractors to develop applications for you, or if your Information Services (IS) department is big enough to develop your own, this is not a consideration for you. If you have more modest means, however, the availability of third-party support is of substantial importance.

Most database vendors are continually forming alliances with hardware and software vendors to assure their customers wide support within the computer industry. Research the industry partners a database vendor has allied with to get an idea of what hardware platforms receive favored status by the database vendor, and which third-party software developers are focusing their efforts on a particular database.

If a hardware vendor is an industry partner, new database products will probably be developed for that hardware platform first, and database upgrades and maintenance patches might be issued to customers using the allied platform first.

If a software developer is allied with a database vendor, look at the products the developer has produced in the past. If they are of good quality and well-respected in the industry, the new software products targeted at a particular database could make your life easier. Just don't forget to check licensing fees and the added expense of a software maintenance agreement, as well as limits on the number of users the software will support.

Determining the Level of Server Administration Required

Database server administration is not limited to watching for the database to crash and restarting it. If this is a full-time job for your administrators, get another database. Database administration starts with database design and implementation and continues through periodic checks for data integrity, performance tuning, error-log monitoring, and many other activities, such as the following:

- Managing user accounts
- Managing database resources
- Monitoring database performance
- Allocating new storage space
- Transporting data between databases
- Performing database backups and restorations

Some database administrators (DBA) prefer to have a few user accounts created in the database and allow users to share the accounts based on the access level assigned to them. Other DBAs assign each user a unique user account in the database and assign access levels individually. Either method requires time to set up the accounts and remove old accounts for departing users. Some sort of automated account-administration program can greatly reduce the amount of time spent working on user accounts, and can help eliminate data entry errors.

A single database server can support many different databases running on the same computer. Doing so, however, increases the amount of administration needed. Different databases are usually dispersed to their own storage devices, and ensuring each database has enough room in temporary storage to perform calculations and other database processes can be a time-consuming issue.

Before choosing a database, check into the level of database administration tools provided by the vendor. Well designed monitoring tools can save you endless hours of hunting for the cause of problems, and can help DBAs catch potential problems before they occur. By intelligently using monitoring tools, your DBAs can reduce costly down time and bring a database back online faster by solving problems more quickly.

Databases from different vendors have their own mechanisms by which new storage space is added or changed. They also provide support for different storage mediums. The ease with which new hard drives or optical drives can be added for the database server to use is an important consideration. Thumbing through a database manual looking for some combination of arcane commands while your database fills up is a gut-churning experience. Adding new storage space should be simple and fast.

Data Portability

When migrating from one database to another or transporting data from the production server to the development server, a database should provide a way to offload data into a file that can be read by any database server (see fig. 4.15). Data dumps and loads should be easy and painless. No one wants to use a cantankerous database engine that requires data to be in some quirky format before it will be accepted. A DBA has more important things to do.

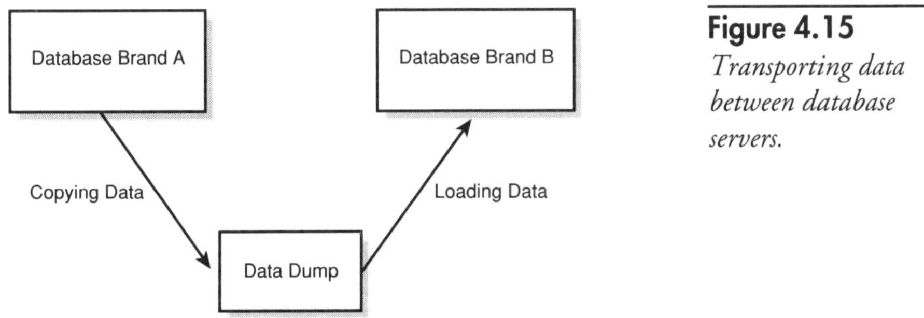

Figure 4.15
Transporting data between database servers.

The usual format is to dump the data from each table into a separate file, with some sort of delimiter symbol inserted between pieces of data. Data dumped from one database should be in a format that can be loaded into another with no changes.

Some database engines dump their data in a proprietary format that can only be read by a database from the same vendor. This can cause a DBA to have a huge headache if you want to move your data from one vendor's database to another vendor's database. A database that uses a proprietary data dump format should be avoided.

Backing Up a Database

The single most important function of a DBA is to develop a comprehensive backup strategy and perform either full or partial database backups on a daily basis. The single most neglected function of a DBA is performing backups. If you were to have a single database crash and discover that the most recent backup was made two days before the latest marketing campaign, which brought in 500 new customers, you would find yourself unemployed.

A common method of performing database backups is to use a five-week system, which could be performed as follows:

- **Daily backups**, also called *incremental* backups, save all changes made since the last daily backup. Daily backups are usually kept onsite. Dailies are made Monday through Thursday.
- **Weekly backups** save the complete database. On the five-week system, as each weekly backup is made, it is stored offsite to protect data against fires or floods on the premises. The last five weekly backups are kept offsite, and as the newest weekly is sent offsite, the oldest weekly is returned to the site to be reused. Weeklies are made on Friday.
- **Monthly backups** save the complete database. As each monthly backup is made, it is stored offsite. Twelve old monthly backups are stored offsite, and the oldest is returned to the site for reuse. Monthlies are made on the last Saturday of each month.
- **Yearly backups** save the complete database. Each yearly backup is stored offsite and old yearly backups are returned to the site for reuse. Yearlies are made at the end of each year.

The purpose of all these backups is to enable you to restore the database to any previous state from the past year. Some people think only the most current data is important, but what happens, for example, if something was deleted from the database and not discovered for several weeks or months? By keeping several weekly and monthly backups, you can pinpoint the missing data and restore it as needed, even if it was deleted a year ago. A comprehensive backup plan is an essential part of database administration. An example of a five-week system is shown in figure 4.16.

	Sun	Mon	Tues	Wed	Thurs	Fri	Sat
Week 1		Daily 1	Daily 2	Daily 3	Daily 4	Weekly 1	Monthly 1
Week 2		Daily 1	Daily 2	Daily 3	Daily 4	Weekly 2	
Week 3		Daily 1	Daily 2	Daily 3	Daily 4	Weekly 3	
Week 4		Daily 1	Daily 2	Daily 3	Daily 4	Weekly 4	
Week 5		Daily 1	Daily 2	Daily 3	Daily 4	Weekly 5	Monthly 2

Figure 4.16
A five-week database backup system.

The most common backup medium is magnetic tapes, which can vary in capacity from a few hundred megabytes to several gigabytes. If you have gigabytes of data to back up to tape, make sure the database engine will support a high-density tape backup machine. No DBA wants to hang around for hours just waiting to change tapes. Making backups too inconvenient might prevent them from happening, which can be a disaster waiting to happen.

Some databases enable you to perform backups and restores on a database-by-database basis, and others require you to back up or restore everything on the server. If only one database develops a problem and has to be restored, it is very time-consuming to reload five databases to temporary space and then copy the data you need into the real database by using SQL select statements. It is even worse to reload all five databases only to discover you just overwrote the data in the other four and you have not backed them up yet. The capability to backup and restore on a database-by-database basis is a real benefit.

A sophisticated backup-and-restore process can make a database administrator's life much easier and can help avert possible disasters. Be sure the backup and restore programs support a wide array of devices in case you want to change from using tapes to using optical drives for your backups. Also look for a tape drive that can handle multiple tapes for making unattended backups of databases that require more than one tape. A sensible backup strategy will pay off many times over, and the easier it is to do, the more confident you can be it will be done.

Determining the Quality of Database Manuals

Nothing separates a good database from a great database like the accompanying documentation. Poorly written manuals can make even a great database impossible to use. It is one thing to have a list of the commands a database engine understands, and another to have extensive, coherent examples of how to use the commands.

A comprehensive set of manuals is essential to manage a large database server. No one person can know everything about the server, no matter how much training she has been through. A quick reference card of the most often used commands is a handy item to have as well. Another useful item is a tutorial manual that offers start-to-finish examples of setting up a database. Any help at all will make database administration that much easier.

It is also much more convenient to have actual books rather than online documentation. Documents on a CD-ROM that use a GUI to display the docs are useless when a DBA is huddled over a VT-100 terminal wondering what error code -540 means. Database manuals are the best place to scribble notes and reminders where you can be sure not to lose them. A CD does not like to be written on.

All of the concepts mentioned in this chapter are meant as a general guide for you to use when evaluating the suitability of a database for your needs. Database vendors offer new products on a regular basis with new features and better performance. By arming yourself with as much knowledge as you can, you can make a more informed decision about which database to choose.

Database Interfaces

This chapter focuses on exactly what a database interface, often called a gateway, *can and cannot do to help you access a database. It is important to know the potential of a tool before you start to use it in order to set realistic expectations for you and your application users.*

These are the main topics covered in this chapter:

- *What do interfaces and gateways do?*
- *Using a database over a network*
- *Using a database interface*
- *Using commercial products*
- *Using freeware or shareware gateways*
- *Supporting software needed*

Please note that there could be some confusing terminology. The software provided by a database vendor to access the database is called an interface. The gateway that connects the Web to your database interface software can also be called an interface. Some gateways require a database-specific module to talk to a database, and the module can be called an interface.

In this chapter, the term *interface* refers to the provided database software, the term *gateway* refers to Web/database connection software, and specific gateway modules are identified as they are used in the gateway software. The common gateway interface provided by HTML is referred to simply as CGI. Hopefully the diagram in figure 5.1 will help eliminate most of the confusion.

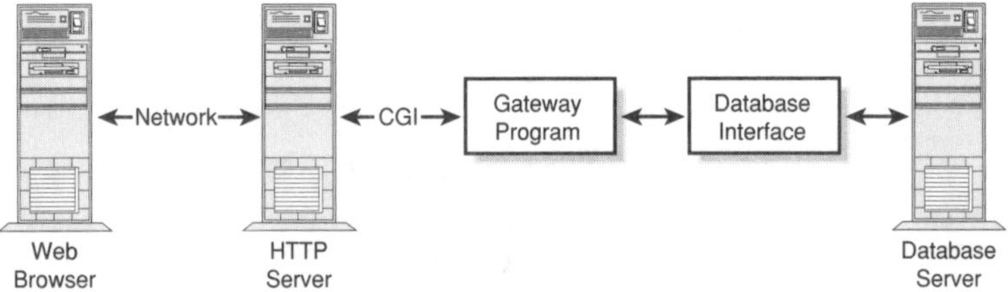

Figure 5.1 *An overview of the pieces required to access a database from the Web.*

Retrieving Database Information

When someone uses a Web browser to access a database, there are several components involved in passing the user query to the database and getting back the results. The action happens as follows:

1. The user calls a gateway program using CGI, usually by clicking on a hyperlink or pressing a button in the Web browser.
2. The Web browser collects the information entered by the user to send to the CGI program.
3. The browser then contacts the HTTP server on the machine where the CGI program resides, asking the server to find the CGI program and pass it the information.
4. The HTTP server checks to see if the requesting machine is allowed to access the CGI program.

5. If the user is allowed access, the HTTP server locates the gateway program and passes the Web browser information to the gateway. Steps 1–5 are shown in figure 5.2.

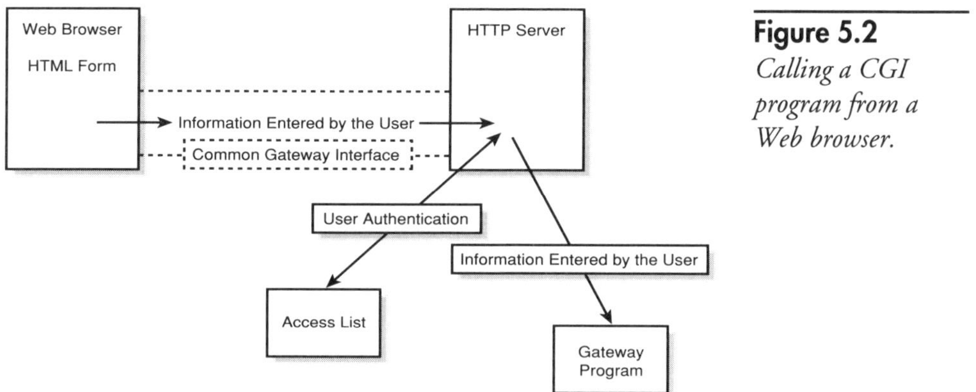

Figure 5.2
Calling a CGI program from a Web browser.

6. The gateway program is executed.

7. First, the gateway processes the passed-in information into a format the database understands.

8. Next, the gateway uses the database module to pass the database query to the database interface.

9. The database interface parses the database query for accuracy.

10. If the interface finds a syntax error in the query, an error message is passed back to the gateway program.

11. The error message is sent to the HTTP server, which sends it back to the Web browser for display to the user, and the process stops here. Steps 6–11 are shown in figure 5.3.

12. If there is no error, the database interface sends the query to the database.

13. The database performs the query and passes back any results to the gateway program, through the database interface.

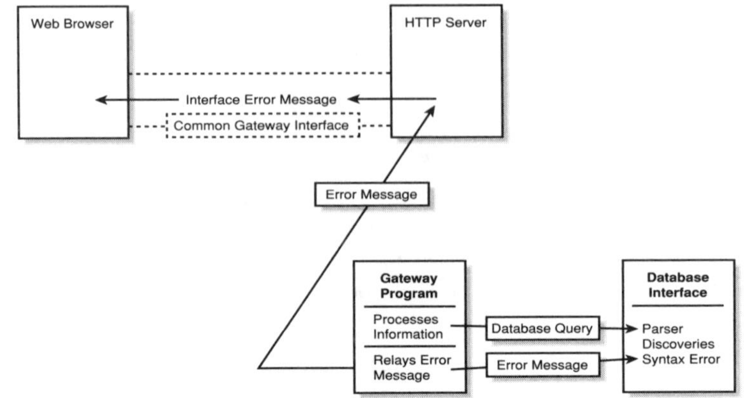

Figure 5.3 *Sending back an error message.*

14. The gateway program formats the results and sends them back through the CGI to the server for relay to the Web browser.

15. The Web browser displays the results. Steps 12–15 are shown in figure 5.4.

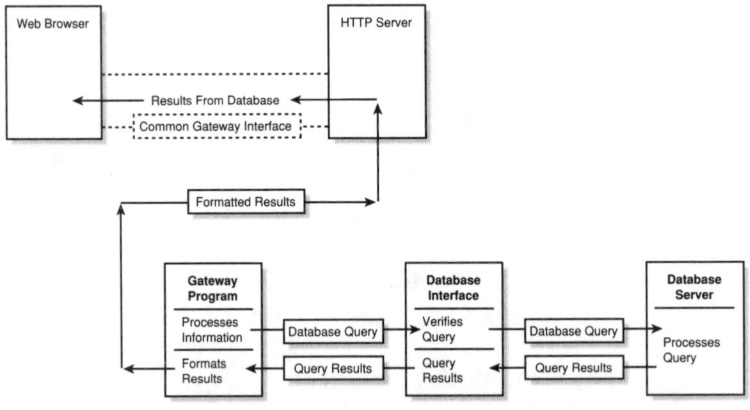

Figure 5.4 *Sending back formatted database query results.*

Despite how the process might sound, it works very smoothly. In many cases, the database module and database interface are integral parts of the gateway software. The module might be a Perl library of subroutines that is parsed as part of the Perl gateway program, or the interface might be a C library that is compiled or linked into an executable gateway program. Although the database module or interface is necessary to provide database connectivity, it does not necessarily exist as a separate program.

When you get to choose an interface, as described in Chapter 7, "Choosing a Database Gateway," you will explore exactly what is needed and how gateways, modules, and interfaces are integrated into a complete system.

If you plan to connect your database to the Web, no matter which gateway product you use—freeware or commercial—most of them will use CGI to send data back and forth between the Web browser and database. Which operating system you use will determine exactly how that is done.

To access a database server running on a Unix platform, for example, there are several options. Freeware and shareware gateways abound for Unix platforms. If you plan to design your own, Perl is a good choice if your database has a command-line interface that will accept commands via standard input. If the added capabilities provided by an API or 4GL are what is needed, using C/C++ for your gateway is a good way to go. If you would rather buy a commercial product, you can find one to support most commercial databases.

For PC or Macintosh platforms, options are more limited because these platforms do not provide the programming freedom present under a Unix operating system. Most databases for these platforms require a proprietary interface that does not provide any way to access the database externally, or they use the *Open Database Connectivity* (ODBC) standard API for database access. Shareware products are rare for these platforms, but several commercial products have arisen to meet the need for Web/database connectivity.

What Do Interfaces and Gateways Do?

Simply put, *interfaces* provide a method to interact with a database. SQL commands that create tables, insert, update, and delete data, return query results, and so on, are passed to the database engine for processing, and the results are passed back. Database vendors can provide interfaces of varying sophistication to meet your needs.

Gateways receive data passed from a Web browser through an HTTP server and convert it into a form the database can understand. The converted data is passed to the database interface and the database executes it. The database results, if any, are returned to the gateway program, which converts the results so the Web browser can display it. The converted results are passed back to the Web browser and are displayed.

A gateway cannot work alone. Database engines are not simple programs, and they require special interface software to talk to the outside world. The gateway requires some sort of channel to talk to the database. This channel is provided by the database interface, which is special software provided by the database vendor. The gateway talks to the interface, which talks to the database.

Exactly how this process works depends on the capabilities of the target database and the type of gateway you use. There are three methods for a Web server to talk to a database engine:

- Using a database without networking capabilities
- Using a database with networking capabilities
- Using third-party networking software

The main consideration in each method is which software is used to handle the network connections for database access from remote computers.

Using a Database Over a Network

Why is it so important to use a network connection? Would it not be easier to have the users on the same machine as the database? Although it would be easier, if the database is relatively large and the number of users is high, performance becomes a big issue. A database server likes to have the total resources of the host computer to itself.

If the database front end is a GUI application, GUIs require a lot of resources such as memory and CPU time. Database performance is directly related to the amount of memory and CPU time the database engine has access to. GUI applications and database servers do not share resources nicely. Some database engines actually "lock" large portions of memory for their exclusive use, preventing any other programs from using the locked memory. This practically requires the database front end applications to run on another machine to give the GUI applications and the database the computer resources they need.

When the database access applications are moved to other machines, this requires some way to access a database across a network. The database queries submitted to the database and the results obtained are passed across the network. This requires software dedicated to handling the information traveling from computer to computer.

Using a Database without Networking Capabilities

In some cases, a database will not have client/server capabilities. A database may be able to handle multiple users at once, but only if the users are on the same machine the database server resides on. Some database vendors offer networking capabilities as an added feature and charge a client licensing fee for every machine that has network access to the database.

In this case, running an HTTP server on the same machine as the database server can alleviate the problem, provided the server machine can handle the double load. As detailed in figure 5.5, this method relies on the Web client and server to provide the networking capabilities.

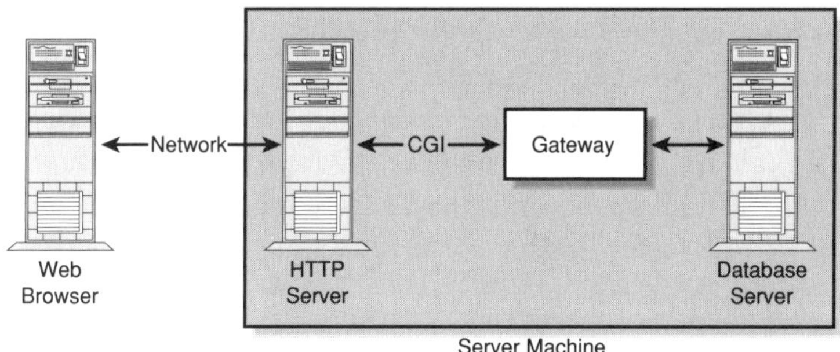

Figure 5.5
Using a database with no networking support.

This method is about as simple as it gets. The HTTP server, CGI programs, and database server all exist on the same machine, giving CGI programs direct access to whatever database interface program you want to use. Database queries and results returned from the database don't travel over the network back and forth to CGI programs, so response time is as good as it can be.

However, this method assumes the Web browsers accessing the data are running on remote machines. If the database is of medium to large size and there are many users, it is definitely *not* a good idea to have the database server, HTTP server, and multiple Web browsers all running on the same machine. This can bring even a powerful machine to its knees.

If you expect a lot of visitors to a Web site, or you have a large amount of data to put on the Web, you will probably end up dedicating a machine to be your server. Most large databases are on a dedicated machine anyway, so if your server can handle the extra HTTP server load, this is the best way to go in most cases.

Even if there currently are machines on your network with client licenses to remotely access the database, the simplicity of this method appeals to a lot of system administrators.

Using a Database with Networking Capabilities

If the target database comes with built-in network capabilities or you have purchased at least one license for remote access, this gives the option of running the HTTP server on a remote machine and accessing the database using the database network software.

Using a database with existing network support presents several options (see fig. 5.6). If the data can be broken into several distinct types, it is a good idea to use a separate HTTP server for each type of data, and even to run each HTTP server on a different machine, if you have the capacity. This reduces the load caused by the HTTP servers and could also reduce bottlenecks on a single node of the network, if the database server machine can serve multiple subnets.

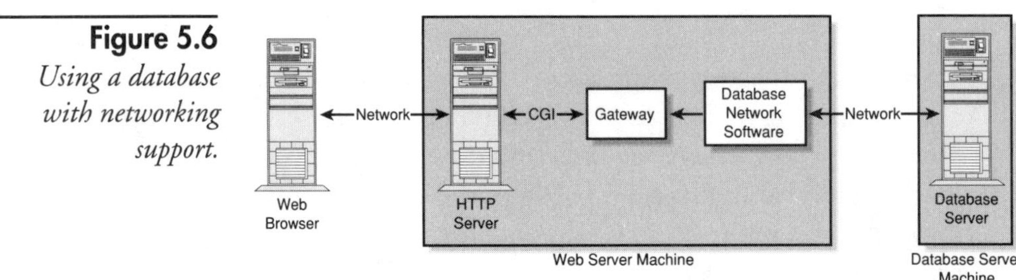

Figure 5.6
Using a database with networking support.

With this method, the CGI programs are located on the same machine as the HTTP server. Many DBAs prefer to have a dedicated machine for the database server to eliminate potential problems with unruly software and to protect their data as much as possible. This method would appeal to them because it moves the HTTP server and CGI programs off the database server machine.

Just remember the database software responsible for network support must be installed on every machine that has access to the database. As mentioned before, this can be expensive due to per-machine licensing fees.

This method also works well if you have more than one database server. A single HTTP server can access multiple database machines through CGI programs, as shown in figure 5.7.

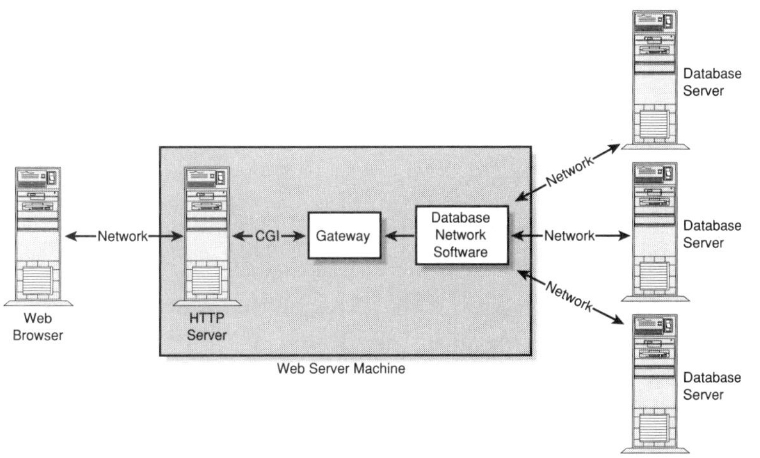

Figure 5.7
Using a Web server to access multiple database servers.

If you can use multiple database servers to lighten the load on any one database, performance can increase dramatically. However, this is only a factor with truly large databases. In most cases, a single database server will handle the load.

Using Third-Party Networking Software

Another way to access a database from a Web server is to use third-party networking software, or even to develop your own. Using software that supports several different databases can offer you the flexibility of talking to databases from different vendors on different kinds of machines (see fig. 5.8).

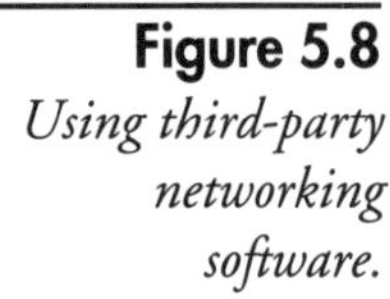

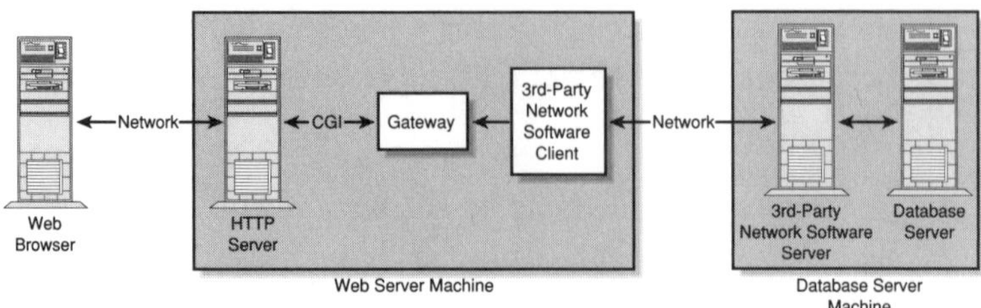

Figure 5.8
Using third-party networking software.

The third-party software must be able to accept database queries from a CGI program on the same machine, pass it over the network to the other half of the network software, submit the query to the database, get the results, and pass the results back over the network and hand them to the CGI program.

In some ways, this functionality is redundant when you consider an HTTP server will do most of what the third-party software does. If you need a way to handle requests for multiple databases, however, using customized networking software as a traffic cop might be the way to go.

As an additional step, the networking software can also be used as database translation software. Database queries can be boiled down to a single set of functions and then no matter what kind of database is used, the programs look the same by using a generic programming interface.

If the networking software is combined with a generic database API, this enables programmers using a single programming interface to submit queries to databases of different kinds. The network/API software translates the queries into database-specific syntax, sends the query over the network to the selected database, and formats the results for relay back to the requesting program.

Using a Database Interface

To use a Web/database gateway, it is necessary to know what kind of interface the database provides. Whether the most simplistic command-line interface or the most sophisticated programming API, the database has to provide some way to get to the data.

> **Note**
>
> The capabilities of your database interface determine the sophistication of your database application. If you choose to use a command-line interface for its simplicity, your application will be limited in what it can do. Command-line interfaces do not allow you to nest database queries or format the database results.
>
> If you choose to use a programming API, on the other hand, your application can do anything the database is able to do, but you will be required to learn how to use the API in your application. The features needed by your database application will determine the interface you use.

Using a database interface requires the user to learn at least a little of the database query language provided by the database vendor. In most cases the language is some flavor of the Structured Query Language (SQL). SQL is a standard query language, but most database vendors have added non-standard extensions to SQL that take advantage of specific features their database offers. This means if you learn SQL for one database, moving to another database can require learning a slightly different syntax or losing some functionality and gaining others.

Using the SQL Language

Although a discussion of the SQL database language is beyond the scope of this book, a brief overview is helpful for understanding some of the examples used in this and other chapters. For more information on SQL, look for New Riders' book, *MSCE Training Guide*, in the Summer of 1996.

SQL (pronounced *sequel*) is used to interact with the database. SQL gives you a way to talk to the database and tell it what to do with your data. There are a host of standard SQL commands, and many databases have their own extensions that differ from other databases, but you can manage almost any database with just the following six SQL commands:

1. **CREATE** creates a new database. Other things can be created, such as tables, indexes, and views. The CREATE command registers a new database with the database server so that new data can be stored.

2. **DROP** destroys a database or elements of it, such as tables, indexes, and views. Once something has been dropped, it cannot be recovered.
3. **SELECT** retrieves selected data out of the database.
4. **INSERT** puts data into the database.
5. **UPDATE** changes data that already exists in the database.
6. **DELETE** removes data from the database.

Each of these commands takes parameters that detail how they behave. As an example, DELETE can be used to remove a single record from the database, or every record in the database. As you can tell, SQL is a powerful language, but can do terrible things to a database in the wrong hands.

For this reason, many database gateways are limited to using the SELECT statement only. This eliminates the possibility of a careless user deleting your database. Gateway products that offer full functionality should also provide some sort of security mechanism to limit who can use commands other than SELECT.

The Command-Line Interface

The command-line interface is the most common and easiest method to use, but it also provides the fewest features. In its simplest form, a command-line interface gives you the ability to enter database query commands and submit them to the database. The results are displayed on-screen, which can be a problem if the results are bigger than your screen.

Following is a representative sample of a command-line interface. The interface shown is *msql*, provided by the shareware database Mini SQL. The database "customer" has already been created, and the command-line interface is being used to create the "customer_info" table.

```
lightspeed:~/msql/bin$ msql customer

Welcome to the MiniSQL monitor.  Type \h for help.
```

```
mSQL > \h


MiniSQL Help!

The following commands are available :-

        \q      Quit
        \g      Go (Send query to database)
        \e      Edit (Edit previous query)
        \p      Print (Print the query buffer)

mSQL > CREATE TABLE customer_info (
    ->   cust_id int primary key,
    ->   first_name char(32),
    ->   last_name char(32),
    ->   middle_name char(32),
    ->   titles char(32),
    ->   address_line1 char(40),
    ->   address_line2 char(40),
    ->   city char(32),
    ->   state char(2),
    ->   zip_code char(10)
    -> )
    -> \g

Query OK.


mSQL > \q
Bye!

lightspeed:~/msql/bin$
```

SQL commands are typed at the prompt, then `\p` tells msql to echo the query, and `\g` tells msql to submit the query to the database. `\q` quits from the interface, and `\e` invokes a text editor to let you make changes to the last command you typed. After you edit your command, you leave the editor and the new command is displayed on the command line, ready to be sent to the database.

Command-line interfaces are commonly used by database administration (DBA) personnel to do routine database administration, such as creating new database tables, inserting a few rows of data, or executing simple queries to get data out of the database. Command-line interfaces are easy to use over a modem line or through a telnet session because they are text-based and require no GUI software, which makes them fast and efficient to use.

Command-line interfaces provided by other databases will differ slightly, but the functionality is the same. You can enter SQL commands, submit them to the database, and use some kind of editor to edit the last command.

Products such as Informix Software's dbaccess take the command-line interface one step further by giving the user a menu-driven interface. Actions are selected from a menu at the top of the screen, which can lead to another submenu of choices or can execute a command. If you prefer the typical text editor to submit SQL commands, there is a menu option to use an editor and create commands for submission to the database. Informix's upgrade to dbaccess called *isql* adds more menu items and form capabilities. Users can create forms for any database table that makes queries, inserts, updates, and deletes much easier than using SQL commands.

Command-line interfaces also have the capability of accepting bulk queries from standard input and emitting the results to standard output. A gateway can make use of this type of database interface by submitting queries via standard input and capturing the results. The query results can be posted as-is to the Web browser, or some minimal amount of processing can be done to format them.

The following is a source code listing of the command file "do_table.sql." Do_table.sql does exactly the same thing as the CREATE command entered in msql from the command line. In addition, it adds a record to the table. (The small arrows indicate the code really exists on a single line.)

```
# Command file for Mini SQL
#
# Command: msql customer < do_table.sql

CREATE TABLE customer_info (
  cust_id int primary key,
  first_name char(32),
  last_name char(32),
  middle_name char(32),
  titles char(32),
  address_line1 char(40),
  address_line2 char(40),
  city char(32),
```

```
  state char(2),
  zip_code char(10)
) \p\g

INSERT INTO customer_info VALUES( 1, 'Jeffrey', 'Rowe', 'Paul',
➥'Webmaster', '1234 Webster Way', NULL, 'Spiderville', 'VA',
➥'123-456-7890')
\p\g
```

A command file is submitted to msql using standard input with this command:

```
msql dbname < do_table.sql
```

`Dbname` is the name of the database the command file should be run against. This command takes the contents of do_table.sql and submits them to the msql interface using standard input. msql reads the commands as if they had been typed on the command line and executes them, one by one.

The results of the command file are printed to standard output as shown here:

```
lightspeed:~/msql/bin$ msql customer < do_table.sql

Welcome to the miniSQL monitor.  Type \h for help.

mSQL >    ->     ->     ->     ->     ->     ->     ->     ->
Query buffer
------------

CREATE TABLE customer_info (
  cust_id int primary key,
  first_name char(32),
  last_name char(32),
  middle_name char(32),
  titles char(32),
  address_line1 char(40),
  address_line2 char(40),
  city char(32),
  state char(2),
  zip_code char(10)
)
[continue]
    ->
```

```
Query OK.

mSQL >     ->     ->     ->
Query buffer
------------
INSERT INTO customer_info VALUES( 1, 'Jeffrey', 'Rowe', 'Paul',
  'Webmaster', '1234 Webster Way', NULL, 'Spiderville', 'VA',
  '123-456-7890')

[continue]
    ->

Query OK.

mSQL >     ->
Bye!

lightspeed:~/msql/bin$
```

The command-line interface works well as a fast, cheap method of accessing a database from the Web. The biggest drawback is the limited ability to format the results for display. Results are returned as a block of text, and, unless the gateway program knows the format, there is little that can be done other than removing leading or trailing lines. Other methods are more complicated, but offer greater flexibility.

Using API Interfaces

Another useful method for accessing a database is to use an application programming interface (API) provided by the database vendor. An *API* is a library of functions that programmers use to write database access programs. In most cases the API recognizes the same SQL statements used by the command-line interface.

The library can be linked into a custom database program to provide direct access to the database. Queries can be constructed ahead of time and presented to the user in a list, or on-the-fly as the program runs, building a query that depends on user input. APIs usually provide access to the data at a lower level than the command-line interface, which makes interface programs using an API faster than submitting bulk transactions through the command-line interface.

Many APIs also contain an extremely useful feature called a cursor. A *cursor* is a data structure that can be used in a program to capture multiple rows of data to be processed one at a time. This enables the programmer to format each row of output, stop processing after a specified number of rows, allow user input as the data is displayed, and so forth. This is distinctly more user-friendly than having to deal with query results as a block of text like the command-line interface gives you.

API programming for different databases works much the same way. A connection is opened to the database engine and a process handle is returned. The *handle* is what identifies a connection to a particular database. Multiple connections can be maintained, and each will have a unique handle.

After the connection is made, queries can be constructed and passed to the database as character strings using a query function. If the query fails, an error code is returned. If the query is successful, another function call can be made to store the returned results in a cursor. Other function calls are used to step through the cursor or to access a particular record directly. After a program has finished processing the data, a function is called to free the memory associated with the cursor, and the database connection is closed.

The following program, msql_api.c, is a simple database access program that uses the Mini SQL API to access data in the customer database, using the customer_info table. The program passes a query string to the database and prints out the results by using a cursor.

```
/*
* msql_api.c - a sample application for using the Mini SQL
* programming API.
 */

#include <stdio.h>
#include <stdlib.h>

/* Needed for the msql API functions and datatypes. */
#include <msql.h>

void main()
{
  m_result *msql_data;  /* an msql cursor for returned data */
  m_row msql_row;       /* a row of data returned from a query */
  m_field *msql_field;  /* a structure of info about a field */
```

```
int result;             /* result returned from function call */
int socket;             /* socket descriptor for db connection */
int numrows;            /* number of rows returned from query */
int numfields;          /* number of fields in a row of data */
int i,j;                /* loop counters */

/* Connect to the database and report an error if necessary */
result = msqlConnect("lightspeed.beowulf.com");

if ( result == -1 ) {
  fprintf(stderr, "Unable to connect to database.\n");
  fprintf(stderr, "  %s\n", msqlErrMsg);
  exit;
}

/* If successful, save the socket descriptor for future use */
socket = result;

/* Select the database to query and report any error */
result = msqlSelectDB(socket, "customer");

if ( result == -1 ) {
  fprintf(stderr, "Unable to find database customer.\n");
  fprintf(stderr, "  %s\n", msqlErrMsg);
  exit;
}

/* Send a query to the database */
result = msqlQuery(socket, "select * from customer_info");

if ( result == -1 ) {
  fprintf(stderr, "Error querying database.\n");
  fprintf(stderr, "  %s\n", msqlErrMsg);
  exit;
}

/* Store the results, if any, in a cursor */
msql_data = msqlStoreResult();

/* Get the number of rows and fields returned */
numrows = msqlNumRows(msql_data);
numfields = msqlNumFields(msql_data);

/* Process each row, field by field */
for (i=0; i<numrows; i++)
{
  fprintf(stdout, "\n");
```

```
    /* Get a row of data */
    msql_row = msqlFetchRow(msql_data);

    for (j=0; j<numfields; j++)
    {
      /* Get information about a field */
      msql_field = msqlFetchField(msql_data);

      /* Print the field name */
      fprintf(stdout, "%15.15s:", msql_field->name);

      /* Determine the type of data in the field and print it */
      switch (msql_field->type)
      {
        case CHAR_TYPE:
          fprintf(stdout, "%s\n", msql_row[j]);
        break;
        case INT_TYPE:
          fprintf(stdout, "%d\n", atoi(msql_row[j]));
        break;
        case REAL_TYPE:
          fprintf(stdout, "%f\n", atof(msql_row[j]));
        break;
      }
    }
  }

  fprintf(stdout, "\n");

  /* Free the memory associated with the cursor */
  msqlFreeResult(msql_data);

  /* Close the connection to the database */
  msqlClose(socket);
}
```

When msql_api is run, it displays the record you entered into the database from your command file in the previous section.

```
lightspeed:~/msql/bin/programs$ msql_api

        cust_id:1
     first_name:Jeffrey
      last_name:Rowe
    middle_name:Paul
         titles:Webmaster
```

```
  address_line1:1234 Webster Way
  address_line2:
           city:Spiderville
          state:VA
       zip_code:12345-6789

lightspeed:~/msql/bin/programs$
```

Some APIs offer a more complicated data structure than the cursor called a descriptor. A *descriptor* is a complicated beast that contains all kinds of information about the data, including the data type, field name, field size, and other pertinent information. Using descriptors, a programmer can query a database without knowing anything about what kind of data will be returned. By using the descriptor information, the data can be identified and processed accordingly.

A lot of databases now offer APIs based on the Open DataBase Connectivity (ODBC) standard. ODBC is important because it is a *standard*, which means an API that declares itself ODBC-compliant must meet certain conditions in relation to how it works. If an API truly meets ODBC standards, programs written to access one database using ODBC should be able to access any other database using the same function calls. This greatly simplifies the task of interacting with multiple databases from different vendors.

Using Commercial Products

There is an old adage that states, "You get what you pay for." This is true among database interfaces as well. Commercial products offer many user-friendly features that make building applications faster and easier, but they don't come cheap.

There are commercial products for constructing database front-end applications, and products are appearing that do the same for constructing gateway programs to use with CGI.

The GUI Interface

These days most users expect some kind of GUI when they use database applications. Using a mouse and text fields, pushbuttons, and menus is far easier than learning SQL and figuring out the underlying structure of the database you want to use so you can reference tables and fields directly.

The same thing applies to designing and constructing a database interface. Database application programmers are used for delving deeply into the database documentation and reading between the lines to figure out how to create database access programs. If GUI tools are available to simplify the process, the programmer's productivity can increase manyfold.

The GUI interface is nice, but GUI-based interfaces have to be developed by programmers who understand the operating system, who know how to incorporate the database API functions with the GUI code, and who know how to develop a new GUI for every different computer that will be used to access the database.

A programmer might know one or two operating systems, but it is rare for any one programmer to know all flavors of Unix, MS Windows, OS/2, and the Macintosh operating system well enough to develop applications under them all. Database vendors have begun to address this cross-platform support issue with builder tools that help programmers port applications to different operating systems.

Builder Tools

To combat the time and expense of developing custom database applications, some database vendors have introduced builder tools that try to automate the development process. By providing users with a selection of controls and text entry fields, prototypes and full-blown applications can be constructed in a fraction of the time it would take to complete a custom application.

In many cases, builder tools can create applications that are more fully integrated with the underlying database functionality, allowing programmers to more fully use the features of a particular database. This locks you into a proprietary scheme that the database vendor controls, but it can maximize the usefulness of your database interface applications.

An ideal product would depict database elements in a visual manner. Table and field names are provided in pull-down menus and forms can be constructed by selecting the tables and fields you want on the screen. Controls such as buttons or scroll bars are selected from a palette and placed on the form, resizing them as needed. After the GUI is constructed, the underlying code is written using a proprietary programming language dedicated to database access.

Some builder tools provide cross-platform support. Some provide more features than others. All of them are relatively expensive and are probably worth more than gold if you need a full-featured database front end constructed by next Tuesday, and you don't want (or can't afford) to hire a cadre of programmers.

Using Freeware or Shareware Gateways

If you want to establish a Web presence with limited funds, the freeware/shareware route probably appeals to you. Some of the gateway products in this category are free to educational or research organizations, but charge a fee for commercial use. The fee is generally far less than most commercial products.

Shareware products appeal to programmers who like to get their hands into the guts of an application, or to organizations with only a small amount of data that doesn't justify a large, commercial database.

Most shareware products are simple, straightforward implementations with limited features and support. They do the job without a lot of fanfare, and most are stable and do what they are supposed to do. By using shareware products, a Webmaster can build a substantial Web site that offers full database access, at a minimum of expense.

Source Code

One of the big attractions of shareware to some programmers is the source code. Many shareware products come complete with the source code used to construct the database interface. In some cases, such as Perl or shell scripts, this is inevitable because the source code is compiled at runtime. In other cases, the C source code is provided for users to compile their own version of a program to run on whatever hardware they use. This can eliminate dependency on vendors to fix bugs in their code, but it also requires more knowledge and programming skill on the user's part.

The availability of the source code allows programmers to customize an application for their particular needs. Most shareware is distributed under the Free Software Foundation's GNU software license, which allows modifications as long as the original copyrights and author names are retained in the source code.

Software Support

Many of the available shareware products are actively supported by the author(s). A polite e-mail message generally produces a timely response. Some products have mailing lists where users exchange bug fixes and ideas on how to best use the software. The Internet is an unending fountain of user experiences, and chances are that someone else has had your problems or questions and an answer is only a few keystrokes away. The shareware concept reflects Internet philosophy at its best.

Supporting Software Needed

To use or develop an interface, you will need some sort of supporting software. Even if the interface is a Unix shell script, the shell software must be present on the machine. Other types of interfaces require specific software to run, or to provide functionality that allows database access. Some of the different kinds of supporting software are listed here, but there are others.

Compilers

A compiler is the most hardware-dependent software there is. If an interface comes with source code that needs to be compiled to run on a specific machine, you will have to have a compiler that matches the language in which the source code is written. If your machine does not have a compiler, there are versions of *Gnu C compilers* (gcc) for virtually every hardware platform, including PCs and Macs.

In addition to standard compilers, some commercial products have their own compiler of sorts. As an example, Informix Software, Inc. has a product called ESQL/C for use with Informix databases. ESQL/C enables database application programmers to create C programs that incorporate database features into their programs. Features such as imbedded SQL statements, cursors, and descriptors can be included without using API function calls.

Programs are written predominantly in C, with language extensions provided by ESQL/C also included in the code. Programs are preprocessed by the ESQL/C compiler, which converts ESQL/C language extensions into C. A normal compiler turns the resultant C code into executable programs. This process is shown in figure 5.9. Source code using ESQL/C is usually easier to read and maintain than code using API function calls. There are also versions of ESQL for COBOL, Ada, and other languages.

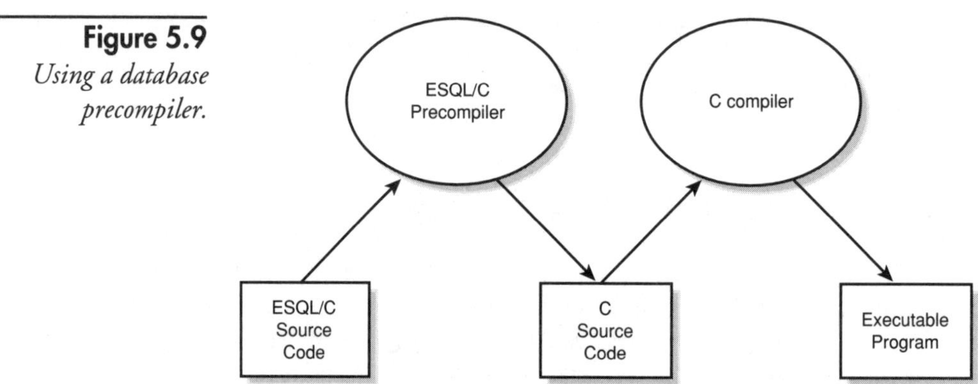

Figure 5.9
Using a database precompiler.

Libraries

Naturally, if you plan to use an API to access a database, the API must be on the system where you do development work. In most cases, the API is provided as a C library file that is linked into your code as it is compiled.

For example, Sybase, Inc. offers an API library called DB-Library as part of their Open Client product. DB-Library is exactly what the name implies: a library of function calls for accessing a Sybase database engine.

Using a library enables programmers to develop multiple database applications using a single set of function calls, and enforces programming techniques common to all applications. This makes it much easier for database application developers to read and maintain code they had no part in writing.

Perl Extensions for Database Interfaces

As mentioned before, one of the most useful programming languages for database access via CGI programs is Perl. By itself, Perl cannot easily access a database, but combined with a compiler or API from a specific database, Perl can make CGI programming a breeze.

There are a lot of products available on the Internet that combine Perl and other database products. IsqlPerl uses Perl libraries and the ESQL/C compiler from Informix to create a database access language for Informix databases. SybPerl does the same with Perl and DB-Library for Sybase databases. OraPerl is used with Oracle databases, pgPerl with Postgres, IngPerl with Ingres, and MsqlPerl with Mini SQL. The list goes on. Chances are if you have a database, there is a Perl-based language to support it.

In addition to Perl programs based on specific database products, there are a host of ancillary Perl programs to make life easier for programmers. Steven Brenner's cgi-lib.pl is one of these. Perl programmers are a vocal and prolific lot, and it is a good bet there are Perl programs already written that will solve database access problems you might be having.

Now that you know what database interfaces do, you are better prepared to explore the issues involved in choosing an interface product, which is covered in Chapter 7, "Choosing a Database Gateway." In the next chapter, "Constructing a Database," you will be shown a practical way of designing your database so that your database server will work less and perform more efficiently.

Constructing a Database

Numerous books have been written on the topic of database construction, and this single chapter certainly does not cover a fraction of the subject, but this is not necessarily a bad thing. Database management classes have been the source of many a long nap. Hopefully, by taking a high-level view of how a database should be put together, you will not be lulled to sleep.

Consider this a beginner's guide to database construction. This chapter gives you some general guidelines to follow, some common sense rules to observe, and a basic understanding of some of the most pressing issues underlying database construction.

These are the main topics covered in this chapter:

- The purpose of a database
- The database structure
- Avoiding data redundancy
- Indexing the database
- Using referential constraints
- Promoting ease of readability
- How will the data be used?
- Recognizing data hierarchies
- Keeping data together
- Storing multi-value data
- There is no substitute for experience
- A complete example

Please keep in mind that the simple examples shown in this chapter are not intended to be finished products, but rather are intended to illustrate points. A lot of information that would be included in a functional database has been excluded for brevity and simplicity. The final example presents a complete solution that includes all pertinent information.

First off, the term *database construction* gives the wrong impression. It makes a database seem like something you can throw together with a hammer and saw, and, as long as it doesn't leak data, it will work fine. While many a database has been done just that way, other problems can arise down the road that will cause a database to break.

Use the term *data modeling* instead. A database should be a recognizable model of the data it contains. If a piece doesn't fit, maybe it doesn't belong in the database, or it needs to be trimmed to fit.

Another point to remember is not to look at your data as an inanimate lump or as a tangled mess. Once you start logically arranging the information you want to model, it will more than likely assume a natural form that will suggest a good first try at piecing the database together.

Determining the Purpose of a Database

Always remember a database must have a purpose. Maybe it has to solve a problem, make data readily available to those who need it, or present information in a way that makes decisions more informed. Whatever the purpose is, it should drive the eventual shape of the database. Think about the database.

- What does it need to do?
- What problem will it solve?
- Whose lives will it make easier?
- Who will use it?
- What point of view should it represent?

Let your knowledge of what the database will contain and how it will be used influence the database structure. Only store the data you need. If you aren't sure what you need, think about it some more. The effort you put into the database now will pay off handsomely in the future. If you just start throwing data around, it will only have to be done again.

In its simplest form, a database should make information available quickly with a minimum of effort. If information is hard to extract or requires users to memorize arcane commands to get to the information, users will not use it. The information should also be complete or as complete as you can make it. If the information presented to the user is not useful because it leaves out important data, users will not have confidence in the database to provide answers to their questions.

The Database Structure

A database is composed of *tables*. Ideally, a table is composed of a single type of information. The information in a table is divided into *fields*. Fields are a logical division of information into its basic parts. A collection of fields that describes a single piece of information is called a *record*. A record can span more than one table.

Figure 6.1 shows a table. If you think of fields as columns, and records as rows, you can imagine how a table is constructed.

Figure 6.1
A generic database table.

	Field 1	Field 2	Field 3	Field 4
Row 1				
Row 2				
Row 3				
Row 4				
Row 5				
Row 6				
Row 7				

In order to more readily locate or identify a single database record, each row in a table should have at least one field that contains a unique value. If the record itself has no identifying information, such as a serial number or social security number, it is a good idea to create an artificial identifier. If the database engine supports serial fields, use that to generate the unique value. A *serial field* is a numerical value that is guaranteed to be unique. This is usually done by assigning an integer value to the field and incrementing the value by one for each successive record. If your database does not support a serial type field, you can create your own unique identifiers, but to understand how to do so, you will need to know more about database construction. Later in the chapter, the "Creating a Unique Key" section examines a way of generating unique identifiers. This unique field is your *primary key* for the table. There can be other key fields in a table, but there should only be one primary key. The primary key is the main identifier for a record and is used in database queries to quickly locate the information you are searching for.

If all databases were made of a single table, this would be all you would need to know to construct a database. However, only in rare cases should all the data in a database reside in a single table. One of the main reasons for this is data redundancy.

Avoiding Data Redundancy

Data redundancy is the storing of data more than once in the same database. Why would this happen and is it a bad thing? The debate rages on. While the database theorists argue, look at a simple example.

Imagine you have a list of computer parts you have purchased. Information about each part will be stored in the database, including part name, cost, serial number, vendor name, address, and phone number. A first impression might be to use the serial number as the primary key, but there is a possibility that two different manufacturers might use the same serial number for two completely different parts.

An obvious database structure is shown as the table labeled "computer_parts" in figure 6.2. The simplest way to model the data is to put everything in a single table. If you look a little more closely at the data, however, you can see a lot of data redundancy in the vendor_name, vendor_address, and vendor_phone fields.

computer_parts

Key	part_name	cost	serial_number	vendor_name	vendor_address	vendor_phone
1	widget X	10	wts143	Circuit Shack	13 M St., New York	123-456-7890
2	widget Y	30	369y	Circuit Shack	13 M St., New York	123-456-7890
3	widget Z	25	ttz4	Radio City	Rt. 5, Dallas	345-678-9012
4	dongle	8	do457	Radio City	Rt. 5, Dallas	345-678-9012
5	whazzit	105	3958275	Circuit Shack	13 M St., New York	123-456-7890

Figure 6.2
The computer_parts table.

If the database contains relatively few records, this redundancy does not waste an appreciable amount of disk space, but as the number of records increases, the amount of wasted space increases. Although one table with repeated data is a small problem, consider the amount of excess space taken up by a database with 200 tables full of redundant data, or even a single table with 50,000 computer parts purchased from the same company.

Breaking Data into Parts

A solution to this problem is to break the computer_parts table into two pieces. Create a new vendors table for the vendor information and give each vendor a primary key. That way a single vendor can be referred to by a number in the computer_parts table. Instead of repeating all the vendor information, only the number gets repeated.

The number that represents a vendor record is called a *primary key* in the vendors table. When that primary key is used in another table, it is called a *foreign key*. Foreign keys are used to link related data together in a database, when the data has been broken into logical parts. The use of two tables is shown in tables 6.1 and 6.2.

Table 6.1
computer_parts

part_id	name	cost	serial_number	vendor_id
1	widget X	10	wts143	1
2	widget Y	30	369y	1
3	widget Z	25	ttz4	2
4	dongle	8	do457	2
5	whazzit	105	3958275	1

Table 6.2
vendors

vendor_id	name	address	phone
1	Circuit Shack	13 M St., New York	1234567890
2	Radio City	Rt 5, Dallas	3456789012

The point of this additional table is to reduce the amount of space wasted by repeating the vendor information for every computer part purchased from them. It gives the added benefit of providing vendor information that is not dependent on computer parts. If you want to see a list of the vendors you buy from, or you need a vendor phone number because the Rolodex got rained on, the vendor information can be retrieved directly, without wading through a ton of unrelated computer parts data.

However, now that the data is in two tables, how do you match the parts to the vendor they came from if you run a query on the database?

Performing a Join

Bringing together the information stored in two or more tables is called *performing a join.* Joins are perhaps the most fundamental concept of a database and can be tough to understand. Normally, a database query is used to select only pieces of data that match certain conditions. A join enables you to do this across multiple tables and piece together the results into a composite whole. When the results are displayed, they look as if they came from a single table.

A *join* involves combining data from different tables using query constraints that dictate how to select the desired data. A *query constraint* is, in effect, a rule that tells the database how to connect the information from multiple tables.

Tables are usually connected in a join by the relation between the primary field in one table and the foreign key in one or more other tables. If the foreign key value in a record in one table matches the primary key value of another record in another table, the corresponding records are related. To understand how to perform a join using a primary key and foreign key query constraint, consider the following example.

Look at tables 6.1 and 6.2 again. Assume you want to generate a report that contains the part name, serial_number, and vendor name for each part in the database. Doing so involves using the database query language SQL. SQL is a vast and complex language and a study of it is beyond the scope of this book, but simple SQL statements will be used to show how to get results out of the database.

First of all, formulate the database query in plain language: You want to select the name and serial_number fields from the computer_parts table, and the name field from the vendors table. The tables are linked by the vendor_id field, so to each computer_parts record, you want to join the matching vendors record using the vendor_id field.

The SQL statement to accomplish this is called a SELECT statement because it selects data from the database, and it looks like this:

```
SELECT computer_parts.name, serial_number, vendors.name
FROM computer_parts, vendors
WHERE computer_parts.vendor_id = vendors.vendor_id
```

The `SELECT` keyword tells the database engine which field data to return as a result of the query. `FROM` tells the engine which tables to get the data from. `WHERE` is the query constraint that gives the database the criteria to determine which data to join. The `vendors.vendor_id` field is the primary key in the vendors table because it uniquely identifies a vendor record. The `computer_parts.vendor_id` field is a foreign key in the computer_parts table because it ties computer parts information to a vendor by using the vendor_id.

Using the primary and foreign key relationships between the tables in tables 6.1 and 6.2, you can tell that widget X, widget Y, and whazzit are provided by Circuit Shack, and the widget Z and dongle are provided by Radio City. The relationship between the information contained in the vendor_id field in the vendors and computer_parts table is used by the SQL query to combine matching data together, as illustrated in figure 6.3.

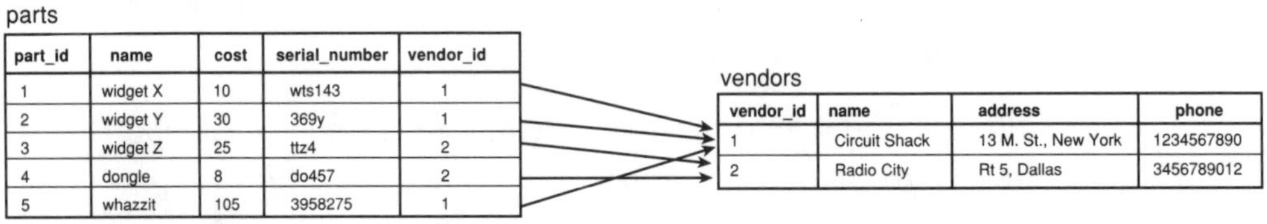

parts

part_id	name	cost	serial_number	vendor_id
1	widget X	10	wts143	1
2	widget Y	30	369y	1
3	widget Z	25	ttz4	2
4	dongle	8	do457	2
5	whazzit	105	3958275	1

vendors

vendor_id	name	address	phone
1	Circuit Shack	13 M. St., New York	1234567890
2	Radio City	Rt 5, Dallas	3456789012

Figure 6.3
Primary and foreign key relationships.

Because the name and vendor_id fields exist in both tables, you must qualify the field names in the SQL query by prefixing the name of the table they are in. Qualifying the field names tells the database exactly which vendor_id field is being referenced. If the field names were not qualified, the database would return an error because the name vendor_id exists in both tables and the database cannot magically decide which field you are trying to access.

Note

Some people think every field should be qualified even if it is unique because it improves readability. This is true, but it can result in a lot more typing when you enter queries. If a query will be saved and reused by many people, the extra typing is justified by the complete information the fully qualified field names provide.

Always give the user as much information about the database as possible so they can understand the structure of the database as much as they want to. Too much information is better than not enough.

The results of the SELECT are shown in table 6.3 and are exactly as expected. The results appear to be from a single table, which is what performing a join does for you. A join combines information from multiple tables as if the information were contained in a single table.

Table 6.3
The SELECT Results

computer_parts	serial_number	vendor name
widget X	wts	Circuit Shack
widget Y	369y	Circuit Shack
widget Z	ttz4	Radio City
dongle	d0457	Radio City
whazzit	3958275	Circuit Shack

As the complexity of a database increases, more tables can be added and more foreign key references added. At some point, database performance will become an issue. If all of the computer parts information is in a single table, searching for information will be faster but more space will be used. If the data is split into two tables, the search speed will decrease slightly, but the database will be smaller. If three tables are used, the speed will decrease a bit more, but the database size will decrease yet again. Don't go overboard eliminating redundant data at the expense of database complexity and performance.

Indexing the Database

After you have the data broken neatly into parts, and all the records have primary and foreign keys, there is one more thing that needs to be done. An *index* should be put on every key.

The database contains keys to let humans identify important data more readily, but the database sees a key as just another field in a table. Indexing the key fields tells the database to build an index that keeps track of the location of every key value in the database. Indexes make it easier to find information in the database and increase performance quite a bit.

Indexes make searches faster and decrease the amount of work the database server has to do when searching for data. Unindexed data requires the database engine to search every record in a table, comparing it to the value you are looking for. An index gives the database a way to get to information with minimal effort, exactly like using the index in a book to find the topic you are looking for, instead of reading the entire book hoping you find the pertinent information.

The concept of an index is shown in figure 6.4. The index itself is sorted so database searches can find the pointer to a record quickly. The data itself does not need to be sorted.

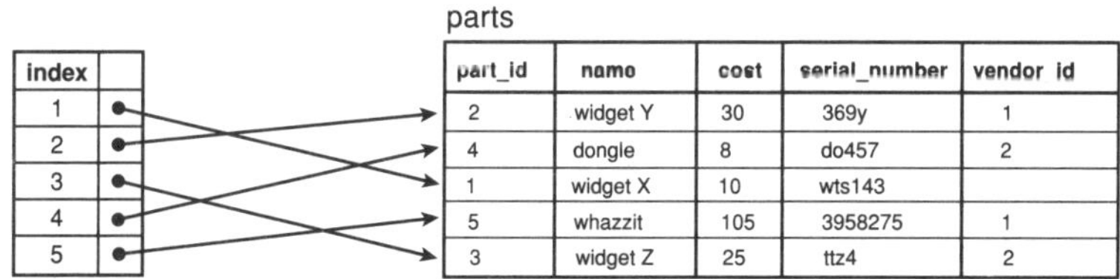

Figure 6.4
An index on the part_id field.

It is a general rule to put an index on every field in a table that users or application programs will perform searches on. If you write a program that searches for ZIP codes in customer addresses, the ZIP code should have an index on it to make the database searches faster and more efficient.

You are not limited to putting indexes on single fields. A *composite index* is one put on multiple fields within a single table. If you want to perform searches on a manufacturer, model, and serial number, you can put a single index on all three fields, and the database will build an index that keeps track of the combination of all three fields.

> **Warning**
>
> Indexes take up disk space. If you index most of the fields in a table or use a lot of composite indexes, the index can easily take more space than the data being indexed. The performance gains are considerable when using indexes, but allow plenty of disk space if you use a lot of them.

Creating a data model, constructing the database, and putting indexes on fields that will be heavily used are the main tasks that should be done when creating a database. With just these basic features, the database will function and answer your queries. There are more in-depth topics, however, that should be considered when building your database and that are discussed in the following sections:

- Using referential constraints
- Promoting ease of readability
- How will the data be used?

- Recognizing data hierarchies
- Keeping data together
- Storing multi-value data

Using Referential Constraints

After you have data in your database, it would be nice to have a way to make sure the data is as accurate and complete as possible. Many databases provide a way for you to create rules that tell the database when the data being entered is complete, and the database will enforce these rules for you. The rules you create are called *referential constraints.*

What are referential constraints? Another term for them is *data dependencies,* which means one piece of information depends on another piece that is somewhere else in the database. Using the database schema for the computer parts database as an example, it would be uninformative to have a record in the computer_parts table but no matching record in the vendors table. It is possible to force records to contain complete information by adding constraints to related data.

To ensure every computer part in the database has related vendor information, two steps should be taken:

1. Put a constraint on the vendor_id field in the computer_parts table so that a NULL value is not allowed in that field. This means the vendor_id field *must* contain a value.

2. Make the vendor_id field in the computer_parts table *dependent* on the vendor_id field in the vendors table. This means the vendor_id value in the computer_parts table must contain a value that already exists in the vendors table.

Taking these steps forces the user to enter the vendor information first, if it does not already exist, and then enter only a valid vendor_id in the computer_parts table. This guarantees the database will contain complete, accurate information.

It is possible to have a computer part that has no associated vendor for various reasons. If you use the preceding constraints, these parts cannot be put into the database unless you create a vendor record for "Unknown Vendor" and let the orphan parts reference it.

Avoiding Referential Loops

Unfortunately, it is possible to have too much of a good thing. If you have three tables, and a field in table1 is dependent on a field in table2, table2 has a dependency in table3, and table3 is dependent on table1, what do you have? You have a problem, as detailed in figure 6.5.

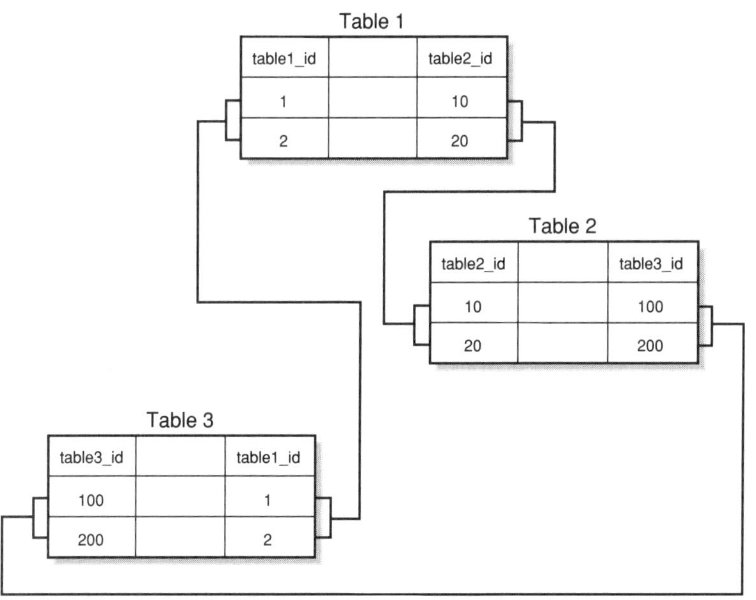

Figure 6.5
A referential loop.

Referential constraints work not only when you insert data, but when you delete data, too. If you try to delete a record from table3, the database will not let you because table2 contains a foreign key reference to table3, and deleting the record from table3 would violate the constraints that have been placed on the data. If you try to delete from table2 first, there is the same problem with table1. Deleting from table1 causes the same problem with table3. Essentially, you have a *deadlock* where nothing can be deleted from any of these tables until you remove one or more of the referential constraints.

This does not happen often, but it is possible if the constraints are not well thought out before being implemented.

Preserving Data Integrity

One of the most vicious problems in database management is ensuring the integrity of the data. Careless deletions or unenforced referential constraints can leave bits and pieces of useless information cluttering up a database, degrading performance and taking up space.

Warning

Just *defining* referential constraints is not enough. You must allow the database to *enforce* them. Otherwise, they do you no good. As you work with a database, the constraints may seem too restrictive, or may seem to make you do too much work to adhere to them. In many cases, the constraints are turned off to make your job easier.

DO NOT REMOVE CONSTRAINTS! If the referential constraints are important enough to define, they are imperative to enforce. What may seem like a harmless way of making your job easier can cause your database to lose any semblance of accuracy. Do not remove referential constraints without a full understanding of what you are doing and the repercussions you might cause.

Assuring data integrity requires discipline and painstaking care when designing a database schema and data dependencies. Inserts, updates, and deletes must be done in the correct order, and must cover all tables and fields that make up a complete record. Otherwise, pieces of unrelated data can be left behind after the process finishes.

Any applications that manipulate the data must execute database transactions meticulously and check each step of a transaction to be sure each separate step has succeeded before proceeding to the next. If any error occurs, the data must be returned to its previous state to avoid inserting or deleting only part of a record.

This might sound unreasonable. Not so. If a database is not continuously checked for problems—and corrected quickly—it is possible for a database to become completely useless because of inaccurate, incomplete, or just plain bad information. If the data is not good, the database loses its purpose.

Wisely used, referential constraints can help enforce data integrity, but be warned: Constraints have a significant impact on database performance. Constraints are not a cure-all panacea, but a tool to be used along with care and common sense.

How Often Will the Data Change?

An important issue to consider as you plan a database schema is how often will the data be changing? Will the data be inserted in the database and remain static, or will the database be very fluid with data constantly inserted, updated, and deleted? This is crucial to consider when deciding how complex to make your database schema. Constant transactions on a complex database can bring a server to its knees, and careless transactions can ruin data integrity.

If you choose to retain some redundant data, every occurrence must be found and processed. This takes processing time as well.

> **Warning**
>
> When data is deleted from some databases, the database may not be able to reuse the empty space until a database backup is performed. In some extreme cases, the empty space is never reclaimed at all and the database must be backed up, dropped, re-created, and restored in order to reclaim the space freed when data is deleted.
>
> Find out if your database has this restriction before implementing a database that will process frequent deletes. You will have to schedule the regular re-creation of your database, or better yet, use a different database server altogether.

Promoting Ease of Readability

Creating an easily readable database can be an impossible task even for small databases because of the complex interaction between the various pieces. There are, however, some simple things to do that can make a database at least *more* readable by someone who is not familiar with the database schema.

One of the most important things to do is keep the names of foreign keys the same as the primary key they reference. Otherwise, there is no easy way to determine relationships among tables. As an alternative, some database designers like to start all the field names in a table with the name of the table. This can lead to long table names that are a royal pain to type in SQL queries, but this method does make it easier to tell which fields belong in which table, plus it ensures unique field names.

Keep abbreviations to a minimum. Is cust_name the customer name or the custodian name? If you do decide to use some abbreviations, use the *same* abbreviation for the same word. Don't use zip, zip_cd, and zip_code. Choose one and stick with it database-wide. Following are some other rules of thumb:

- Make table and field names meaningful. The table name should reflect the contents of the table. Ditto for the field names.
- Use plurals. If a table will contain customer names, call the table "customer_names," not "cust_name." This does a better job of demonstrating the contents of the table.
- Use underscores (_) as spaces in table and field names. Scrunching words together makes them unreadable.
- Avoid mixing uppercase and lowercase letters in names. It is very frustrating to have to remember which letters are capitalized and which aren't if you don't have it written down in front of you.

In general, the labels that are put on the database parts can make the job of maintaining a database easier. Think of the poor soul who has to figure out field names at 3:00 a.m. because the automatic letter printing program went stupid. He'll thank you later.

How Will the Data Be Used?

As you work out a database schema, ask yourself how the data will be used. If you know parts of the database will be used more heavily than others, use that knowledge to influence how the database is structured. Even if you can divide some of the information into three tables with no problems, if half the database accesses do a join on those three tables to bring information back together have you done yourself any favors?

If you have large text fields that logically belong with other data, manipulating free-form text is one of the toughest things a database has to do, so consider putting the text fields in their own table if the data is needed infrequently. If the text fields are needed in most queries, keep them in the same table as the other data. Eliminating a join will save processing time.

If your database will host only an occasional user, and the database can devote all of its resources to one user at a time, the database design is not so critical. As the number of users increases, however, database design flaws will become apparent. You would be wise to design your database for the worst case. Some things you can do to improve performance include the following:

- *Keep joins to a minimum.* In many cases, breaking data into separate tables is necessary, but don't go overboard. Every table added to a join increases the time it takes to process every query. A three-table join can take 10 times longer to complete than a two-table join, if you have thousands of rows of data.
- *Use referential constraints sparingly.* Every time the database has to check data validity or examine the relationship between data, database resources have to be devoted to the task. Use the constraints you need, but don't overdo it.
- *Use as many indexes on your data as is practical.* If you have the disk space to spare, index everything. Indexes expedite database queries and reduce the work your database has to do. If you can't spare the disk space to index every field, make sure all the important fields are indexed. It is in your best interest to make your database as fast as possible.

Recognizing Data Hierarchies

As you lay out your database, keep in mind a lot of data falls into a natural hierarchy. Some of the data is the "main" data, and other information is in the database to support the main data. The main data should be at the "top" of the chain when designing primary and foreign key relationships. The *top of the chain* is the table that contains the main data, and contains the primary key data for the database. Other tables that contain supporting data contain foreign key references to the main table. Not all of the tables in a database key off from a single table. It is possible to have several tables that are the top of a separate chain.

In each chain, the most important data tables should contain the primary keys, and the supporting data tables should contain the foreign key references. This helps define the information flow of a database and can make database application development easier. Knowing which data to insert first or delete last during a transaction can reduce debugging time.

Insert data at the top of the chain and work out from the main table to the other tables. If the first insert fails, none of the other inserts can proceed. Delete data starting at the outer tables, and work up to the main table. Referential constraints may force you to remove data that refers to a primary piece of data before the primary piece can be deleted.

An Example of Organizing Data

As an example of deciding information importance, consider a taxicab company that wants to keep track of its cars and who is driving them. The data would need to reside in two tables, one for drivers and one for the cabs, as shown in tables 6.4 and 6.5. Because the cab company assigns its own unique cab identification number, that can be used as the primary key for the cabs. A natural primary key for the drivers is the social security number.

Table 6.4

computer_parts

cab_id	mileage	year	make	model
ca111	18700	96	chevy	caprice
ca112	12500	96	pontiac	bonneville

cab_id	mileage	year	make	model
ca113	8500	96	ford	taurus
ca114	6000	96	dodge	intrepid

Table 6.5
vendors

ssn	name	hire_date	phone	route	cab_id
111-111-1111	abdul ahmad	11/92	1234567	7	ca114
222-222-2222	frank chin	7/94	2345678	14	ca111
333-333-3333	joe smith	3/93	3456789	8	ca113
444-444-4444	jose alveraz	8/93	4567890	3	ca112

Although both might seem equally important, to the cab company dispatcher or scheduler, the cab information might be the most important, so a database the dispatchers would use should have the cabs in the top-level table.

If a mail-order catalog company has a database of customer information and orders, the distinction might depend on the point of view of a person accessing the data. Although the shipping warehouse would consider the order information the most important, the billing office would consider the order information the most important. In this case, both would want much of the same information, such as the customer address to send the products and bill to, and the actual order and billing information might become the subsidiary tables.

Keeping Data Together

It is easy to see certain data in only one way and never think twice about it. Yet, some information that seems to belong in pieces might not need to be kept separate.

Consider the shipping warehouse mentioned previously. The customer address would certainly be needed, but in what form? If the only use for the information is printing shipping labels, do the city name, state, and ZIP code need to occupy separate fields in the database, or could they be stored together? Storing them in a single field would simplify the database structure and make printing labels a bit easier, as well.

On the other hand, the marketing department might want to be able to search the database by ZIP code to see if the company gets more orders from particular areas of the country so they can concentrate advertising there to maximize sales.

If you are positive the data will not be used in pieces, by all means simplify whenever possible. If you aren't sure, use common sense and an eye to future uses to decide how to store the data.

Storing Multi-Value Data

It is possible for one field in a database table to contain more than one value at a time. Obviously, all the information can't be stuffed into a single field, so how do you handle this case?

Consider the cab and drivers table example again. The front office is complaining that some drivers are abusing the cabs even beyond normal cabby behavior. As a solution, the cab company has decided to designate some drivers to be responsible for several cabs apiece, and hold them responsible for unnecessary damage.

Where the database schema shown in tables 6.4 and 6.5 works fine for associating one driver to a cab, there is no way to link a driver to more than a single cab. Instead of redesigning the database, a simple addition would provide the necessary functionality.

You will create an "assignments" table in the cabby database that consists of only two fields: cab_id and driver_id. As you might have guessed, both of these fields are foreign key references to the cabs and drivers tables. The assignments table will be used as a *link table*, whose sole purpose is to associate a single record in one table with multiple records in another. The link table will allow the links to go either way—that is, associating multiple cabs with a single driver, or assigning multiple drivers to a single cab. The new database is shown in tables 6.6, 6.7, and 6.8.

Table 6.6
cabs

cab_id	mileage	year	make	model
ca111	18700	96	chevy	caprice
ca112	12500	96	pontiac	bonneville
ca113	8500	96	ford	taurus
ca114	6000	96	dodge	intrepid

Table 6.7
assignments

cab_id	driver_id
ca111	111-111-1111
ca112	333-333-3333
ca113	333-333-3333
ca114	111-111-1111

Table 6.8
drivers

driver_id	name	hire_date	phone	route	cab_id
111-111-1111	abdul ahmad	11/92	1234567	7	ca114
222-222-2222	frank chin	7/94	2345678	14	ca111
333-333-3333	joe smith	3/93	3456789	9	ca113
444-444-4444	jose alveraz	8/93	4567890	3	ca112

Now Abdul and Joe have been made responsible for multiple cabs, and the link table will allow the other drivers to be made responsible for other cabs if necessary, but how can you get the information out of the database? That requires another SQL query. The data connected by the link table is shown in figure 6.6.

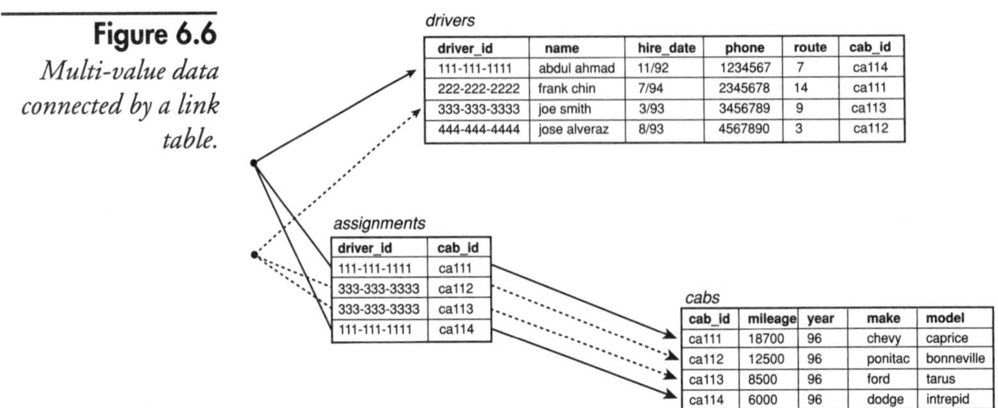

drivers

driver_id	name	hire_date	phone	route	cab_id
111-111-1111	abdul ahmad	11/92	1234567	7	ca114
222-222-2222	frank chin	7/94	2345678	14	ca111
333-333-3333	joe smith	3/93	3456789	9	ca113
444-444-4444	jose alveraz	8/93	4567890	3	ca112

assignments

driver_id	cab_id
111-111-1111	ca111
333-333-3333	ca112
333-333-3333	ca113
111-111-1111	ca114

cabs

cab_id	mileage	year	make	model
ca111	18700	96	chevy	caprice
ca112	12500	96	ponitac	bonneville
ca113	8500	96	ford	tarus
ca114	6000	96	dodge	intrepid

Figure 6.6
Multi-value data connected by a link table.

Formulating the SQL Query

First formulate the query in plain language. You want a list of driver names and the cab information of the cabs for which they are responsible. In other words, you want to select the driver name and the cab information from the drivers and cabs tables, where the assignments table contains links for them. The query looks like so:

```
SELECT drivers.name,
       cabs.cab_id, cabs.mileage, cabs.make, cabs.model
FROM drivers, cabs, assignments
WHERE assignments.cab_id = cabs.cab_id
      AND assignments.ssn = drivers.ssn
```

The SELECT clause chooses the field information you want. The FROM clause contains the names of all the tables needed for the query, so even though no data is selected from the assignments table, the WHERE clause references it so it must be included. The WHERE clause details the join conditions required to select the proper data. You want all the cabs and drivers that are linked by the assignments table.

A big advantage of this method is that when the links change, none of the data in either the cabs or drivers tables changes. New assignments can be made without affecting existing data. Old assignments can be updated or deleted, and no other data in the database needs to reflect the change. This method is clean, precise, and affects a minimum of data.

A Complete Example

Talking about these issues is fine, but without a comprehensive example, it is hard to see how some of them come into play. The rest of this chapter is dedicated to constructing a complete database, with some of the reasoning behind the design decisions made. Keep in mind there can be more than one "right" way to design any database. The following database model is merely a way that works.

This is a database intended to contain restaurant information for the purpose of informing Web visitors where to go for a good place to eat. Because this will be on the Web, the information will not be limited to any local area, but should be applicable to anyone who can access the database. It is intended that Web users from around the world can add their own favorite restaurants and the database will grow as more and more people add to it.

In addition to basic information about restaurants, such as address and phone number, other information about the atmosphere, services, favorite menu items, hours of operation, and so forth, will be included. Also, there will be the capability to give reviews of the food and service.

Identifying the Data

First you should identify what data Web visitors will enter about the restaurant itself. There are some obvious items to include, as well as things that involve the services and facilities the restaurant provides:

- Name
- Address
- Telephone number
- Hours of operation
- Salad bar
- Drinks bar

- Handicapped access
- Non-smoking section
- Smoking section
- Do they offer takeout?
- Do they require a reservation?
- Do they take reservations?
- Type of cuisine
- Type of dress required

If parents with small children are looking for a kid-friendly place to go, there is specific information of interest to them:

- High chairs
- Booster seats
- Kids' menu
- Crayons and coloring books or other items to occupy short attention spans
- Diaper-changing table in rest rooms

If a strapped college student or a senior citizen on a fixed income is looking for a good place to eat, the payment options and discounts offered would be an important item to include:

- Senior citizen discount
- Do they take checks?
- Do they take credit cards? Which ones?
- Do they have any specials? What and when?

Of course, information about visitors' favorite menu items should be included:

- Food or meal name
- What food does the entree come with?
- Description
- Price
- Notes, such as dietary information, and so forth

And to provide some sort of subjective opinions about the food and the service, the following items should be included:

- The menu item being reviewed
- Serving size
- Food quality
- Comments
- Rating
- Service speed
- Service quality
- How long is the average wait for a table?
- Is the place crowded?
- Lighting
- Atmosphere
- Music
- Comments

This information covers just about everything a Web visitor would want to know about a restaurant in order to make an informed decision about where to eat. If anything is missing, visitors will be provided a way to e-mail comments and suggestions.

Breaking the Data into Parts

Looking through the information, some things naturally separate into pieces, such as reviews about food, services, and the menu. Other topics need to be expanded beyond a single field.

The hours of operation, for example, would not fit well in a single field. Some restaurants have different hours on the weekend or are open late on selected nights. Some are open for lunch and not dinner or vice versa on specific days. This suggests a way is needed to individually list each day and its hours of operation, or a range of days and hours.

The restaurant address needs to be in multiple fields to enable users to search by city, state, or even country. In many cases, a single line for the street address is not enough so an extra line should be included to allow for unusual addresses.

You must also expand the credit card information. Should there be a list to select from or just a text field to enter credit card names into? In order to make data entry as quick and easy as possible, a list of major credit cards with a yes or no selection would be best. To catch any credit card missed in the list, a text box will be included for other credit cards.

The restaurant specials should probably be a separate entity as well, or included in the menu. Some specials are not regular menu items or are just an item at a special price and the item is decided daily. This kind of thing would not fit in a regular menu, so would probably be best in its own table.

The food and services review could be stored together or individually. Service and food quality generally do not affect one another, so they will be modeled in separate tables.

The same goes for basic restaurant information, the kid stuff information, and the types of payment accepted. Users will be given the option of what information to query on, depending on what they care about. The most basic data would be the name, address, phone, and the type of cuisine and dress required. The services provided, kids information, and payment information could be included in the main table or broken into individual tables. To make the database as simple as possible, all of this data will be stored in the same table.

The food reviews, service reviews, and specials all have comments associated with them, and so could go into a separate comments table. However, the comments are integral to the tables and would probably be accessed almost every time the main tables are. Adding a comments table would increase the complexity of the database, which would adversely affect database performance.

So what kind of database structure does that provide? The information is grouped as follows:

- Restaurant Information:

  Name

  Address

  Phone

  Type of cuisine

  Type of dress

  Salad bar

  Drinks bar

  Handicapped access

  Non-smoking section

  Smoking section

  Do they offer takeout?

  Do they require a reservation?

Do they take reservations?

High chairs

Booster seats

Kids' menu

Kid toys?

Diaper-changing table in rest rooms

Senior citizen discount?

Do they take checks?

American Express

Visa

Master Card

Discover

Other credit cards

Other payment method

- Hours of Operation:

  Day or range

  Open time

  Close time

- Menu Items:

  Food or meal name

  What food does the entree come with, if any?

  Description

Price

Notes, such as low in fat and/or sodium, etc.

- Food Reviews:

  Menu item

  Serving size

  Food quality

  Rating

  Comments

- Service Reviews:

  Service speed

  Service quality

  How long is the wait for a table?

  Is the place crowded?

  Lighting

  Atmosphere

  Music

  Comments

- Specials:

  Description

  When offered

  Price

  Comments

The Data Model

The tables will be constructed as the information is grouped above. The next thing to do is determine the data types and field sizes for each data item. This is an inexact science at best, so the field sizes usually have to come from previous experience or an educated guess.

Pieces of names and addresses would rarely go beyond 32 characters each, and a telephone number with area code and extension should fit in 20 characters. Description and note fields can be limited to 64 characters to prevent them from taking up too much space in the database and force users to be succinct when entering information. Comments are limited to 128 characters for the same reasons.

The character fields with a single character are for simple yes or no entries (Y/N). Some databases provide a Boolean data type that allows true or false entries, or some database designers use an integer that is set to 0 or 1 for true/false or yes/no. Using a Boolean or integer value can be confusing to a user not familiar with those types of values and usually requires the front end program to do some kind of translation. Using a Y or N character provides a method to show the user the value that actually exists in the database, and it takes less storage space than an integer. The final database model is detailed as follows:

Table name: restaurants

Field Name	Data Type
restaurant_id	Serial integer, primary key
name	Character(32)
address1	Character(32)
address2	Character(32)
phone	Character(20)
cuisine	Character(16)

Field Name	Data Type
dress	Character(16)
salad_bar	Character(1)
bar	Character(1)
handicapped_access	Character(1)
non_smoking_section	Character(1)
smoking_section	Character(1)
takeout	Character(1)
reservation_required	Character(1)
reservation_taken	Character(1)
highchairs	Character(1)
booster_seats	Character(1)
kids_menu	Character(1)
kid_toys	Character(1)
diaper_table	Character(1)
senior_discount	Character(1)
personal_checks	Character(1)
american_express	Character(1)
visa	Character(1)
master_card	Character(1)
discover	Character(1)
other_credit_cards	Character(32)
other_payment_method	Character(32)

Table name: hours

Field Name	Data Type
hour_id	Serial integer, primary key
when	Character(16)
open_time	Character(8)
close_time	Character(8)
restaurant_id	Integer, foreign key

Table name: menu

Field Name	Data Type
menu_id	Serial integer, primary key
name	Character(32)
side_dishes	Character(32)
description	Character(64)
price	Real
notes	Character(64)
restaurant_id	Integer, foreign key

Table name: food_reviews

Field Name	Data Type
food_review_id	Serial integer, primary key
menu_item	Character(32)
serving_size	Character(16)
food_quality	Character(16)
rating	Integer
comments	Character(128)
restaurant_id	Integer, foreign key

Table name: service_reviews

Field Name	Data Type
service_review_id	Serial integer, primary key
service_speed	Integer
service_quality	Integer
wait_time	Integer
crowd	Integer
lighting	Integer
atmosphere	Integer
music	Integer
comments	Character(128)
restaurant_id	Integer, foreign key

Table name: specials

Field Name	Data Type
special_id	Serial integer, primary key
when	Character(16)
description	Character(64)
price	Real
restaurant_id	Integer, foreign key

The restaurants table is the primary table in the database, and all the other tables contain foreign key references to the restaurants table, as shown in figure 6.7.

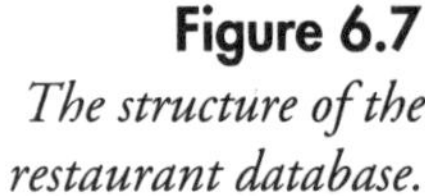

Figure 6.7
The structure of the restaurant database.

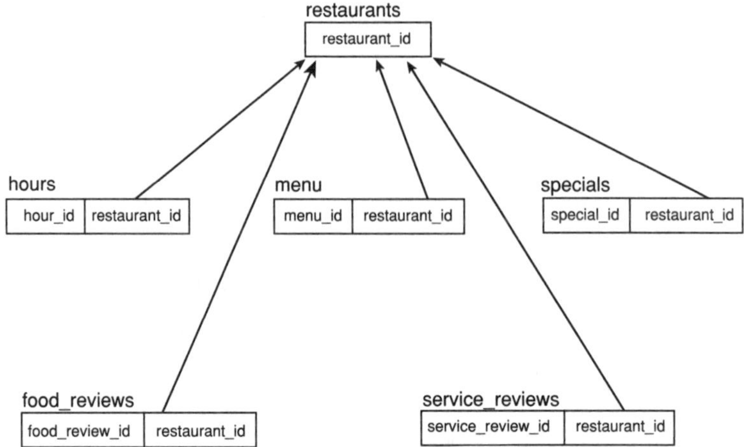

This database implementation will be seen again. Chapter 8, "Putting It All Together," details the actual construction of this database schema using different types of databases and the specific issues that arise. Changes may be made to accommodate database limitations, or to take advantage of a special feature provided by a database. One such limitation is the lack of a serial key data type. A possible solution is detailed in the next section.

Creating a Unique Key

If your database does not support a data type similar to the serial field, you can create your own unique identifier. One way to do this is to create a table in your database called "unique_keys." The table has two fields, "table_name" and "key_value." The unique_keys table holds a value for every table in the database that needs a unique identifier. The value is one larger than the current largest serial key value in a particular table. As an example of using the unique_keys table, consider the following example.

You have three tables in your database called "widgets," "gadgets," and "dongles." Each record in all three tables needs a unique identifier, but the database has no serial data type. The unique_keys table is created, and you create three records in the table, one for each table. There are no records in your database yet, so the number 1 is inserted into the key_value field as an initial value for all tables. The unique_keys table is shown in table 6.9.

Table 6.9
unique_keys

table_name	key_value
widgets	1
gadgets	1
dongles	1

You first enter information into the widgets table. As you insert each new record into the table, you must follow these steps:

1. Select the current unique key_value of the widgets table by querying the unique_keys table.
2. Because the widgets table is currently empty in this example, the value of the first unique key is 1. Use this value as the unique identifier for the first widget inserted into the widgets table.
3. Use the key value as the unique identifier for the current widget.
4. Increment the value by 1.
5. Replace the old key_value for the widgets table in the unique_keys table with the new number. In this example, that number is 2.

As each new record is inserted into the widgets table, the value in the key_value field in the unique_keys table continues to grow, as shown in figure 6.8.

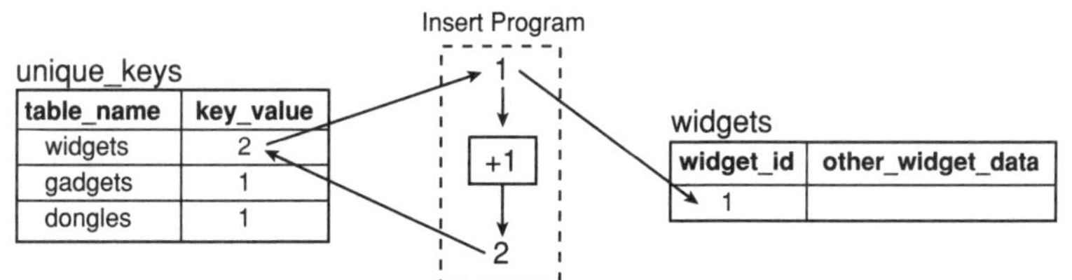

Figure 6.8
Generating a unique key value.

If 20 widget records are inserted into the widgets table, the unique_keys table will look like table 6.10.

Table 6.10
unique_keys

table_name	key_value
widgets	21
gadgets	1
dongles	1

As each new record is added to the gadgets and dongles tables, the corresponding key value in the unique_keys table is incremented the same way as for the widgets table.

Warning

The key_value in the unique_keys table cannot be used as anything but a unique identifier. Subtracting 1 from the value in the key_value field might seem like a good way to find out how many records are in the widgets table, but this only works if you never delete any records from the widgets table.

The unique identifier values are not reused. If you insert 20 records and delete 19, the next record inserted will get the unique identifier value of 21. This does not accurately reflect the number of records in the widgets table.

As you can tell, this method requires more care on your part to make it work correctly. If you want to insert more than a few records into a table that uses the previous method, you will want to write an insertion program that uses the unique_keys table. Inserting records one at a time, then incrementing the key value by hand, would be maddening.

There Is No Substitute for Experience

All these issues might seem overwhelming to someone who has never constructed a database. Those who design databases as part of their job know these are only some of the issues that can have a significant impact on a database.

No matter where you start, start small. The first database you design will probably not be perfect, but it will work, at least for a while. Be prepared to do it over. Everything you do right or wrong will help you in subsequent designs. Do not be afraid to fail, or you can deadlock looking for the perfect database and never produce anything.

Using the database on a daily basis will point out things that were missed and things that were done well. Learn from them and do better next time. Do not worry about creating a perfect database. If it does what you need, you have succeeded.

CHAPTER 7

Choosing a Database Gateway

Whether you choose to use an existing Web-database gateway product or to create your own, the gateway you eventually use is determined by several factors.

If you have already chosen a database or will use an existing database engine, your choice of which gateway product to use is narrowed considerably. The gateway chosen must support the database, regardless of the other features it offers.

If you have yet to pick a database but have decided on the hardware and operating system to use, the list of products available are similarly confined. Different operating systems support different products.

If you have not chosen the hardware or a database, this presents you with the opportunity to see what is available and to make your choice of hardware, database, and gateway as a unit.

To choose a gateway or to decide which features your homegrown application will provide, consider the following factors:

- Database compatibility
- Platform support
- Providing query support only
- Providing full functionality
- Gateway program speed
- Method of database access
- List of available products

Database Compatibility

The gateway you use must support the database in which the data resides. This might seem obvious, but it is easy to lose sight of what you are looking for in a gateway when faced with a large number of choices and features.

Is the Gateway Database-Specific?

Some gateway products are made to support one database. A product might use the database system tables to read information about the database, or it might create tables in the database for its own use.

If you plan to develop your own gateway and you design it to support a specific database, you can use features of the database to increase performance. If you plan to closely couple the gateway to an existing database schema, the gateway can process data much more easily by knowing ahead of time how the data is constructed by using the database system tables to get information about the database structure, or by using template files that describe the database.

Not only do you need to consider which database(s) the gateway supports, but also the method used to access the database. Most databases have their own proprietary interface software, such as a command-line interface or an *Application Programming Interface* (API) that a gateway might require before it will support a database. Other gateways might use the *Open Database Connectivity* (ODBC) interface to access your database.

Other products offer support for multiple databases. This might be accomplished by using a standard API, such as ODBC, or by the use of interchangeable code modules that contain a database-specific access code. This makes a gateway more flexible by providing access to multiple brands of databases.

The development plan for your own gateway would do well to follow this model, even if you will use a specific database. By isolating the database-specific code into function calls, future changes to an upgraded version of the database or migration to another database will be made much more easily.

Some database vendors sell a database with a basic set of features and then charge extra for added functionality, such as ODBC support or a programming API. Client/server network software and multi-user licenses often fall into that category as well.

Database Licenses

Every remote machine that accesses a database server across a network requires a user license. Each machine also needs a copy of the network software provided by the database. If you plan for your gateway to access the database across a network, keep this in mind.

Also, many databases only allow a certain number of user connections at any time. If more users need access, you are required to buy more user licenses. Multiple simultaneous connections are usually not a problem when you use a gateway, but if you have a popular Web site, the number of database connections can increase dramatically, requiring more user licenses.

A Web-database gateway using CGI accesses a database in a different manner than human users do. A user will usually make a connection to the database and stay connected for an extended period of time, executing multiple transactions. This long-term connection requires a user license for as long as the user remains connected to the database.

A gateway program, on the other hand, is required by the limitations of CGI to open a connection to the database, process one or more transactions, and close the database connection. The connection maintained by the gateway rarely takes more than a few seconds, so a single-user license is required for only a short period of time. Even if several people are accessing a database at the same time, the short duration of their connections enables a few user licenses to support many more people. This is one of the important attractions of using a Web-based solution to access a database.

Examining Gateway Platform Support

Unix platforms support different kinds of software than PC or Macintosh platforms. Each operating system offers freedoms a gateway program can exploit and limitations that a gateway must be aware of. The gateway you choose or develop will be limited to the hardware your database runs on and the operating system that you use.

Almost every gateway requires some kind of support software. The supporting software can be generic, such as a C compiler, or specific, such as Oracle's PRO*C programming language. Make sure the support software will run on your chosen platform, and that you have the required support software, before choosing a gateway that requires it.

Many gateways require Perl to operate. Perl has extensions that have been used to develop interface software for virtually every type of database, such as isqlperl for Informix, oraperl for Oracle, sybperl for Sybase, and so on. Each of these interfaces also requires some sort of programming API provided with the target database. Be certain your platform supports Perl if you choose a gateway that requires it.

Note

Perl has been ported to many operating systems, including MS-DOS and the Macintosh, but because of operating system limitations, Perl may not offer the full set of features from one platform to the next. This means Perl programs written on one platform may not behave the same way on another.

Before starting a large project involving Perl on a platform you are not familiar with, do some research and experimentation to be sure the version of Perl you plan to use will support the features your gateway program requires.

A lot of new gateway programs make use of the ODBC interface that lets you access any ODBC-compliant database using the same program. This feature is extremely useful if you have multiple databases that support ODBC because you can buy or write one gateway to handle all database requests.

Note

If your gateway needs ODBC interface software for database access, finding it for some platforms can be hard, unless your database vendor can provide them. Under Microsoft Windows, ODBC drivers are included with some compilers and databases. Just be sure they are 16- or 32-bit as required.

Determining Gateway Functionality

A big issue when choosing or designing a gateway is what kind of database access should be provided. All gateways offer query support, but is more complete database access needed for inserts, updates, and deletes? Another issue is how well the gateway protects your data. When selecting a gateway, there are a few things to consider:

- Data safety
- Gateway features
- Gateway security
- Gateway execution speed

Data Safety

The main thing to consider is the safety of the data. If your gateway provides no support for deletes, users cannot delete data from the database accidentally or on purpose. The same applies to inserting new data or changing existing data.

Making your database available on the Internet is not something to be taken lightly. Most Internet users are pleasant people who do not attempt to misuse the computers connected to the Internet. There are others, however, who take malicious pleasure in damaging everything they can. By restricting database access to query only, you eliminate a possible avenue for hackers to do unpleasant things to your database.

Another thing to consider is gateway simplicity. The SQL Select statement is fairly standard among databases. Database vendors have added extensions to support different feature sets, but for simply getting data out of a database, the same select statement will work for a majority of databases.

Additionally, the fewer features the gateway provides, the less source code is involved. In the case of a Perl program, every time the program is run, the entire source file code is loaded and compiled. The shorter the program, the faster it is executed.

By limiting the features provided by a gateway, your data is safer, and the gateway program runs faster. If added functionality is needed, however, many gateways support most or all of the features of a database.

Gateway Features

If you have users who need to enter new data into the database or a DBA who needs to create new database tables and fields, you can provide full functionality through the Web at the expense of a bit more processing time.

Performing inserts, updates, and deletes on a database requires more complex processing than simple queries. The insert code must check to see if the data already exists in the database before attempting to insert it to prevent duplication of data. The update code has to make sure the data exists before trying to change it or a database error will occur. Deletes are generally restricted to a trusted few to prevent eliminating needed data.

Another feature to consider is the amount of freedom you are given to determine how users access your data. When using a commercial product, you must work within the limitations of the product because you cannot rewrite its processing code. A product that gives you more ways to access your data is easier to use and allows you to present your database information to the user in different ways. A full-featured gateway, such as dbWeb, shown in figure 7.1, gives you the option of using simple queries or the freedom to join several tables using custom query constraints, depending on how you want your data to look. dbWeb is discussed in Chapter 8, "Putting It All Together," where you will be shown how to publish a Microsoft SQL Server database on the Web using dbWeb.

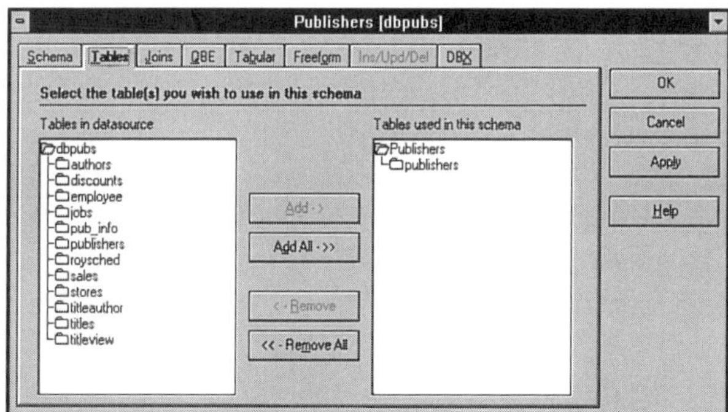

Figure 7.1
The dbWeb gateway provides many nice features.

A fully functional gateway not only contains more processing code, but, in many cases, database transactions have to be carefully written to make sure multiple users are not able to change the same data at the same time. This usually involves the use of database transactions that lock data so only one user at a time can alter the data. If the transactions performed by the gateway involve more than a single database table or require multiple actions, such as inserts and updates within the same transaction, the affected data in all tables must be locked for the duration of the transaction to prevent database corruption.

It does not matter if two users query the same data at the same time because the data is not changing, but in the case of an update, one user's changes can overwrite another user's changes, or part of the data can reflect one set of changes while the rest reflects another. For a more thorough discussion of database access control, see Chapter 4, "Choosing a Database," in the sections "Database Locking Levels" and "Transaction Support."

Gateway Security

When processing anything more than simple queries in a multi-user environment, some kind of access control is a necessity, whether it makes use of the native database capabilities or is incorporated into the software. If a gateway offers full database access, it is important that the gateway software provide some sort of access security to limit what users can do to your database. Some of the possible security arrangements follow:

- Checking a user's login id against a list of users who are allowed to use a particular database function, such as the insert, update, or delete functions.

- Requiring every user to have a login id and password that is maintained by the gateway program, and assigning an access level to each user based on the functions they are allowed access to.

- Using the user authentication provided by the operating system, such as Windows NT. The gateway program assumes the user id of the current user and is granted access to the database based on user privileges.

- Using the password authentication of the target database to validate user access levels. This requires you to create usernames and passwords for all users in the database.

The method you use may depend on how you plan to use the gateway program. Security is one of the nice features of WebDBC, shown in figure 7.2. WebDBC gives you a choice of the method to use for validating users.

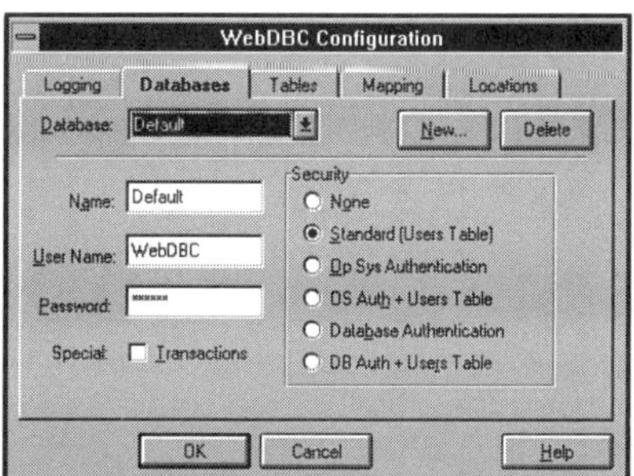

Figure 7.2
The WebDBC gateway provides several user authentication methods.

If your database exists on an internal Web server and is available only to company personnel, you can tightly control database access. If the database is accessible from the Internet, all users come into the database by way of the username assigned to the Web server, and that might require you to create passwords for Internet users, or restrict Internet users to performing only queries.

Warning

Some gateway products may use passwords embedded in HTML files as their method of providing security. As a Web browser loads the HTML page and the embedded SQL commands are passed to the database for execution, the password is passed over the network along with the SQL commands. This is a very insecure method of user authentication. Password schemes that keep the passwords on the same machine as the database or in the database itself are much more secure because they do not send passwords across the network where a hacker might be able to intercept them. Verify the method of security used by a gateway before buying the product.

Gateway Execution Speed

Most of the time involved in a database query is spent either in the database performing the query itself, or in transporting the query and results across the network to and from the database. The size and type of gateway you use, however, can add to this processing time.

Executable programs, such as those compiled from C source code, are inherently faster than scripts that are *interpreted*, or compiled at runtime, such as Perl or Bourne shell scripts. The compiled programs are created by a compiler that can take as long as necessary to create the program, and a compiler can optimize the code to take maximum advantage of the hardware the program runs on.

Interpreters must be fast, or the time spent compiling will render the program unusable. The interpreter cannot spend as much time optimizing as a compiler so the code will be slower. Also, the size of the source code will affect the processing time by requiring the interpreter to do more work.

Both compiled and interpreted code take longer when performing complex database queries. Constructing long involved SELECT statements to send to the database, or performing elaborate formatting of the results can increase processing time appreciably. Performance and features need to be balanced to provide the functionality you need with acceptable response time. The gateway Cold Fusion gives you the option of caching the Cold Fusion executable code, which can increase database access speed (see fig. 7.3).

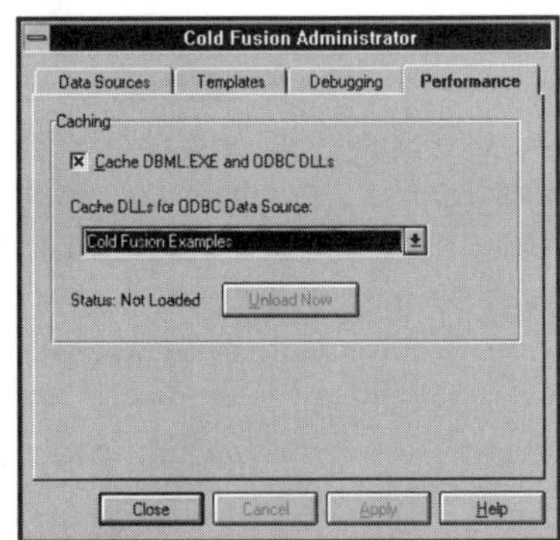

Figure 7.3
The Cold Fusion gateway provides a caching option to increase performance.

Choosing a Database Access Method

Gateways use a variety of methods to access a database. If you use a commercial product, much of the interaction between the gateway and the database is often hidden from the user and the gateway vendor provides tools to construct and maintain Web pages for database access.

If you choose a free or shareware product, it is usually necessary to become familiar with the way the product works because you are responsible for setting it up correctly.

The following are the main methods used to access a database from a gateway:

- *Embedding SQL statements in HTML files.* The HTML files are passed to a CGI program that reads the embedded SQL commands and replaces them with the results of the command. The resulting HTML file is passed to the Web browser for display.
- *Template files that describe the tables and fields in a database.* A CGI program reads the template files and presents the user with a query form tailored for a particular database.
- *A CGI program which calls database stored procedures.* A *stored procedure* is a collection of SQL commands that are stored in the database and can be called by external programs. The results are passed back to the Web browser for display.
- *Using the ODBC API to connect to a variety of databases using the same database access program.* ODBC is a programming library of function calls that can be used for any database that is ODBC compliant and offers an ODBC driver.
- *Using the proprietary API provided by the database vendor.* Proprietary APIs differ from the ODBC API in that they only provide access to a single brand of database.

The two methods most often used by free gateway products are embedded SQL and template files, which are examined more fully in the following sections.

Embedded SQL in HTML Documents

In this method, SQL statements are included as part of the HTML document. You might think that would be confusing for the HTTP server because it doesn't know anything about SQL. This would be true if the SQL statements were sent to the HTTP server directly, but they are not.

An *enhanced* HTML document containing embedded SQL statements is first sent to a CGI database gateway. The gateway program parses the document and looks for statements to execute. The embedded statements are constructed using a syntax similar to HTML, but are specific to the gateway. The statements include SQL commands to be sent to the database, but can also include other commands to process the results returned from a query. By processing the results, the data can be formatted to construct HTML elements such as scrollable lists, pull-down lists, labels, or any other elements. This gives you the capability to generate dynamic HTML pages based on user input.

After the gateway has sent the SQL query to the database and formatted the results, what is sent to the HTTP server is a standard HTML document. The data generated by the embedded SQL has been incorporated into the HTML tags as if it were an ordinary part of the document, so the http server is not required to process the embedded SQL statements.

We will look at an example using a gateway called W3-msql, which is a product created by the author of the Mini SQL database software. W3-msql is a CGI gateway program designed to be used with Mini SQL that includes mSQL commands for database queries and results formatting. The following is an HTML document that uses W3-msql.

```
<HTML>
<HEAD>
<TITLE>Employee Lookup Page</TITLE>
</HEAD>
<BODY>
<H1> Employee Lookup Page </H1>
```

```
<BR>
<BR>
<FORM ACTION="http://lightspeed.beowulf.com/cgi-bin/get_info.cgi">
<! msql connect lightspeed >
<! msql database employee_info >
<! msql query "select id, name from employees order by name" names
>
Select the employee for whom you want information:
<BR>
<BR>
<SELECT NAME="namelist" SIZE=4>
<! msql print_rows names "<OPTION> @names.1\n">
</SELECT>
<! msql free names >
<! msql close >
<BR>
<BR>
<INPUT TYPE="submit" VALUE="Look up">
<INPUT TYPE="reset">
</FORM>
</BODY>
</HTML>
```

Figure 7.4 shows how the preceding HTML code is displayed by a Web browser. Note the URL in the Web browser window. The document is called as a CGI program and the name of the enhanced document is passed to it as additional path information.

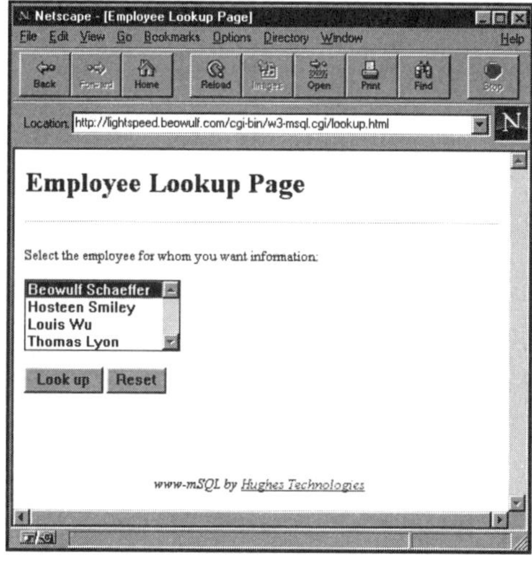

Figure 7.4
The Web page after processing the embedded mSQL commands.

After the user selects a name to look up, the form information is passed to the get_info.cgi CGI program which then gets data about the person from the database.

Using embedded SQL commands provides you with a simple way to use any database command. The commands are included in your HTML files so there are no other files to keep track of, and the CGI gateway program provides the interface to the database.

External Template Files

Another common method of interacting with a database is using external template files. After a database is created, a template file is constructed for each table in the database. The template files contain information about the table name, the fields in the table, the data type of each field, and so on. Some gateways that use template files also enable you to include additional information, such as these:

- Labels
- Instructions on how to format and display the data
- URL information for hyperlinks to help pages or other documents
- Many other features

The template file is used by the gateway program to create HTML pages for querying a database, construct the query statement based on user input, and format the results. The gateway program uses the template file to know ahead of time which fields exist in the database and what kind of data is in each one, making constructing dynamic SQL queries possible.

As an example, we will use a product called the Web Database interface (WDB). WDB is a Perl program that uses templates called *Form Definition Files* (FDF) that contain the database information. WDB is called as a CGI program and the name of the template file is passed as additional path information. WDB parses the template file and uses the database information to construct an HTML page on the fly. The HTML page is a query form displayed by the Web browser.

The user makes use of the query form to select which fields to include in the output and can enter query constraint information to narrow the database search. WDB is called once again and the form information is passed to the program using standard input. WDB constructs an SQL statement to select the fields specified by the user and includes the query constraints. The SQL query is sent to the database and the results are formatted into another dynamic HTML page and displayed by the Web browser.

The following is a sample WDB FDF file that details the same database as used in the W3-msql example.

```
NAME         = employees
TABLE        = employees
DATABASE     = employee_info
TITLE        = employees
Q_HEADER     = employees Query Form
R_HEADER     = employees Query Result
#DOCURL      = # URL to documentation.

#JOIN        = # Join condition ..
#CONSTRAINTS = # Extra query constraints ....
#ORDER       = # ORDER BY columns ...

#RECTOP      = # Record title ....
#PERL        = # Extra perl commands ....
#COMMENTS_TO = # Your e-mail address ....
#-----------------------------------

FIELD   = more
label   = More
from_db = "<i>MORE</i>"
url     = "$WDB/$form{'DATABASE'}/$form{'NAME'}/query/$val{'id'}"
length  = 4
computed
forcetab
no_query
no_full

FIELD  = id
label  = Id
column = id
type   = int
length = 6
key
```

```
FIELD  = name
label  = Name
column = name
type   = char
length = 32

FIELD  = office
label  = Office
column = office
type   = char
length = 32

FIELD  = phone
label  = Phone
column = phone
type   = char
length = 32
```

There are global parameters displayed at the top of the file. If you don't need to use a specific parameter, it can be commented out with a pound sign (#). The # is Perl's comment delimiter. Anything following the # is not executed as part of a Perl program.

Following the global parameters at the top of the file are specifications for fields. The "more" field is a WDB link that enables the user to get more detailed information about any record that is displayed. Following the "more" field are all of the fields in the database table and the specifications for each.

After WDB parses the preceding FDF file, it generates an HTML document that is displayed by a Web browser, as shown in figure 7.5.

All fields are selected for display by default, and if no additional query constraints are entered, information is returned from the database and formatted by WDB as in figure 7.6.

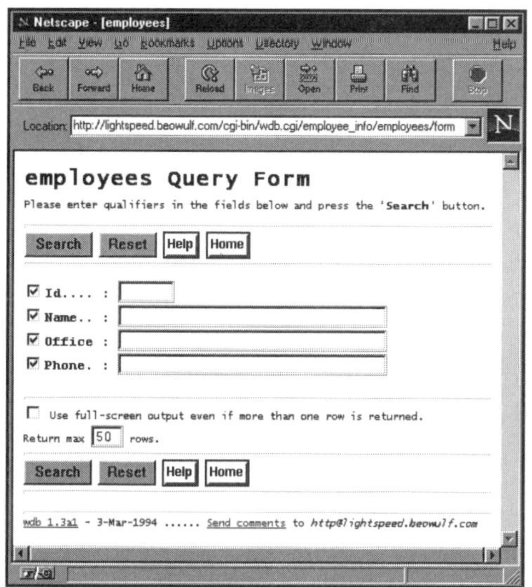

Figure 7.5
A query form generated by WDB.

Netscape - [employees]
Location: http://lightspeed.beowulf.com/cgi-bin/wdb.cgi/employee_info/employees/query

employees Query Result

Query Home

More	Id	Name	Office	Phone
MORE	1	Beowulf Schaeffer	1313 B Fred Building	804-123-4567 ext 13
MORE	2	Hosteen Smiley	265 Stats Bldg.	512-567-8901
MORE	3	Louis Wu	14 Ringworld Bldg.	210-543-0978
MORE	4	Thomas Lyon	6 Steeplechase Hall	501-123-4567

A total of 4 were retrieved

wdb 1.3a1 - 3-Mar-1994 ...... Send comments to http@lightspeed.beowulf.com

Figure 7.6
The WDB query results.

If a user clicks on the "More" hyperlink for Beowulf Schaeffer, the single record is displayed as in figure 7.7.

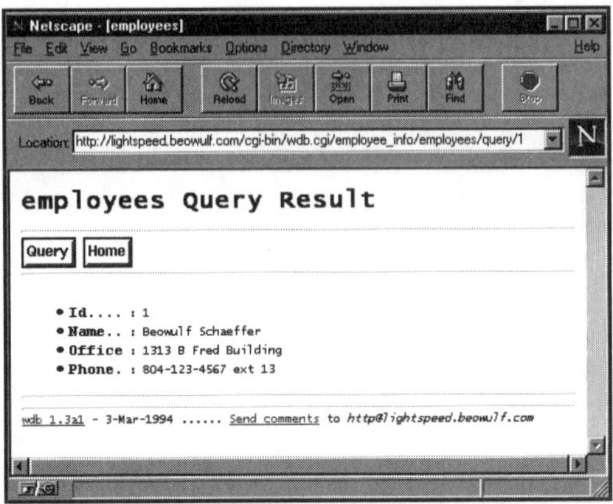

Figure 7.7
A single record displayed by WDB.

FDF files can be customized to a great extent. Join conditions can be specified, HTML tags can be added for any field, and additional Perl instructions can be specified for any field.

The Future of Gateway Products

Like any other realm of the technological world, the World Wide Web is undergoing rapid growth and change. Gateway programs that are on the cutting edge today will be average performers in a few months. This should not discourage you from choosing a gateway for your database now, but it should prepare you for the new products that will arise in the future. As a taste of things to come, this section briefly touches on some of the new Web-based developments that have come about as this book was being written.

Netscape Communications Corporation, which produces the most popular Web browser on the Web, also offers a line of Web servers. A major enhancement to their Web servers is the Netscape Server API (NSAPI), which gives programmers an alternative to CGI when using a Netscape Web server. NSAPI is a programming interface that offers better performance than CGI, and also provides a way to interact with the Netscape Web server directly, with access to many of the internal functions of the server. External programs called by the Web server have greater flexibility and can do more things than programs that use the narrowly defined CGI.

Another Netscape innovation to be released soon involves their popular Web browser. The Live Wire Pro software package offers a new Web browser that has the capability to access Oracle, Informix, Microsoft, and Sybase databases built into the Web browser itself. In addition, Live Wire Pro will provide a single-user version of a relational database for developers to use when designing database access programs from the Web browser. Netscape Corporation recognizes the importance of putting databases on the Web and is creating tools that will make the process easier.

Not to be outdone, Microsoft Corporation has developed its own Web browser, the Internet Explorer, and Web server, the Internet Information Server. Initially surprised by the phenomenal growth of the Web, Microsoft has been making up ground in a hurry. The Internet Information Server has its own programming API called the Internet Server API (ISAPI), which offers yet another alternative to CGI and to the Netscape Server's API. In fact, Microsoft has announced that when Windows NT Server 4.0 comes out sometime this year, the Internet Server will be bundled with it free of charge. Windows NT will be a big player in the future of the World Wide Web.

Microsoft also announced recently they would be making free software available on their Web site that will make their popular FoxPro database software Web-aware and provide FoxPro users a way to put FoxPro databases on the Web. Obviously, Microsoft is making a big charge at owning a piece of the Web.

As you browse through the list of available gateway products in the next section, keep in mind the current pace of development will continue to produce new products that will offer more features and better performance. Get what you need today, but keep an eye out for the future as new products emerge.

A List of Available Products

The rest of this chapter is a listing of Web-database gateway products with a brief description of each. Nothing that deals with the World Wide Web can claim to be exhaustive, but the following list is as complete as possible. New products arise frequently, and established products change features with each new version, but as of this writing, the following descriptions and feature lists are correct. The product descriptions have been gleaned from the associated Web pages. The URL for each product's Web page is included for you to do further research.

Most of these are gateway products designed to facilitate connecting your database to the Web. Others are tools you can use to build your own gateway. In some cases, the tools do not have a Web site, but are readily available for download at an ftp site, so the ftp site is listed instead.

Each product is marked as follows:

- Free (F)
- Shareware (S)
- Commercial (C)
- Unknown (U)

The products are broken into categories based on what operating system they support, either Unix, Microsoft Windows, Macintosh, or Other. Some products may be listed multiple times if they support more than one platform.

This information is maintained on the Web at the following address. Look there for the most recent information regarding Web/database gateway products and tools.

`http://cscsun1.larc.nasa.gov/~beowulf/db/existing_products.html.`

Unix

dbCGI (F) uses embedded SQL in HTML documents to execute database queries and format the results. Support for Informix and Progress requires ESQL/C. Sybase support requires DB-Library. Oracle and Ingres support requires similar software. You can port dbCGI to other databases by writing your own interface module. dbCGI has support for BLOB data, such as images, sound, and video.

`http://www.progress.com/webtools/webtools.htm`

DBperl (F) is a database Application Programming Interface (API) for the Perl language. The DBperl API Specification defines a set of functions, variables, and conventions that provide a consistent database interface independent of the actual database being used.

`http://www.hermetica.com/technologia/DBI/`

Decoux (F) is an Oracle-specific gateway written in Oraperl or Oracle's PRO*C programming language. Decoux opens an HTML document that contains pseudo-HTML tags with SQL statements in the tags. The SQL statements are executed and the pseudo-tags are replaced by the data retrieved from the database and the document is displayed.

`http://dozer.us.oracle.com:8080/sdk10/decoux/`

GemStone WWW Gateway (F) is a gateway between the GemStone Object Oriented DBMS and the World Wide Web. It is implemented entirely in GemStone Smalltalk and supports forms and user authentication.

`http://ftp.tuwien.ac.at/~go/Implementation.html`

Genera (F) is a Sybase-specific gateway that uses a proprietary syntax to create a database or use an existing one. Genera language text files are parsed to get a description of a database and the format it should have when displayed as a Web page. Genera also supports form-based queries. Genera is written in Perl and Sybperl and provides query-only capability.

`http://gdbdoc.gdb.org/letovsky/genera/genera.html`

GSQL (F) is a C program that is specific to the Mosaic Web browser. It is called by a shell script which is called by the HTTP server. GSQL uses processing files—PROC files—which contain HTML tags that map database components to HTML elements. User input is sent to the database, and the results are converted to HTML using the PROC file formatting instructions. GSQL is a query-only gateway.

`http://www.santel.lu/SANTEL/SOFT/gsql_new.html`

HyperSTAR Web Developer's Kit (C) enables any HTML browser to dynamically interact with a wide variety of relational and legacy databases. The WDK is based upon an object-messaging middleware product, HyperSTAR. It is compatible with all Web servers that support the CGI standard. Each kit contains a visual query builder, a C-language API, a database-specific access server, and documentation. Access servers are currently available for Oracle, Sybase, Informix, uniVerse, Ingres, and Micro Focus Cobol ISAM. Future releases will support IBM's DB2 for MVS.

`http://www.vmark.com/products/wdk/index.html`

Informix CGI Interface Kit (F) is a C library of function calls that require the Informix ESQL/C or 4GL programming languages. The kit gives the developer a set of Web-database development tools that offers full database functionality including BLOB management routines.

`http://www.informix.com/informix/dbweb/grail/freeware.htm`

Ingres Tools Archive (F) is a collection of tools for using Ingres databases. There are a few Web-oriented tools on this Web site that provide query-only support, but you have to search for them.

`http://www.adc.com/ingres/iua/naiua-tools.html`

isqlperl (F) is an Informix/perl interface language. It requires Perl 4.036 and the Informix ESQL/C compiler.

`ftp://ftp.demon.co.uk/pub/perl/db/isqlperl/isqlperl-1.1.shar.Z`

KE Texpress (C) is an object-oriented database system that can handle formatted text and multimedia objects (jpegs, mpegs, and so forth). Together with Texhtml, a proprietary WWW database gateway, users can publish Web pages with query and update capabilities.

`http://www.dingo.com/`

Mini SQL (S) is a lightweight database engine written in C that has very low memory requirements. It offers a limited subset of the SQL database language, but comes with utilities that enable you to administer your database, as well as enforce access control. Also included is a good user's manual in PostScript format.

`http://AusWeb.com.au/computer/Hughes/`

MORE (F) is a meta-data based repository using the Mosaic Web browser as the only GUI. MORE's meta-data contains information about "artifacts," which can be on the file system, in another database, or even another software package. Access is controlled through user groups. The meta-data is displayed with a hypertext link to the data itself. MORE is Oracle-specific, but support for other databases is forthcoming.

`http://rbse.jsc.nasa.gov:81/DEMO/`

MOWI (F) is a replacement executable for the wowstub.c program released as part of Oracle's WOW package. MOWI also includes the MOWI interface, which is an html forms-based SQL prompt. It enables you to type arbitrary SQL commands and have them executed by the Oracle database server.

`http://gserver.grads.vt.edu/mowi.tar.gz`

MsqlPerl (F) is a Mini SQL/perl interface language that requires Perl 5.001m or later and the Mini SQL API library.

`ftp://Bond.edu.au/pub/Minerva/msql/Contrib/MsqlPerl-1.03.tar.gz`

NeXT WebObjects (C) is an object-oriented Web development platform that runs under Windows NT and various flavors of Unix, as well as the NeXT Mach OS. It is database independent and adds a dynamic HTML presentation layer to data stored not only in object-oriented applications but also in industry standard relational databases.

`http://www.next.com/WebObjects/`

O2Web (C) is a fully modular object database system that integrates a powerful database engine with a graphic programming environment, a complete set of development tools, and programming languages. O2Web provides O2DBAccess, an SQL gateway enabling your O2 applications to manipulate information managed by any kind of SQL server on any kind of platform (AS/400, DB2, Oracle, Ingres, Sybase, Informix, OS/2 database, RDB database, SUPRA server, and so forth).

`http://www.o2tech.com`

Oracle WebServer (C) is a Web server integrated with an Oracle 7 database server. It supports standardized secure authentication mechanisms, encrypted data streams, scalability and support for very many concurrent users.

`http://www.oracle.com/mainEvent/webServer/ois1.html`

Oracle WWW Interface Kit (F) is a collection of tools for accessing Oracle databases from the WWW.

`http://dozer.us.oracle.com:8080/`

Oraperl (F) is an Oracle/Perl interface language that requires Perl 5.001m or later and Oracle's PRO*C compiler.

`http://dozer.us.oracle.com:8080/ftp/util/perl/oraperl-v2.4.tar.Z`

OrayWWW (F) is an Oracle-specific gateway written in Oraperl that lets you generate HTML forms on the fly, based on user input. OrayWWW creates template files that you can reference by calling them in other HTML documents after they are created.

`http://dozer.us.oracle.com:8080/sdk10/oraywww/`

pgperl (F) is a Postgres95/Perl interface language that requires Perl 5.001m or later and the Postgres95 API library.

Postgres95 (F) is a freeware database management system. Postgres95 grew out of the POSTGRES project at the University of California at Berkeley. If you need a database and want the source code for it, this might be the one for you. Postgres95 has more features than Mini SQL, but requires more resources. It has C, Perl, and Tcl programming APIs.

`http://s2k-ftp.CS.Berkeley.EDU:8000/postgres95/`

Sapphire/Web (C) is a GUI-based development tool that creates applications designed to use HTML as the front end. It comes with support for Informix, Oracle, and Sybase databases. Sapphire/Web generates CGI programs in C or C++ source code to which you can add your own processing code. It runs on several Unix platforms, as well as Windows 95 and NT, and the DEC Alpha.

`http://www.bluestone.com/products/sapphire/`

Sibylla (C) is a Web/database gateway that supports Mini SQL and Basis Plus under SunOS 4.1.3, HP-UX 9.0, OSF1 1.3, Linux, and VMS. (mSQL doesn't work under VMS.) Version 2.0 supports ODBC connections to Oracle, Sybase, Informix, SQL Server, and FULCRUM.

`http://www.cib.unibo.it/guests/ariadne/sibylla/sibyllaeng.html`

Software Engine (C) runs on SUN Unix platforms and requires a Sybase database because it uses Sybase database tables to store information about your forms. You define what you want and Software Engine creates the database tables for you.

`http://www.engine.com/`

Spider (C) consists of two modules: Spider Development, which is a GUI-based Web-database interface development tool, and Spider Deployment, which executes applications. Users can link HTML forms to a database using drag-and-drop. Spider supports Informix, Oracle, and Sybase servers.

`http://www.w3spider.com/website/product.html`

SQLGate (F) is a gateway for Mini SQL that uses embedded commands in HTML files. The executable is only available for the Linux operating system.

`http://think.ucdavis.edu/~cgi/SQLGate/index.html`

Sybase WWW Tools (F) is a collection of tools for accessing Sybase databases from the WWW.

`http://www.sybase.com/WWW/`

sybperl (F) is a Sybase/Perl interface language that requires Perl 5.001m or later and Sybase's DB-Library.

`http://www.sybase.com/WWW/Sybperl/sybperl-2.0.tar.gz`

TEXIS WWW Bridge (C) is a Web gateway for the TEXIS RDBMS. Supports Query, Insert, and Update transactions, as well as multimedia delivery.

`http://198.49.220.90/sqlbridge.html`

TILE (C) is a software program for creating World Wide Web sites using Lotus Notes.

`http://www.tile.net/tile/info/about.html`

UMASS Information Navigator (F) is a tool that enables a user to navigate around a relational database. The Navigator is based on a meta-database that contains information about the real data. A configuration file contains the opening screen information, including the views contained in the meta-database. The Navigator presents the user with a choice of these views to search within. Once in a view, the user continues to make choices narrowing the search until a specific query form is generated. This product supports Oracle and Basis+ databases.

`http://info.oit.umass.edu/navigator.html`

W3-msql (F) is a gateway written for Mini SQL that enables a developer to embed any mSQL commands in HTML files and perform database queries on the fly, processing the returned results in a variety of ways.

`http://AusWeb.com.au/computer/Hughes/w3-msql`

WDB (F) is a query-only gateway written in Perl. It comes with modules that support Informix, Mini SQL, and Sybase. A script determines your database table structure and creates a file definition form (FDF). By customizing the FDFs, you can perform joins, constrain queries to specified fields, format the input and output, and so on.

`http://arch-http.hq.eso.org/bfrasmus/wdb/`

WDB-p95 (F) is a version of WDB written for Postgres95.

`http://www.eol.ists.ca/~dunlop/wdb-p95/`

WebDBC (C) runs on Windows 95 and NT, Macintosh, and Sparc Solaris platforms. It uses ODBC and CGI to provide complete functionality and access to any ODBC compliant database.

`http://www.ndev.com/`

WebinTool (F) is a generic WWW to SQL-database interface building tool. Only the INGRES DBMS is supported in this version (v1.0), but it can be ported (without too much effort) to other databases.

`http://www.ri.bbsrc.ac.uk/webintool.html`

WebLogic dbKona (C) is a vendor-independent, high-level, object interface for accessing an Oracle, Sybase, or Informix database from any non-applet Java program. dbKona is used to develop stand-alone, "two-tier" client-server Java applications. dbKona/T3 enables Java applets to access relational databases using a scalable "three-tier" architecture implementation.

`http://weblogic.com/`

WORA (F) is a form generator written in Oracle PRO*C and uses the Oracle system tables to get table and view information, and enables you to set query conditions for the finished form. WORA can dynamically find new tables with no setup. It cannot use multiple WHERE conditions, GROUP BY or ORDER BY, DISTINCT, and other SQL parameters.

`http://dozer.us.oracle.com:8080/sdk10/wora/`

WOW (F) is a gateway that uses a cgi-script as a stub to call Oracle stored procedures, then processes the output.

`http://dozer.us.oracle.com:8080/sdk10/wow/`

WWWBase (U) is a Web server and database combination written entirely in Perl 5. The database portion can be used alone with a regular Web server using CGI.

`http://fxfx.com:8080/`

Windows 3.1/95/NT

4w Publisher (C) runs under Windows (3.1/95/NT) and uses Microsoft's Access Jet Engine as its underlying database. Generates static Web pages that can be stored on any Web server. A CGI version of 4W Publisher will be released soon.

`http://www.4w.com/4wpublisher/`

AXONE'S dbWeb 2.0</A> (F) is a freeware professional tool for designing, implementing and maintaining huge hypertexts in a platform independent format (SQL database). This product is not related to the commercial dbWeb. MS Windows 3.1x and MS Access 2.0 are required.

`http://www.axone.ch/dbWeb/`

A-XOrion (C) runs under Windows 3.1, 95, or NT. It requires Microsoft Access 2.0 to be installed because it is built around Access tools. A-XOrion is a CGI gateway that can access most brand-name PC databases. It has full Query, Insert, Update, and Delete support. A-XOrion requires a Pentium CPU and 16 MB of RAM.

`http://www.clark.net/infouser/endidc.htm`

Cold Fusion (C) runs under Windows 95 and Windows NT and can access any database that is ODBC compliant. Cold Fusion is a CGI program that sends queries to the database. Template files determine how output is presented to the user. Cold Fusion can create dynamic HTML pages in response to user input by mixing HTML tags and Database Markup Language (DBML) to dictate how the results are displayed.

`http://www.allaire.com/cfusion`

DataRamp (C) comes in two parts. DataRamp Client enables you to connect your ODBC-enabled tool to a database anywhere on the Internet. DataRamp Server is a Windows NT service that listens for requested ODBC connections and passes them to your ODBC-compliant database.

`http://dataramp.com/`

DB Gateway (C) enables you to access MS Access and FoxPro databases directly. You don't need anything but the "mdf" or "dbf" files. Queries can be RQBE, internal Access, or external sql files. Query results can be returned in raw tabular form or piped into external report templates that use HTML-like syntax. The addition of external report templates means that you can build virtual www-db applications (that is, the returned report can be itself a form that is resubmitted back to the gateway).

`http://fcim1.csdc.com/dbgate.htm`

dbWeb (C) runs under Windows NT as a multithreaded NT service and can use any ODBC-compliant data source. dbWeb provides full insert/update/delete capabilities. Graphical administration tools help you set up and maintain a repository database that stores the information dbWeb needs to create dynamic HTML forms to access a database.

`http://www.aspectse.com/Product/dbWeb/dbWeb.html`

FoxPro/HTML Internet Project (U) isn't exactly an interface product, but is a project to develop Web accessible databases using FoxPro. If that's what you're looking for, check this site out.

`http://www.waterware.com/mark/foxhtml.html`

FoxWeb (C) is a software tool that allows World Wide Web servers to interface with FoxPro data and programs.

`http://www.intermedia.net/aegis/`

NeXT WebObjects (C) is an object-oriented Web development platform that runs under Windows NT and various flavors of Unix. It is database independent and adds a dynamic HTML presentation layer to data stored not only in object-oriented applications but also in industry standard relational databases.

`http://www.next.com/WebObjects/`

ORALink (F) is freeware product for Windows NT that works with Oracle 7 Server for NT. ORALink is a multithreaded, CGI 1.1 compliant, Windows NT console application that uses the POST method to get output from forms.

`http://oradb1.jinr.dubna.su/Software/ORALink/`

R:WEB (C) is an Internet version of R:BASE that is designed to run under Windows NT Server. It has a Form Designer tool to create forms and link them to the database. When the form is run, R:WEB converts it into HTML. No knowledge of HTML or CGI is required by the programmer. R:WEB requires RBASE 5.5 and provides full database functionality.

`http://www.microrim.com/RBASE_Products/Software/RWeb.html`

Sapphire/Web (C) is a GUI-based development tool that creates applications designed to use HTML as the front end. It comes with support for Informix, Oracle, and Sybase databases. Sapphire/Web generates CGI programs in C or C++ source code to which you can add your own processing code. It runs on several Unix platforms, as well as Windows 95 and NT, and the DEC Alpha.

`http://www.bluestone.com/products/sapphire/`

TEXIS WWW Bridge (C) is a Web gateway for the TEXIS RDBMS. Supports Query, Insert, and Update transactions, as well as multimedia delivery.

`http://198.49.220.90/sqlbridge.html`

TGate (C) allows information to be added to Lotus Notes databases by Internet users on the World Wide Web.

`http://www.shelby.com/pub/shelby/tgate.html`

TILE (C) is a software program for creating World Wide Web sites using Lotus Notes.

`http://www.tile.net/tile/info/about.html`

Tool Kit Internet (C) is a set of Visual Basic procedures that enable users of the O'Reilly WebSite Web server to create their own database systems on the World Wide Web.

`http://highsierra.com/highsierra/products.htm`

Web2SQL (C) is a gateway interface between Microsoft SQL Server and Netscape Server under Microsoft Windows NT that uses the Netscape API instead of CGI.

`http://www.nutech.com/products/`

WebBase (C) runs under any Microsoft Windows platform and accesses data in Microsoft SQL Server, Access, FoxPro, or Excel, as well as dBASE III and IV, Btrieve, Paradox, and Oracle 6 or 7. WebBase uses embedded SQL statements in HTML documents, and includes a full-featured macro language, mathematical functions, and database logging features, among others.

`http://www.webbase.com/`

WebDBC (C) runs on Windows 95 and NT, Macintosh, and Sparc Solaris platforms. It uses ODBC and CGI to provide complete functionality and access to any ODBC-compliant database.

`http://www.ndev.com/`

Worb Web (C) uses a database back end to provide an application framework for multiple users to design their own Web applications with database access, but without knowing anything about how to connect a Web page to a database. It currently only works with Oracle databases, including Personal Oracle 7, but is being ported to other databases.

`http://www.indra.com/plusplus/worbweb.html`

Macintosh

NetLink/4D (C) connects 4th Dimension (4D) databases to a WebSTAR Web server. NetLink/4D handles all events between 4D and WebSTAR including multiple simultaneous events, and multiple 4D processes.

`http://www.fsti.com/productinfo/netlink.html`

ROFM CGI (F) connects FileMaker Pro databases to the Web using WebSTAR or MacHTTP Web servers. ROFM CGI supports multiple databases with add, find, and get capabilities.

`http://rowen.astro.washington.edu/`

Tango (C) integrates Butler SQL and the WebSTAR Web server. It comes in two parts: Tango CGI, which is a CGI interface to link Butler SQL to WebSTAR, and Tango Editor, which is a GUI environment used to create query documents.

`http://www.everyware.com/Tango_Info/default.html`

WebDBC (C) runs on Windows 95 and NT, Macintosh, and Sparc Solaris platforms. It uses ODBC and CGI to provide complete functionality and access to any ODBC-compliant database.

`http://www.ndev.com/`

Web FM (C) is a CGI program that links FileMaker Pro database to WebSTAR Web servers. Web FM supports most FileMaker Pro database operations, and accessing multiple databases from a single Web server.

`http://macweb.batnet.com/webfm/`

Other (OS/2, NeXT, DEC Alpha)

DB2WWW (F) is IBM's WWW interface to their DB2 database product. It uses standard HTML and SQL. The HTML forms and SQL queries are stored as macro files on the Web server machine. The macro files are processed by DB2WWW when the user requests data, and performs variable substitution to access the requested data. DB2WWW also facilitates access to Oracle and Sybase servers. It can include secure data transfer when used with other IBM products. It runs on OS/2, AIX, and some AS/400 servers.

`http://www.software.ibm.com/data/db2/db2wfac2.html`

NeXT WebObjects (C) is an object-oriented Web development platform that runs under Windows NT and various flavors of Unix, as well as the NeXT Mach OS. It is database independent, and adds a dynamic HTML presentation layer to data stored not only in object-oriented applications but also in industry standard relational databases.

`http://www.next.com/WebObjects/`

Sapphire/Web (C) is a GUI-based development tool that creates applications designed to use HTML as the front end. It comes with support for Informix, Oracle, and Sybase databases. Sapphire/Web generates CGI programs in C or C++ source code to which you can add your own processing code. It runs on several Unix platforms as well as Windows 95 and NT, and the DEC Alpha.

`http://www.bluestone.com/products/sapphire/`

Putting It All Together

Now that you have mastered the WWW, learned how to use CGI to access a database, chosen a database engine, modeled a database schema, constructed a database, and picked an interface, how do you put all of them together and put your database on the Web?

No single chapter can cover every possible combination, so the examples are limited to two completely different platforms: Unix and Windows NT. Most Web and database servers on the Internet use one of these two operating systems.

Unix is the traditional Internet operating system, and the advent of public domain Unix clones, such as Linux and FreeBSD, has made the power of Unix readily available as a Web and database server to anyone who has an Internet connection.

Windows NT is the hot new platform for Web servers. No other platform has experienced such an explosive growth in users and support software. Commercial products that connect databases to the Web using ODBC have found a home on Windows NT.

The following sections guide you step by step through installing the software necessary for putting a database on the Web, from installing the database to compiling and installing any supporting software. By the end of the chapter, you should have a good idea of what is involved in putting a database on the Web and which platform can best serve your needs.

Case Study 1: Linux, Mini SQL, WDB

The first case study focuses on showing you how to put a database on the Web as cheaply as possible, using free and shareware products that meet most of your needs. It also intends to give you an idea of the types of problems and difficulties that can arise when you use products that have little or no technical support behind them.

This case study covers the following topics:

- The hardware for Case Study 1
- The software needed for Case Study 1
- Building and installing the software
- Constructing the Mini SQL database
- Creating FDF files
- Creating Web pages
- Modifying WDB

Even if you plan to use an expensive Unix machine and a commercial database, much of this example still applies. You can use all the products used in this case study on many versions of commercial Unix, and the basic principles of connecting a database to the Web apply no matter what hardware and software you use.

One thing to keep in mind when using public domain software is the constant change in version numbers. Because public domain software is not subject to the rigid testing standards of commercial software, new versions can appear literally overnight. This is a good way to add new features and fix bugs in the old versions, but being on the "bleeding edge" of technology has its price.

All too often, a major new release of a public domain software package has a few rough edges that will take several more versions to polish off. If you like having the newest of everything, public domain software is what you want.

If, on the other hand, you depend on free software to power a Web site that must be dependable, automatically updating every new version that comes out isn't wise. Wait out major new improvements and stay with a tested, more stable version. You can get a good idea of which versions are regarded as ones to keep by reading newsgroups or subscribing to mailing lists.

Unfortunately, the prudent path also poses obstacles. Software developers must stay up with the market and might not want to support older versions of their software. Staying with an older version of one software package can limit what other software you can use because the other applications might require a newer version of the stable software you use.

Like any other public domain software, all the packages used in this example have version requirements. Each one is identified and any possible consequences are mentioned. The main idea here is to use the most stable set of applications possible while taking advantage of as many new features as possible.

The Hardware for Case Study 1

The computer used in this example is a Gateway 2000 486/66 with 16 megabytes of RAM. The 486/66 is relatively slow compared to the new Pentium machines on the market, but remember, you're trying to minimize spending and a 486 can be had quite cheaply. When running the Linux operating system, a 486/66 operates surprisingly fast and handles moderate loads easily.

If your database will be fairly large, buying more RAM will help more than upgrading your CPU, but the Gateway motherboard has only four RAM slots, which limits total RAM to 64 MB. If you require more than 64 MB and find another brand of computer that offers more available RAM slots, check the size of memory chips the motherboard will accept. Some computers are limited to 4-MB memory chips, which don't do you any good. To maximize the amount of RAM a computer can hold, 16-MB chips are the size you need.

The Linux operating system is installed on a SCSI hard drive and is dual-booted with Windows 95. This means the computer can run Windows 95 or Linux, depending on which one you choose when you start the computer. If you can afford to dedicate a machine to running a Web server, you can remove any other operating system and make Linux the only operating system. If you plan to run the server only part of the time and need another operating system for daily use, Linux can coexist with all popular operating systems. Just be sure you have enough hard drive space to support multiple systems and the applications for each.

The Software Needed for Case Study 1

Several software packages are needed to construct this case study. The software needs to be compiled, configured, and installed in order for all the pieces to work together. The software needed are listed here:

- The Linux Operating System
- The NCSA Web Server
- The Mini SQL Database Server
- The Perl Language
- The Web Database Interface (WDB)
- The MsqlPerl Extensions

The following sections discuss each software package, the version number required, where to get the software, and some resources available on the Internet to learn more about each software package.

The Linux Operating System

The Linux operating system has been around for several years and has gone through literally hundreds of version numbers. Version 1.2.13 is used in this example, and is widely considered to be one of the most stable versions of Linux ever developed. After the 1.2.x development, the new versions of Linux have moved to an experimental kernel that is the heart of the operating system.

As a testament to the stability of version 1.2.13, the new 1.3.x version has already gone beyond 1.3.45, or 45 releases, as of this writing and new releases in the series have come out literally overnight. The new 1.3.x kernel offers some excellent new features, but other pieces of the operating system continue to undergo severe growing pains.

The major new upgrade to the Linux kernel changes the *Executable and Linking Format* (ELF) so that using shared system libraries is much easier and more efficient. This in itself is no reason to upgrade to the 1.3.x series, but because Linux is moving to ELF, other applications will be also.

The gcc compiler, which is essential to compiling software under Linux, is moving to the ELF format, as are the C libraries gcc uses to compile programs. This will encourage other application developers to move to the ELF format as well.

What does this mean if you choose version 1.2.13 as your development platform? It means you have a stable operating system as the basis of your platform. It also means you probably will eventually upgrade to a 1.3.x or higher version somewhere along the line. The key is to wait long enough to get a stable version in which all the applications you need are compatible with the new format, but not so long you have to discard everything you have done and start over.

If you're adventurous, you can convert the 1.2.13 kernel to the ELF format. One problem you face taking that approach is that you need both old and new versions of many system libraries, and because some software (most notably the Mosaic and Netscape Web browsers) is not ELF compatible, you would be forced to run a mixed old and new system. You could do it, but doing so might not be worth the trouble.

The best way to stay abreast of the changes in the Linux operating system is to subscribe to related Usenet newsgroups. A quick newsgroup search for the keyword "linux" brings up the following newsgroups:

- alt.os.linux
- alt.uu.comp.os.linux.questions
- comp.os.linux.hardware
- comp.os.linux.help
- comp.os.linux.misc
- comp.os.linux.networking
- comp.os.linux.setup
- comp.os.linux.x

Others undoubtedly exist as well. Periodically scanning the posts in these newsgroups can acquaint you with the newest versions of Linux and the Internet community's opinions of them. The newsgroups also serve as an excellent source of experience and information should you ever need help.

The NCSA Web Server

The Web server, or http server, used in this example is the version developed by the National Center for Supercomputing Applications (NCSA). Why? It's free, for one, and for another, it's one of the most widely used HTTP servers on the Internet and has become a de facto standard.

The latest version is 1.5a. For an explanation of the version numbers, the following is from the http README file:

```
Version Number Defined
-------------------------
1.5.1a
| | ||
| | | - Portability and typos.  ie, not anything special, but just to keep
| | |   us honest
| |  -- Bug fixes, minor features (as requested or provided)  Also security
| |     fixes.
| |
```

```
¦  ---- Major revisions.  Probably not going to be another until 2.0
 ------ Really major revisions, code overhauls, goal changes, language
        changes
```

You can obtain httpd_1.5a at the following site:

```
ftp://ftp.ncsa.uiuc.edu/Web/httpd/Unix/ncsa_httpd/httpd_1.5/
```

The distribution version of 1.5a available for Linux is for version 1.2.13 with ELF support, as indicated by the names on the files:

```
httpd_1.5a-export_linux1.2.13_ELF.Z

httpd_1.5a-export_linux1.2.13_ELF.tar.Z
```

The file ending `.tar.Z` contains all the source code you need to compile your own version. The file ending with `.Z` is a binary already compiled for you. Before you can use this version, you need an ELF-based system. If you don't have ELF, just download the following file:

```
httpd_1.5a-export_source.tar.Z
```

The generic version of 1.5a enables you to compile a Linux version that doesn't require ELF support.

HTTP servers of all kinds are discussed in the following newsgroups:

- comp.infosystems.www.servers.mac
- comp.infosystems.www.servers.misc
- comp.infosystems.www.servers.ms-windows
- comp.infosystems.www.servers.unix

The Mini SQL Database Server

Mini SQL, also referred to as *mSQL*, is a lightweight database engine that implements a subset of the ANSI SQL standard. mSQL is a shareware product authored by David J. Hughes, and is free to educational and research organizations but requires a fee for commercial use. (The fee is insignificant compared to the cost of a commercial database server.)

By implementing only a subset of the available SQL commands, mSQL requires very little in the way of computer resources and is easy to set up and use. The features and data types it supports are limited, but do meet most applications' needs. Most people don't need a full-blown database server, and Mini SQL was developed to give users a slimmed-down relational database server. For more information on Mini SQL, see the Mini SQL documentation included in the book's appendix.

mSQL comes with a nice user's guide (in PostScript format) that covers the basics of the available SQL commands, the included C programming API, the command-line interface, and the various administration tools provided with the database engine.

mSQL is written in C and distributed with the complete source code. You have to compile the executables yourself, but the mSQL configuration program is one of the easiest-to-use packages available on the Internet.

Mini SQL is available for ftp from Bond University in Australia:

`ftp://Bond.edu.au/pub/Minerva/msql`

The version used here is msql-1.0.10, which is the latest version as of this writing. David Hughes currently is working on a version 2 release, but it probably won't be backward compatible. David currently is supporting version 1 with patches and maintenance releases while he works on version 2.

For problems that might arise, whether they be questions on how to do something using mSQL or discovering a possible bug in the database software, you can use an active mailing list dedicated to mSQL users. The author is a regular poster, as are other Mini SQL "experts" familiar with the source code, SQL, and many other aspects of database use.

To subscribe to the mSQL mailing list, send a message to `msql-list-request@bunyip.com`, using the word **subscribe** as the body of the message. To send a message to the mailing list, address it to `msql-list@bunyip.com`.

The Perl Language

Perl is fast becoming the programming language of choice for shell programmers and people who used to use awk and sed. Quite a few C programmers are migrating to Perl as well because the syntax is similar and it can do some things C cannot.

Perl is free software distributed under the GNU Public Software License, and some versions of Perl run on practically every type of machine in the universe, including DOS, Windows NT, and the Macintosh, not to mention every flavor of Unix (where Perl was born).

Perl is available all over the place. A more useful list of ftp sites follows:

`ftp://ftp.cis.ufl.edu/pub/perl/CPAN/src/5.0/`

`ftp://ftp.netlabs.com/pub/outgoing/perl5.0/`

`ftp://ftp.metronet.com/pub/perl/source/`

`ftp://sunsite.doc.ic.ac.uk/pub/computing/programming/languages/perl/perl.5.0/`

The version of Perl used in this example is 5.001m. The "m" patchlevel is important because the other software used in this example requires version 5.001m. As of this writing, 5.001n has been released, but commonly is referred to as a "developers version" and isn't really intended for public consumption. Perl 5.002 is currently in beta, but the latest stable full production release is 5.001m, so that's the one used here.

Perl is discussed in the following newsgroups, among others:

- comp.lang.perl.announce
- comp.lang.perl.misc

Numerous books have been written about Perl, and more are on the way owing to Perl's immense popularity among programmers. Two very good Perl manuals are *Learning Perl* and *Programming Perl*, published by O'Reilly & Associates. *Programming Perl* is co-authored by the author of Perl, Larry Wall. Unfortunately, these books only cover Perl through version 4, but a version 5 rewrite is in development.

The Web Database Interface (WDB)

WDB is a public domain CGI gateway written in Perl. WDB comes with modules that support Sybase, Informix, and mSQL, providing you have the appropriate interface software. There will be more discussion about interface software in a later section, "The MsqlPerl Extensions." WDB is a query-only gateway, but the majority of database access is limited to select statements.

WDB uses template files called *Form Definition Files* (FDF) to define the database schema. The FDF is used to generate HTML forms on-the-fly, which is nice because no HTML files clutter up your hard drive. The FDF can be customized to change the way the HTML form is used.

WDB was developed at the Space Telescope—European Coordinating Facility (ST-ECF) in Europe. The original programmer has moved on to other things, and the author does not actively support WDB. Developers (including the author of this book) still use WDB and continue to expand its functionality, but no organized support framework exists for it, such as does for Linux, Mini SQL, and Perl. WDB has been chosen as a representative sample of how free Web-to-database gateways work and because of the ease with which it can be modified, as you will be shown later in the section "Modifying WDB."

WDB can be downloaded from the following URL:

```
http://arch-http.hq.eso.org/wdb/html/wdb.html
```

The version used for this example is wdb1.3. The ST-ECF reports they have version 1.4, which they use internally, but which they will not make publicly available until they replace the original WDB developer.

The MsqlPerl Extensions

When using Perl and WDB to access an mSQL database, one element is missing: the piece that passes SQL commands to the database and gets back the results. That missing link is MsqlPerl.

MsqlPerl is a Perl extension written by Andreas Koenig that uses the mSQL API to access a Mini SQL database. MsqlPerl bridges the gap between Perl and mSQL by defining a set of function calls that a Perl program can load and use to call mSQL database functions.

You can find Perl extensions for virtually every kind of Unix-based database, such as isqlperl for Informix, oraperl for Oracle, and sybperl for Sybase. A software application currently under development, called Dbperl, is intended to replace all the various flavors of database Perl extensions.

Dbperl eventually will become a generic Perl interface to any database, including those that use ODBC. Mini SQL is one of the databases that Dbperl supports, but the full product will take some time to complete. Until then, MsqlPerl will support mSQL just fine.

MsqlPerl can be found at the same ftp site as Mini SQL:

```
ftp://Bond.edu.au/pub/Minerva/msql/Contrib/
```

The latest version is MsqlPerl1.03, which is the one used in this example.

MsqlPerl has a low-volume mailing list that you subscribe to by sending a message that contains the word **subscribe** as the body of the message to the following address:

```
msqlperl-request@franz.ww.tu-berlin.de
```

You can send messages to everyone subscribed to the mailing list by sending mail to the following address:

```
msqlperl@franz.ww.tu-berlin.de.
```

Note

The mailing address for subscribing to the mailing list, and the address to post messages to the mailing list are not the same. Pay attention to the address you send your messages to and do not send a subscribe or unsubscribe message to the mailing list by mistake.

It is embarrassing when your lack of attention is broadcast to a mailing list read by people all over the world.

The mSQL mailing list also discusses some MsqlPerl topics, and the MsqlPerl author commonly posts there.

Building and Installing the Software

After you have all of the software listed previously, you must compile most of it and install all of it. This section discusses possible methods of deploying all of the software, depending on what level of access you have to the server machine. As a reminder, the software used in this case study is listed below, along with the required version numbers:

- Linux 1.2.13
- NCSA Web server 1.5a
- Mini SQL 1.0.10
- Perl 5.001m
- MsqlPerl 1.03
- WDB 1.3

The following sections take you through the installation and configuration of each software package, with the exception of the Linux operating system, with an eye toward making the software work best for publishing your database on the Web.

Although including directions on how to install and set up the Linux operating system probably would prove useful, doing so goes far beyond the scope of this book, owing to the many different types of computers and an endless array of configurations that would require individual instructions on how to set up each one. For more information on installing Linux, try reading *Building a Linux Internet Server*, by New Riders Publishing.

Several different distributions of Linux are available. All the software is freely available at ftp sites, but requires considerable patience and time to download it all. Some of the commercial distributions available on CD include Slackware, Red Hat, Yggdrasil, and Debian. Each one has varying amounts of installation instructions and accompanying software packages, but all enable you to install Linux from the CD, which is much nicer than feeding 40 floppy disks to your computer as Linux is installed.

If you don't already have Linux or are looking for a newer version, you should read the previously mentioned Linux-oriented newsgroups to find the distribution that is best for you or attend a local computer show and see what's available. Vendors on the Web offer Linux packages on CD.

Installing the Web Server

Some system administrators vehemently oppose setting up a user account to run an http server. Some system administrators, on the other hand, wouldn't do it any other way. If you don't have root access to the server machine, you have no other choice but to run the http server under your username. If you do so, please be sure your system administrator approves.

Choosing a Username

If you have root access, you can choose between two main ways to run the HTTP server. The "default" method is to start up the server as root and then after it is bound to the default http port number 80, it changes to another username, such as "nobody" or "daemon." Changing usernames prevents hackers from using the HTTP server to gain root access to your machine. The nobody or daemon user has very little system privileges, so a security break-in can do only miniscule damage.

The other method is to create a user, such as HTTP, and keep all related software under the HTTP username. You still can start the HTTP server as root, so it still has access to port 80. No user other than the root user can access port numbers below 1023. After the HTTP server is bound to port 80, it changes to the HTTP username. If you place related software, such as CGI programs, the database server, and so on, under the HTTP username, you don't encounter problems with file permissions and several Web administrators can share the http account.

The one drawback to this approach is the possibility that anyone who breaks into your system via the Web server would have access to all the HTTP user's privileges, which would include wiping out any files or directories HTTP owns—which is a bad thing.

HTTP servers in general are not easy to use as break-in vehicles, however, and whether any serious damage could be done in that manner is problematical. A break-in is also a consideration if you are running an HTTP server under your username. A lucky hacker would have access to any of your files, not just those associated with the HTTP server. The decision is up to you.

For this example, the username HTTP is the owner of all files associated with putting the database on the Web and the home directory of HTTP is /home/http.

Unpacking the Web Server Software

The first thing to do is construct an orderly plan concerning where you want to put everything. Most of the necessary software will be compiled in one place and then installed in another, which lets you tinker with the original software without changing the executable version of the program that others are using. After you have the configuration or features you want, you can install the new version of the software over the first version for everyone on the system to use.

All of our software packages will be unpacked into their own subdirectories under the /home/http directory. The first package to be installed is the HTTP server distribution package. The httpd_1.5a-export_source.tar.Z file is placed into the /home/http directory. The following commands uncompress and unpack the httpd distribution into the directory /home/http/httpd_1.5a-export/, respectively:

```
uncompress httpd_1.5a-export_source.tar.Z

tar -xf httpd_1.5a-export_source.tar
```

Tip

You can save yourself some typing time by creating a symbolic link to this directory using a shorter name.

The following command creates a link called "httpd" that you can use as the directory name:

```
ln -s httpd_1.5a-export httpd
```

When you enter the httpd directory, you see several files and subdirectories laid out for you. This is the home directory for your HTTP server.

Execute the command **make linux**, and the gcc compiler goes to work, compiling several files and then generating the executable program, httpd. Running the **httpd** program starts up the HTTP server.

Running the Web Server

When you run the httpd program for the first time, it generates the following error message:

```
httpd: could not open server config. file /usr/local/etc/httpd/
➥conf/httpd.conf
fopen: No such file or directory
```

The error message appears for two reasons:

- The HTTP server is looking in the wrong directory for the HTTP server configuration files.
- The HTTP server configuration files have not yet been set up.

The default home directory for the HTTP server is /usr/local/etc/httpd. If you don't have root access to your host machine, or you choose to put the HTTP home directory somewhere else, as in this example, you need to invoke the httpd program using a command-line flag to tell it where its new home is. The following command uses the -d command-line flag to tell the server where to look for the startup configuration files:

```
httpd -d /home/http/httpd
```

> **Tip**
>
> The preceding command is required every time you start up the http server. To make your life easier, create a simple command script, containing the single line:
>
> ```
> httpd -d /home/http/httpd
> ```
>
> If you call the script "run_http," just entering **run_http** starts the HTTP server correctly.

Notice that the name of the symbolic link is used rather than the longer httpd_1.5a-export directory name. This works fine, unless you move the HTTP directory somewhere else without updating the directory to which the link points.

Using the -d command-line flag doesn't fully resolve the problem if you haven't set up the HTTP server configuration files. Although you might expect the distribution to include some sort of instructions on setting up the HTTP server, the documentation is available only on the Web at `http://hoohoo.ncsa.uiuc.edu/`. This might seem inconvenient, but when you consider how often the HTTP server software is upgraded, it makes sense—the latest documentation always is available on the Web and the software developers only need to update one copy (and this update is essentially instantaneous).

Setting Up the Web Server Configuration Files

For your convenience, the necessary configuration files are identified and the parameters that might need to be changed are shown, along with comments on some possible configuration options. A mindboggling number of possible settings are available for the HTTP server, but a basic setup requires only a few changes to the template configuration files provided with the server software.

All of the HTTP server configuration files have a warning similar to the following at the beginning, which you would do well to read closely:

```
#========================================================================
# NCSA HTTPd (comments, questions to httpd@ncsa.uiuc.edu)
#========================================================================
# See URL http://hoohoo.ncsa.uiuc.edu/ for HTTPd Documentation.
# Information specific to this file can be found at
# http://hoohoo.ncsa.uiuc.edu/docs/setup/srm/Overview.html
# Do NOT simply read the instructions in here without understanding
# what they do.  If you are unsure, consult the online docs.  You
# have been warned.
#========================================================================
```

Warning

Indiscriminately setting the config file parameters can result in strange HTTP server behavior, and might create security holes you won't know about until after damage is done. Be careful.

You can find the first configuration file to edit in the /home/http/httpd/conf directory. In this directory, copy the file http.conf-dist to the name "http.conf" because the HTTP server expects a file named http.conf to be in the /home/http/httpd/conf directory. By copying the original file instead of changing the name, you can mess up the copy and still have an original file with which you can start over.

The http.conf file configures how the HTTP server will run. The following listing includes changes to the http.conf file. You must change only a few parameters in the http.conf file. The rest are preferences you can choose to use after you become familiar with the server software.

If you run the HTTP server without root access, the port number will need to be changed. Port number 8080 is a common selection.

```
# Port: The port the standalone listens to. For ports < 1023, you
# will need HTTPd to be run as root initially.
# Default: 80 (or DEFAULT_PORT)

Port 80
```

In previous versions of NCSA's HTTP server, only one server was used until more were needed, at which time another HTTP server instance was started. Instead of the overhead of constantly starting new servers, the HTTP server program starts up StartServer servers, and, as more are needed, they are created up to MaxServers. New servers are not shut down, but remain in the server pool until needed again. Having a pool of servers greatly increases server performance and response time.

```
# StartServers: The number of servers to launch at startup. Must be
# compiled without the NO_PASS compile option
# Default: 5 (or DEFAULT_START_DAEMON)

StartServers 5
```

```
# MaxServers: The number of servers to launch until mimicking the 1.3
# scheme (new server for each connection).  These servers will stay
# around until the server is restarted.  They will be reused as needed,
# however. See the documentation on hoohoo.ncsa.uiuc.edu for more infor-
# mation. If compile option RESOURCE_LIMIT is used, HTTPd will not mimic
# the 1.3 behavior, and MaxServers will be the maximum number of servers
# possible.
# Default: 10 (or DEFAULT_MAX_DAEMON)

MaxServers 20
```

This example uses the username "http." You will need to change the User parameter to the name of the process your server will run under. The default is "nobody."

> **Warning**
>
> Do not run the HTTP server as "root."

```
# If you want HTTPd to run as a different user or group, you must run
# HTTPd as root initially and it will switch.
# User/Group: The name (or #number) of the user/group to run HTTPd as.
# Default: #-1 (or DEFAULT_USER / DEFAULT_GROUP)

User http
Group #-1
```

Change the following e-mail address to that of your Web administrator.

```
# ServerAdmin: Your address, where problems with the server should be
# e-mailed.
# Valid within <VirtualHost>
# Default: <none> (or DEFAULT_ADMIN)

ServerAdmin http@lightspeed.beowulf.com

#======================================================================
# File Locations
#----------------------------------------------------------------------
# ServerRoot: The directory the server's config, error, and log files
# are kept.
# Note: All other paths will use this as a prefix if they don't start
# with / Default: /usr/local/etc/httpd (or HTTPD_ROOT)

ServerRoot /home/http/httpd
```

Not all Web browsers can use this paramcter, but if they can, the time required to load a Web document can decrease dramatically. Each piece of a Web page, text, background images, images for buttons or bars, and so on, requires a request to the Web server. In the past, each piece required a separate connection, but the KeepAlive parameter enables a Web browser to get all of the pieces with a single connection.

```
#===========================================================================
# KeepAlive Directives
#---------------------------------------------------------------------------
# The directives below configure keepalive, the capability of the server
# to maintain a persistent connection with a client at the client's
# request

# The following line turns keepalive on. The default is off, so
# you can omit this line, or change 'on' to 'off'

# KeepAlive on
```

To get the HTTP server to run, this section needs to be commented out or the /local directory changed or created. If you use the VirtualHost option, the file localhost_srm.conf-dist needs to be copied to the name localhost_srm.conf and the options set. The localhost_srm.conf file is not used for our example.

```
# VirtualHost allows you to look differently depending on the hostname
# you are called by.  The parameter must be either an IP address or a
# hostname that maps to a single IP address.  Most of the normal httpd.
# conf commands are available, as well as the capability to denote a
# special ResourceConfig file for this host.
# You can also specify an error level with this setting, by denoting
# the VirtualHost as Optional or Required.

#<VirtualHost 127.0.0.1 Optional>
#DocumentRoot /local
#ServerName localhost.ncsa.uiuc.edu
#ResourceConfig conf/localhost_srm.conf
#</VirtualHost>
```

The next file to edit also is contained in the same /home/http/httpd/conf directory. Copy the file srm.conf-dist to the name "srm.conf." The following listing includes changes to the srm.conf file. You must make four changes. Any other preferences are up to you.

DocumentRoot is the name of the directory in which requested documents will be searched for, unless a full path name is given. For example, just opening the URL `http://lightspeed.beowulf.com/` will look in DocumentRoot as the default. The htdocs directory does not exist, so needs to be created. The name you choose may be different.

```
#===========================================================================
# Name Space Options
#---------------------------------------------------------------------------
# DocumentRoot: The directory out of which you will serve your
# documents. By default, all requests are taken from this directory, but
# symbolic links and aliases may be used to point to other locations.

DocumentRoot /home/http/httpd/htdocs
```

If other users will be allowed to serve Web pages from this HTTP server, they can create a "public_html" directory in their home directories, and the HTTP server will automatically look there for user documents.

```
# UserDir: The name of the directory which is appended onto a
# user's home directory if a ~user request is received.

UserDir public_html
```

Aliases enable you to put things in one place and reference them from HTML documents somewhere else. The HTTP server knows where the real location is by using the alias.

```
# Aliases: Add here as many aliases as you need. The format is
# Alias fakename realname

Alias /icons/ /home/http/httpd/icons/
```

ScriptAlias is *very* important because it is the place your CGI programs will be kept.

```
# ScriptAlias: This controls which directories contain server
# scripts. Format: ScriptAlias fakename realname

ScriptAlias /cgi-bin/ /home/http/httpd/cgi-bin/
```

The `AddType application/x-httpd-cgi .cgi` line is important if you plan to allow other users to run CGI programs from your server. This example requires all CGI programs outside the ScriptAlias directory to end with the file extension .cgi before the HTTP server will attempt to execute them.

```
# The following are known to the server as "Magic Mime Types."  They
# enable you to change how the server perceives a document by the exten-
# sion. The server currently recognizes the following mime types for
# server side includes, internal imagemap, and CGI anywhere.  Uncomment
# them to use them. Note: If you disallow (in access.conf) Options
# Includes ExecCGI, and you uncomment the following, the files will be
# passed with the magic mime type as the content type, which causes
# most browsers to attempt to save the file to disk.

#AddType text/x-server-parsed-html .shtml
#AddType text/x-imagemap .mapAddType application/x-httpd-cgi .cgi
```

The last file to edit also is contained in the /home/http/httpd/conf directory. Copy access.conf-dist to the name “access.conf.” The following listing includes changes to the access.conf file. You must make two changes.

ServerRoot is in the http.conf file.

```
# /usr/local/etc/httpd/ should be changed to whatever you set
# ServerRoot to.

<Directory /home/http/httpd/cgi-bin>
Options Indexes FollowSymLinks
</Directory>
```

DocumentRoot is in the srm.conf file.

```
# This should be changed to whatever you set DocumentRoot to.

<Directory /home/http/httpd/htdocs>
```

After you create the HTTP server, be sure to create the /home/http/httpd/htdocs and /home/http/httpd/logs directories—otherwise, the HTTP server will not run.

If you use port 80, change to the root user before you start the HTTP server. Execute the following command (your location may be different):

```
/home/http/httpd -d /home/http/httpd
```

Assuming you performed the changes correctly, the HTTP server will run. To make sure the server started, execute the following command:

```
ps -ax | grep httpd
```

You should see something similar to the following:

```
934  ?  S     0:00 /home/http/httpd/httpd -d /home/http/httpd
935  ?  S     0:00 /home/http/httpd/httpd -d /home/http/httpd
936  ?  S     0:00 /home/http/httpd/httpd -d /home/http/httpd
937  ?  S     0:00 /home/http/httpd/httpd -d /home/http/httpd
938  ?  S     0:00 /home/http/httpd/httpd -d /home/http/httpd
939  ?  S     0:00 /home/http/httpd/httpd -d /home/http/httpd
```

The ps command shows you one parent process that controls five http servers. Your http server is up and running!

Installing Mini SQL

Compared to the HTTP server, Mini SQL is a cinch to configure and install. In our example, the mSQL source files are untarred into the /home/http/msql-1.0.10 directory. After you compile the software, the executables and any databases reside in the /home/http/msql directory, unless you put them elsewhere.

Unpacking the Database Software

The msql-1.0.10.tar.gz file is placed in the /home/http directory and the following commands uncompress and unpack the mSQL source code into the /home/http/msql-1.0.10 directory, respectively:

```
gunzip msql-1.0.10.tar.gz
```

```
tar -xf msql-1.0.10.tar
```

Mini SQL has a nice configuration program that detects the type of operating system you have and sets itself up accordingly. The README file that comes with the Mini SQL distribution gives you instructions on how to compile Mini SQL.

To begin the process, enter the /home/http/msql-1.0.10 directory and enter the command **make target**. The following information appears during the configuration of the Mini SQL package:

```
Making target directory for Linux-1.2.13-i486
Building directory tree.
        Adding common
        Adding sample
        Adding conf
        Adding makegen
        Adding msql
        Adding regexp
        Adding tests
        Adding tests/rtest.src
        Adding makedepend

Adding sym-links
.................................................................
.....................

Build of target directory for Linux-1.2.13-i486 complete
```

The target directory is targets/Linux-1.2.13-i486/. Entering this directory puts you where the software will be compiled. Enter the command **setup**. The configuration program asks the following questions. The answers may differ for your system, depending on where you put things.

```
Interactive configuration section
        Top of install tree ? [/usr/local/Minerva] /home/http/msql
        Will this installation be running as root ? [y] n
        What username will it run under ?  http
        Directory for pid file ? [/var/adm] /home/http/msql
```

After you answer these questions, the configuration software determines various things about the system and what features Mini SQL can use.

After the configuration program ends, enter the command **make all**. New makefiles are generated by the make utility based on your system parameters, and the compiler goes to work compiling the Mini SQL source files.

After the compilation finishes, you need to copy the Mini SQL software to the /home/http/msql directory. Enter the command **make install** to create all the necessary subdirectories, copy all the necessary files to the appropriate places, and set the correct permissions on files and directories.

The executable programs are not the only Mini SQL files you need. Any application software that takes advantage of the Mini SQL programming API will need the include files and the API programming library. All of these files also are copied to the appropriate destination under the /home/http/msql directory.

Running the Database Server

Go to the /home/http/msql/bin directory and enter the following command:

```
msqld &
```

If the software compiles correctly, the following message appears:

```
mSQL Server 1.0.10 starting ...
Warning : Couldn't open ACL file: No such file or directory
```

This warning message isn't a problem. The access control list file tells the Mini SQL database server which users have access to which database. Access control isn't used in this example, so no ACL file is needed. The Mini SQL database server is now up and running.

You should test the server to make sure everything is working correctly. The Mini SQL software includes several test programs for this purpose. The first step is to create a database named "test" by entering the following command, which creates the test database:

```
msqladmin create test
```

You also use the msqladmin program to shut down the database, as follows:

```
msqladmin shutdown
```

Just shutting down the computer without neatly terminating the mSQL server is not a good idea because database corruption can result in rare circumstances.

The first database test script is located in the /home/http/msql-1.0.10/targets/Linux-1.2.13-i486/msql directory. Enter this directory and execute the following command:

```
msql test < sample.msql > test_result
```

The test generates about 300 lines of output, so the output is redirected into the file "msql_result." Look through msql_result to make sure everything is working correctly. A couple of error messages are generated, but they indicate the database is working correctly by preventing illegal commands from being executed.

Other, more severe, test scripts can be found in the /home/http/msql-1.0.10/targets/Linux-1.2.13-i486/tests directory. Run those if you want to produce benchmarks for your database server, or if you want to be really sure the server is running correctly.

Patching the Database Software

One of the nice things about subscribing to the Mini SQL mailing list is that users occasionally report a bug. When this occurs, the mailing list subscribers usually discuss whether it really is a bug or the user is doing something wrong. If the problem turns out to be a bug, someone figures out a patch to the source code and posts it to the mailing list. The following mail message is from the Mini SQL author, David Hughes, and offers a simple patch to a problem that causes Mini SQL to lock up on rare occasions. (Some of the mail header information has been changed to protect the innocent.) This mail message gives you an idea of the type of message posted to the mailing list, as well as shows you how Mini SQL patches are posted.

```
Date: Thu, 30 Nov 1995 11:30:54 +1000 (EST)
X-Sender: bambi@glen
To: <deleted>
Cc: msql-list@bunyip.com
Subject: [mSQL] re: weird mSQL freezing
Sender: owner-msql-list@bunyip.com
Precedence: bulk
Reply-To: "David J. Hughes" <bambi@Hughes.com.au>
Errors-To: owner-msql-list@bunyip.com

OK, problem solved.

The problem is a 1 liner in bSort() where it recurses once too far and
ends up calling itself with an upper bound of MAX_UINT (i.e. unsigned 0 -
1).  The problem is solved by the following patch.


*** src/msql/msqldb.c    Thu Nov 30 11:28:25 1995
--- src/msql/msqldb.c.new        Thu Nov 30 11:27:41 1995
***************
*** 5170,5176 ****
                else
```

```
                        bSwap(entry,high,newHigh);
        }
!       bSort(entry, order, olist, low+1, high-1);
  }


--- 5170,5179 ----
                else
                        bSwap(entry,high,newHigh);
        }
!       if (high != 0)
!       {
!               bSort(entry, order, olist, low+1, high-1);
!       }
  }
Bambi
...

   /   /            /               David J. Hughes      Bambi@Hughes.com.au
  /___/        ___  /__  ___  ___   Managing Director    Hughes Technologies
 /   / /  /  /  / /  / /__/ /__     Ph: 0412 644 078       Fax: 07 3302 2199
/   / /__/  /__/ /  / /__  ___/     WWW: http://AusWeb.com.au/computer/Hughes
           __/

---------------------------------------------------------------------------
To remove yourself from the Mini SQL mailing list send a message containing
"unsubscribe" to msql-list-request@bunyip.com.  Send a message containing
"info msql-list" to majordomo@bunyip.com for info on monthly archives of
the list. For more help, mail owner-msql-list@bunyip.com NOT the msql-list!
```

To apply the patch, cut the patch information out of the preceding mail message so you are left with the following in a file by itself:

```
*** src/msql/msqldb.c    Thu Nov 30 11:28:25 1995
--- src/msql/msqldb.c.new        Thu Nov 30 11:27:41 1995
***************
*** 5170,5176 ****
                else
                        bSwap(entry,high,newHigh);
        }
!       bSort(entry, order, olist, low+1, high-1);
  }


--- 5170,5179 ----
                else
                        bSwap(entry,high,newHigh);
```

```
        }
!       if (high != 0)
!       {
!               bSort(entry, order, olist, low+1, high-1);
!       }
  }
```

Assuming the name of the file into which you put the patch information is called "msql_patch," you can apply the patch by going to the directory that contains the mSQL source code (in this case, /home/http/msql-1.0.10/src/msql) and using the "patch" program.

The following command runs the patch program and feeds it the patch file:

```
patch -l < msql_patch
```

The -l parameter causes the patch program to ignore all blank lines when trying to figure out where to apply the patch. This eliminates problems with source code formatting.

When the patch program runs, it returns the following message:

```
Hmm...  Looks like a new-style context diff to me...
The text leading up to this was:
--------------------------
|*** src/msql/msqldb.c    Thu Nov 30 11:28:25 1995
|--- src/msql/msqldb.c.new        Thu Nov 30 11:27:41 1995
--------------------------
Patching file msqldb.c using Plan A...
Hunk #1 succeeded at 5170.
done
```

This message indicates that the patch was applied successfully. After you patch the source code, you should recompile the source code, as well as any application programs that use mSQL libraries.

Installing Perl

Installing Perl is not hard, but can be quite time-consuming. You will have to answer so many questions of the configuration program that your hair might fall out from old age, if you don't pull it out from frustration. Hang in there. After you finish, your answers are saved, so if you need to change anything, you need enter only the changes the next time you run the configuration program.

Unpacking Perl

The Perl distribution is untarred into the /home/http/perl5.001m directory using the following commands:

```
gunzip perl5.001m.tar.gz

tar -xf perl5.001m.tar
```

Enter the /home/http/perl5.001m directory and read the README file. README tells you far more about configuring and installing Perl than you will ever need to know, but the information is useful.

Configuring Perl

The first thing to do is enter the **Configure** command, and be prepared to answer questions. Most of the questions have default answers that the Configuration program supplies. Although the defaults usually are correct, you will need to change some of them, based on how you install Perl.

Some of the notable questions asked of you and appropriate answers are detailed as follows.

On the Linux system used in this example, gcc is aliased to cc. Configure is smart enough to figure that out. The compiler used makes a difference on how the Perl programs should be compiled.

```
Use which C compiler? [cc]

Checking for GNU cc in disguise and/or its version number...
You are using GNU cc 2.6.3.
```

If you do not have root access on your machine, you will need to install Perl somewhere other than in the system directories. Configure figures out where Perl is currently installed on your system and gives you the option of replacing the current version with the new version. For our example, that is what will be done. Another possible installation prefix to use would be /home/http/perl. The configure program uses your answer and prefixes all other install directories with the directory name you give it.

```
By default, perl5 will be installed in /usr/bin, manual
pages under /usr/man, etc..., i.e. with /usr as prefix for
all installation directories. Typically set to /usr/local, but you
may choose /usr if you want to install perl5 among your system
```

```
binaries. If you wish to have binaries under /bin but manual pages
under /usr/local/man, that's ok: you will be prompted separately
for each of the installation directories, the prefix being only used
to set the defaults.

Installation prefix to use? (~name ok) [/usr]
```

Answering "no" to the next question is one of the unfortunate consequences of using a version of Linux without ELF support. Perl 5.001m has a nice feature called "dynamic loading" that is only supported under Linux versions that support ELF. Dynamic loading allows Perl to load a minimum of program code into memory when invoked, and load other Perl modules dynamically as they are needed. This reduces Perl's memory usage and makes it run faster as well. By not using dynamic loading, all Perl modules are compiled into a single executable and are all loaded into memory when Perl is run. It works just fine, but is not as elegant.

```
Do you wish to use dynamic loading? [n]
```

In order to use Perl's setuid feature, you have to have root access to install the Perl executables. If you don't have root access, answer "n" to the following question.

```
Some systems have disabled setuid scripts, especially systems where
setuid scripts cannot be secure.  On systems where setuid scripts have
been disabled, the setuid/setgid bits on scripts are currently
useless.  It is possible for perl5 to detect those bits and emulate
setuid/setgid in a secure fashion.  This emulation will only work if
setuid scripts have been disabled in your kernel.

Do you want to do setuid/setgid emulation? [y]
```

If you do not use dynamic loading, it is a good idea not to use Perl's malloc function either.

```
Do you wish to attempt to use the malloc that comes with perl5? [n]
```

If you see a warning message such as the following, this is Perl's way of telling you there might be a compatibility problem with a particular feature on your machine. In the following case, the dbm functions do not work under Linux, so Perl is letting you know there is a problem with this feature. Perl keeps a collection of hint files with possible problems for many different operating systems, and provides warnings for each.

```
*** WHOA THERE!!! ***
    The recommended value for $d_dbm_open on this machine was
    "undef"!
    Keep the recommended value? [y]
```

If you have other extensions to add to Perl, this is where to add them. For Perl to find an extension program automatically, create a directory for the program in the /home/http/perl5.001m/ext directory and put the source code there. If Configure finds the new source code, it will be added to the list presented here. If you were using dynamic loading, you would have the choice of statically compiling the extensions into Perl by listing them here, or you could answer “none” here and list them all later when asked which programs to load dynamically.

```
Looking for extensions...
A number of extensions are supplied with perl5.  Answer "none"
to include no extensions.

What extensions do you wish to include?
[DB_File Fcntl GDBM_File ODBM_File POSIX SDBM_File Socket]
```

If you encounter any question not mentioned here, accepting the default the Configure program presents should work fine. After you answer all questions, Configure writes many configuration files and allows you to run the **make depend** command to propagate the configuration files throughout the Perl source code tree.

After Configure is done, just enter the **make** command and then go get something to eat. Unless you have a fast machine with no other users on it, compiling Perl takes a long time. Compiling Perl for this example took about 12 minutes on an unloaded system—an eternity in computer time.

Testing Perl

After Perl finishes compiling, enter the command **make test** to run a series of tests on the Perl executable before you install it to make sure everything compiled correctly. The test should conclude with `All tests successful.` If not, see the README file for possible solutions.

If all the tests are passed, enter the command **make install** to install all the Perl programs, include files, and libraries. If you replace the existing Perl files, you need to be the root user to install Perl. This also takes time, but not as much as the source code compile.

If you did not install Perl in the system directories, you need to enter the full path to your version of Perl (such as /home/http/perl/bin/perl) before you can use the correct version. Entering the command **perl -v** should result in the following message:

```
This is perl, version 5.001

        Unofficial patchlevel 1m.

Copyright 1987-1994, Larry Wall

Perl may be copied only under the terms of either the Artistic License
or the GNU General Public License, which may be found in the Perl 5.0
source kit.
```

If you see the correct message, you have successfully configured and installed Perl 5.001m.

Installing MsqlPerl

MsqlPerl is an extension to the Perl language that provides a Perl-based interface to a Mini SQL database server. The MsqlPerl package effectively links the mSQL programming API library into Perl and provides a set of Perl subroutines to call the API functions. This gives any Perl program access to an mSQL database by including the MsqlPerl package in the Perl code. MsqlPerl version 1.03 requires version 5.001m of Perl.

Unpacking MsqlPerl

Unpack the MsqlPerl-1.03.tar.gz file into the /home/http/MsqlPerl-1.03 directory using the following commands:

```
gunzip MsqlPerl-1.03.tar.gz

tar -xf MsqlPerl-1.03.tar
```

From here, the installation of MsqlPerl gets complicated. If the version of Perl used here supported dynamic loading, following the README instructions and installing the MsqlPerl package into the Perl library directory would work. If you were to do that here, however, the first attempt to use MsqlPerl would give you the following error message:

```
Can't load module Msql, dynamic loading not available in this perl.
  (You may need to build a new perl executable which either supports
  dynamic loading or has the Msql module statically linked into it.)
 at /usr/lib/perl5/Msql.pm line 56
```

Because the version of Linux used in this example does not support dynamic loading, and Perl was compiled without dynamic loading support, you must statically link MsqlPerl into Perl the same way as the other extensions. Doing so can be done in more than one way.

Configuring MsqlPerl

One way is to create the directory /home/http/perl5.001m/ext/Msql (or wherever you install Perl) and move everything the MsqlPerl-1.03 directory contains, including its subdirectories, into it. When you rerun Perl's Configure program, Configure automatically finds MsqlPerl as an extension. Recompiling Perl combines the MsqlPerl code into Perl's code and works exactly as if you were to dynamically load MsqlPerl. Statically linking MsqlPerl into the system version of Perl provides all users on your system (who have Perl) access to write programs that access your Mini SQL database server.

The other way works even if you don't have access to Perl's system directories. The README file contains three steps for configuring and installing MsqlPerl.

1. Enter the command **perl Makefile.PL**. The setup program asks the following question:

   ```
   Where is your msql installed? Please name the directory that
   contains the subdirs lib/ and include/. [/usr/local/Minerva]
   ```

   The msql installation directory for this example is /home/http/msql, so respond accordingly. This generates the MsqlPerl Makefile.

2. Enter the command **make**, which generates the appropriate Perl files.

3. Enter the command **make test**. Before the tests are run, the *make* utility creates a new version of Perl in the MsqlPerl directory. The new Perl executable contains the MsqlPerl code statically linked into it. This

version of Perl is used by the make utility to run the MsqlPerl tests. If any of the tests fail, it may be time to post a message to the MsqlPerl mailing list.

If you want a version of Perl that will execute Perl programs that use MsqlPerl, you have it. Just put it somewhere where others have access to it, and MsqlPerl is installed. Using a separate version of Perl for Mini SQL access enables you to control access to your database, instead of allowing everyone on your system to write mSQL access programs. Regardless of which method you use, MsqlPerl now should be installed and available for use.

Installing WDB

In contrast to the preceding programs, WDB is written in Perl, so it doesn't need to be compiled. All you have to do is change some pathnames and parameters in the WDB configuration and CGI script files so the WDB program can get the information it needs about your database and directory system.

The WDB distribution wdb1-3a.tar.gz is one of those nasty tarfiles that does not create a subdirectory for what it unpacks. Unpacking the distribution in your home directory creates several files and subdirectories in your home directory (and finding all the pieces of WDB might take a while).

Unpacking WDB

Create a directory and move the wdb1-3a.tar.gz file into it. You will move WDB into the /home/http/wdb1-3a directory and unpack it there. The following commands unpack all the files and create the WDB directory structure for you:

```
gunzip wdb1-3a.tar.gz

tar -xf wdb1-3a.tar
```

All the documentation is available as HTML files and distributed throughout the directory structure. If you are the type of person who likes a hard copy of documentation to hold in your hand, use your Web browser to contact the following URL, which is a Web page constructed by the original WDB developer and offers links that enable you to download the documentation in PostScript format:

```
http://arch-http.hq.eso.org/bfrasmus/wdb/alpha1.3.html
```

Most Linux distributions offer the "ghostscript" program, which enables you to view the documentation without a PostScript printer.

Note

The documentation is oriented toward the Sybase database, which is the database for which WDB was originally developed. Appendix D of the PostScript documentation contains the mSQL-specific instructions, or if you don't have that, the README.html file in the wdb1-3a/contrib/msql directory contains the same information.

Configuring WDB

WDB is a CGI program that resides in the httpd/cgi-bin directory. The other files WDB requires must also reside under the httpd directory so the HTTP server can find them. WDB requires a configuration file, database template files, an HTML help file, and some GIF images used as buttons. The HTML language affords no way for a user to define their own buttons, so WDB has GIFs that look like buttons.

Tip

Stay alert here because this can get confusing. The directories and pathnames used here are just suggestions. You are free to do things your own way, but if you do, the configuration files must then reflect your choice of directory structure, not the structure shown in this example.

From the directory /home/http/wdb1-3a/cgi-bin, copy the Perl scripts "wdb" and "comments" into the /home/http/httpd/cgi-bin directory. The WDB program is the main WDB CGI program. If you can't put the WDB program in the httpd cgi-bin directory and must use another directory, remember to rename wdb to wdb.cgi so the HTTP server can recognize it as a CGI program. Do the same to the comments program, which is a program that enables users to send suggestions and bug reports to the Webmaster.

Create the directory /home/http/httpd/wdb. From the /home/http/wdb1-3a/conf directory, copy the files wdb.conf and msql_dbi.pl into the new directory. The wdb.conf file contains configuration information about your system and the type of database you use. The msql_dbi.pl file is a Perl program that serves as the interface between WDB and an mSQL database.

Create the directory /home/http/httpd/htdocs/wdb. Copy all files in the /home/http/wdb1-3a/html directory to this new directory. These files are the GIF button images and the HTML help file for WDB.

Copy the file /home/http/wdb1-3a/perl-lib/cgi-lib.pl to the /home/http/httpd/cgi-bin directory. The file, cgi-lib.pl, is Steven Brenner's Perl library for reading HTML form data passed to Perl programs via standard input.

The msqlfdf program in the /home/http/wdb1-3a/contrib/msql directory is a utility WDB provides to create the template files needed for WDB to generate HTML forms for database access. You should put msqlfdf in a directory (perhaps /home/http/bin), so that anyone who needs to create WDB template files has access to it. In the example here, it is installed in the /home/http/bin directory.

All necessary WDB files now are in place and need to be configured.

Edit wdb in the /home/http/httpd/cgi-bin directory. The first two lines should be changed from

```
#!/usr/server/arc/bin/sybperl
$CONFIG_DIR = '/usr/local/etc/httpd/wdb';
```

to

```
#!/usr/bin/perl
$CONFIG_DIR = '/home/http/httpd/wdb';
```

The preceding two lines are the only ones you need to change in WDB.

Edit the wdb.conf file in the /home/http/httpd/wdb directory. At line 7, set the variable $server to the name of your database server machine, such as lightspeed.beowulf.com. At line 20, the variable $DBI_FILE should be changed from syb_dbi.pl to msql_dbi.pl. Throughout the rest of wdb.conf, change any reference to `bfrasmus@eso.org` to the e-mail address of the person responsible for WDB support; here, `http@lightspeed.beowulf.com`.

For compatibility with Perl, you must "escape" the `@` symbol so that Perl can recognize it as a symbol rather than a formatting command. If you see the following message when you try to use WDB, you have forgotten to escape the `@` symbol:

```
Error reading configuration file /home/http/httpd/wdb/wdb.conf:
Literal @eso now requires backslash at /home/http/httpd/wdb/
wdb.conf line 30, within string
```

Perl uses the @ symbol as a formatting instruction. In order to use the @ symbol and tell Perl not to use it as a formatting instruction, put a '\' character in front of it. This is called escaping the @ symbol, and it tells Perl to treat the @ as a simple character. The e-mail address becomes `http\@lightspeed.beowulf.com`. At line 49, the reference to `arch-http.hq.eso.org` should be replaced with the name of your HTTP server; in this case, `lightspeed.beowulf.com`.

That is all that needs to be changed in wdb.conf.

Edit "comments" in the /home/http/httpd/cgi-bin directory. Line one should be changed to read:

```
#!/usr/bin/perl
```

At line 34, you should set the variable $HTTPUSER to the e-mail address of the person responsible for WDB; in this case, `http\@lightspeed.beowulf.com`. At line 35, $LOGO refers to an image file on a computer in Europe, so you should change it to the name of a local image file or comment it out.

If you put the WDB files in the directories as suggested here, these should be the only necessary changes.

To test WDB, use the test database constructed when you ran the mSQL and MsqlPerl software tests. Create the directories /home/http/httpd/wdb/fdf and /home/http/httpd/wdb/fdf/test. WDB searches for all database template files in the fdf directory. Each database will have a directory named after it, such as "test" here, in which all template files associated with the database will reside.

Enter the /home/http/httpd/wdb/fdf/test directory and use the msqlfdf program to create a template file. Here, /home/http/bin is used, so execute the following command:

```
/home/http/bin/msqlfdf -d test -t test
```

The preceding command tells msqlfdf the name of the database and the table for which to create a template. Doing so generates an incomplete template file—incomplete because WDB was developed using MsqlPerl version 1.01. The new version 1.03 uses a different method to access the database. You need to patch msqlfdf before it will work correctly.

Patching WDB

Edit msqlfdf and look at line 127, which reads as follows:

```
$sth = $dbh->ListFields($opt_t);
```

You should change it to read as follows:

```
$sth = $dbh->ListFields($opt_t)
        or die "Can't find table $opt_t ...\n";
die "Error getting columns for $opt_t" unless $sth->numfields;
```

This patch gives you error checking if the script fails to find the table for which you search. Throughout the rest of the file, you should change the following code:

```
$sth->{NUMFIELDS} should be $sth->numfields,
$sth->{'NAME'} should be $sth->name,
$sth->{'TYPE'} should be $sth->type, and
$sth->{'LENGTH'} should be $sth->length.
```

Replacing these values corrects the problem and msqlfdf now runs correctly. Go to the /home/http/httpd/wdb/fdf/test directory and execute the following command again:

```
/home/http/bin/msqlfdf -d test -t test
```

This time a complete "test.fdf" file is created and should appear as follows:

```
NAME          = test
TABLE         = test
DATABASE      = test
TITLE         = test
Q_HEADER      = test Query Form
R_HEADER      = test Query Result
#DOCURL       = # URL to documentation.

#JOIN         = # Join condition ..
#CONSTRAINTS = # Extra query constraints ....
#ORDER        = # ORDER BY columns ...

#RECTOP       = # Record title ....
#PERL         = # Extra perl commands ....
#COMMENTS_TO = # Your e-mail address ....
#-----------------------------------

FIELD    = more
label    = More
from_db  = "<i>MORE</i>"
url      = "$WDB/$form{'DATABASE'}/$form{'NAME'}/query/$val{'name'}"
length   = 4
computed
forcetab
no_query
no_full

FIELD  = name
label  = Name
column = name
type   = char
length = 10
key

FIELD  = age
label  = Age
column = age
type   = int
length = 6
from_db= sprintf("%6d", $val{'age'} );

FIELD  = phone
label  = Phone
column = phone
```

```
type   = char
length = 20
```

If you get a test.fdf file that looks like the preceding file, you have patched msqlfdf correctly. If your test.fdf file does not have any Field listings, go back and carefully check the edits you made to the msqlfdf file. WDB requires the Field information in order to work.

To test WDB and be sure it is installed and configured directly, start up your Web browser and open the following URL:

```
http://lightspeed.beowulf.com/cgi-bin/wdb/test/test/form
```

Replace `lightspeed.beowulf.com` with the name of your own HTTP server machine. This URL tells WDB to look in the test database directory for the test.fdf template file and display it as a form. If you have set up everything correctly, you will load something similar to what is shown in figure 8.1 with your Web browser.

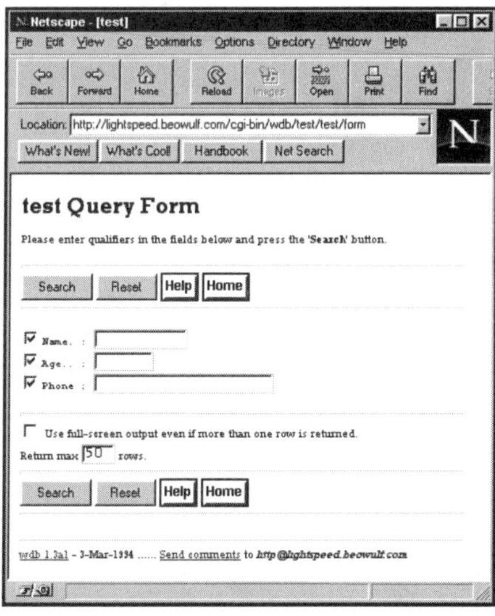

Figure 8.1
A query form for the test database.

If you see the Web page shown in figure 8.1, congratulations! You are ready to construct a database and put in on the World Wide Web. If you do not, go back and check your WDB configuration files very carefully. Setting up WDB is tough compared to Perl and Mini SQL, but after you get it right, you are ready to create a new database.

Constructing the Mini SQL Database

For this example, you implement the restaurant database designed in Chapter 6, "Constructing a Database." The safest way to construct a database is to use command files that automate the process, so if the database needs to be reconstructed, the command files can rebuild the database quickly and precisely without depending on any one person's memory to get it right.

You construct a command file for each table, based on the database schema constructed in Chapter 6. Mini SQL's msql program is used to create the tables and load the database information, so the command files for this database are stored in the directory /home/http/msql/bin/databases/restaurant. This directory does not exist, so you must create it.

First, you use the msqladmin program to create the restaurant database. The following command initializes the database files for mSQL to use and enters "restaurant" into the system tables:

```
msqladmin create restaurant
```

Creating mSQL Database Tables

The first command file to write is for the table "restaurant." Keep in mind that Mini SQL does not support serial data types, so you must artificially generate the values in the primary key field restaurant_id, or enter them by hand. The create_restaurant.msql command file and the command files for the other tables in the database are as follows:

create_restaurant.msql:

```
create table restaurant (
   restaurant_id        int primary key,
   name                 char(32),
   address1             char(32),
   address2             char(32),
   phone                char(20),
   cuisine              char(16),
   dress                char(16),
   salad_bar            char(1),
   bar                  char(1),
   handicapped_access   char(1),
   non_smoking_section  char(1),
   smoking_section      char(1),
```

```
    takeout              char(1),
    reservation_required char(1),
    reservation_taken    char(1),
    highchairs           char(1),
    booster_seats        char(1),
    kids_menu            char(1),
    kid_toys             char(1),
    diaper_table         char(1),
    senior_discount      char(1),
    personal_checks      char(1),
    american_express     char(1),
    visa                 char(1),
    master_card          char(1),
    discover             char(1),
    other_credit_cards   char(32),
    other_payment_method char(32)
)
\p\g
```

create_hours.msql:

```
create table hours (
    hour_id       int primary key,
    when          char(16),
    open_time     char(8),
    close_time    char(8),
    restaurant_id int
)
\p\g
```

create_menu.msql:

```
create table menu (
    menu_id       int primary key,
    name          char(32),
    side_dishes   char(32),
    description   char(64),
    price         real,
    notes         char(64),
    restaurant_id int
)
\p\g
```

create_food_reviews.msql:

```
create table food_reviews (
    food_review_id int primary key,
    menu_item      char(32),
```

```
   serving_size   char(16),
   food_quality   char(16),
   rating         int,
   comments       char(128),
   restaurant_id  int
)
\p\g
```

create_service_reviews.msql:

```
create table service_reviews (
   service_review_id int primary key,
   service_speed     int,
   service_quality   int,
   wait_time         int,
   crowd             int,
   lighting          int,
   atmosphere        int,
   music             int,
   comments          char(128),
   restaurant_id     int
)
\p\g
```

create_specials.msql:

```
create table specials (
   special_id    int primary key,
   when          char(16),
   description   char(64),
   price         real,
   restaurant_id int
)
\p\g
```

You can write a master command file as a shell script that creates all the tables at once by using the individual command files. The master command file, create_restaurant_database.msql, is as follows:

```
#!/bin/sh
../../msql restaurant < create_restaurant.msql
../../msql restaurant < create_hours.msql
../../msql restaurant < create_menu.msql
../../msql restaurant < create_food_reviews.msql
../../msql restaurant < create_service_reviews.msql
../../msql restaurant < create_specials.msql
```

The following command makes the shell script into an executable program:

```
chmod 744 create_restaurant_database.msql
```

Running the master file program creates the entire database, and now you're ready to load data into the database.

Loading Data into mSQL

For this simple example, the database is loaded using command files, just as the table creation was done. If you have a lot of data to load, writing a command file for all of it can be tedious.

> **Tip**
>
> Many databases have load programs that load the data from a file in a specified format very quickly. Mini SQL, unfortunately, is not one of those databases. For an mSQL loader program, connect to the ftp site where Mini SQL is available and look in the Contrib directory, in which you should find an msql_load program that might work for you.

The data for this example is noticeably fake, but illustrates how to use primary and foreign key values to connect the information in different tables together, and how to display the database information on the Web.

The command file, load_restaurant.msql, contains the following SQL statements:

```
insert into restaurant
   values ( 1, 'Bubba\'s BBQ', '1234 Redneck Rd', 'Next to the outhouse',
            '(100) 200-300', 'American', 'Required', 'N', 'Y', 'Y', 'N',
            'Y', 'Y', 'N', 'N', 'Y', 'Y', 'N', 'N', 'Y', 'N', 'N', 'N',
            'N', 'N', 'N', 'None', 'Cash'
          )
\p\g

insert into restaurant
   values ( 2, 'Joe\'s Bar and Grill', '5 Grease Ave', '', '(200) 300-4000',
            'American', 'Casual', 'Y', 'Y', 'Y', 'Y', 'Y', 'Y', 'N', 'Y',
            'Y', 'Y', 'Y', 'N', 'Y', 'Y', 'N', 'Y', 'Y', 'Y', 'N', 'None',
            'Cash'
          )
\p\g
```

```
insert into hours
   values ( 1, 'Monday-Friday', '10:00 am', '10:00 pm', 1 )
\p\g

insert into hours
   values ( 2, 'Saturday', '10:00 am', '12:00 am', 1 )
\p\g

insert into hours
   values ( 3, 'Sunday', 'Closed', '', 1 )
\p\g

insert into hours
   values ( 4, 'Monday-Friday', '9:00 am', '11:00 pm', 2 )
\p\g

insert into hours
   values ( 5, 'Saturday', '10:00 am', '2:00 am', 2 )
\p\g

insert into hours
   values ( 6, 'Sunday', '12:00 pm', '9:00 pm', 2 )
\p\g

insert into menu
   values ( 1, 'BBQ Beef', 'Fries, Beans, Slaw', 'Good BBQ', 5.99, '', 1 )
\p\g

insert into menu
   values ( 2, 'BBQ Pork', 'Fries, Beans, Slaw', 'Good BBQ', 5.99, '', 1 )
\p\g

insert into menu
   values ( 3, 'BBQ Fish', 'Fries, Beans, Slaw', 'Good BBQ', 5.99, '', 1 )
\p\g

insert into menu
   values ( 4, 'Chicken Fried Steak', 'Mashed Potatoes, Peas, Roll',
            'Covered with gravy', 7.49, '', 2 )
\p\g

insert into menu
   values ( 5, 'Chicken Salad', 'Crackers and dressing', '', 7.99,
            'Low fat', 2 )
\p\g

insert into food_reviews
   values ( 1, 'BBQ Fish', 'Huge', 'Swallow-able', 6,
```

```
            'Lots of grease and BBQ sauce.  Yum', 1 )
\p\g

insert into food_reviews
   values ( 2, 'Chicken Fried Steak', 'Big', 'Excellent', 8,
            'Juicy and crisp.', 2 )
\p\g

insert into food_reviews
   values ( 3, 'Chicken Salad', 'Average', 'Adequate', 7,
            'Ok for diet food.  I wanted a hamburger.', 2 )
\p\g

insert into service_reviews
   values ( 1, 4, 4, 0, 5, 1, 1, 0,
            'Lousy place for a family, great for truck drivers', 1 )
\p\g

insert into service_reviews
   values ( 2, 8, 9, 3, 5, 8, 8, 0,
            'Good service, good atmosphere.', 2 )
\p\g

insert into service_reviews
   values ( 3, 6, 7, 5, 7, 8, 9, 0,
            'Slow service, but a big crowd.  Quiet.', 2 )
\p\g

insert into specials
   values ( 1, 'Weekdays', 'BBQ Whale Deal with fries', 4.99, 1 )
\p\g

insert into specials
   values ( 2, 'Thursday 11-1', 'Lunch seafood buffet, all you can eat.',
            5.99, 2 )
\p\g

insert into specials
   values ( 3, 'Monday 7-9', 'Prime rib dinner', 9.99, 2 )
\p\g
```

From the directory /home/http/msql/bin/databases/restaurant, enter the following command to load the data into the restaurant database and capture the output to a file called msql_output:

```
../../msql restaurant < load_restaurant.msql  > msql_output
```

Be sure to scan the output file "msql.output" to make sure all commands were processed correctly.

After loading the database, you are ready to construct an FDF for each database table.

Creating FDF Files

Use the WDB utility msqlfdf, which you patched earlier, to create a *Form Definition File* (FDF). The raw files work just fine, but with some editing designed to make cosmetic differences in the way the HTML forms appear, the effect becomes more pleasant and professional looking.

In this example you use the restaurant table. Create the directory **/home/http/wdb/fdf/restaurant** and enter the new directory. Execute the following command to create the restaurant.fdf file:

```
/home/http/bin/msqlfdf -d restaurant -t restaurant
```

The restaurant.fdf file is the template WDB uses to generate HTML code. In its raw state, selected pieces of it look like this:

```
NAME          = restaurant
TABLE         = restaurant
DATABASE      = restaurant
TITLE         = restaurant
Q_HEADER      = restaurant Query Form
R_HEADER      = restaurant Query Result
#DOCURL       = # URL to documentation.

#JOIN         = # Join condition ..
#CONSTRAINTS = # Extra query constraints ....
#ORDER        = # ORDER BY columns ...

#RECTOP       = # Record title ....
#PERL         = # Extra perl commands ....
#COMMENTS_TO = # Your e-mail address ....
#-----------------------------------

FIELD    = more
label    = More
from_db  = "<i>MORE</i>"
url      = "$WDB/$form{'DATABASE'}/$form{'NAME'}/query/
➥$val{'restaurant_id'}"
```

```
length   = 4
computed
forcetab
no_query
no_full

FIELD  = restaurant_id
label  = Restaurant Id
column = restaurant_id
type   = int
length = 6
from_db= sprintf("%6d", $val{'restaurant_id'} );
key

FIELD  = name
label  = Name
column = name
type   = char
length = 32

FIELD  = address1
label  = Address1
column = address1
type   = char
length = 32

FIELD  = address2
label  = Address2
column = address2
type   = char
length = 32

.
.
.

FIELD  = salad_bar
label  = Salad Bar
column = salad_bar
type   = char
length = 1

FIELD  = bar
label  = Bar
column = bar
type   = char
length = 1

.
```

```
.
.

FIELD  = other_credit_cards
label  = Other Credit Cards
column = other_credit_cards
type   = char
length = 32

FIELD  = other_payment_metho
label  = Other Payment Metho
column = other_payment_metho
type   = char
length = 32
```

This is a large FDF. When created, the msqlfdf program prints a comment that you probably should add some "no_query" attributes. Exactly that is done in this exercise, among other things. Some of the longer field names have been truncated (as you might have noticed) because Mini SQL has a 20-character limit on field names. The shorter field names don't affect the way the database works, but keep them in mind as you develop database applications.

The Web browser displays the raw FDF query form as shown in figure 8.2, and the results as in figure 8.3. Note labels not capitalized, fields taking up the wrong amount of space on the output form, and other minor formatting problems.

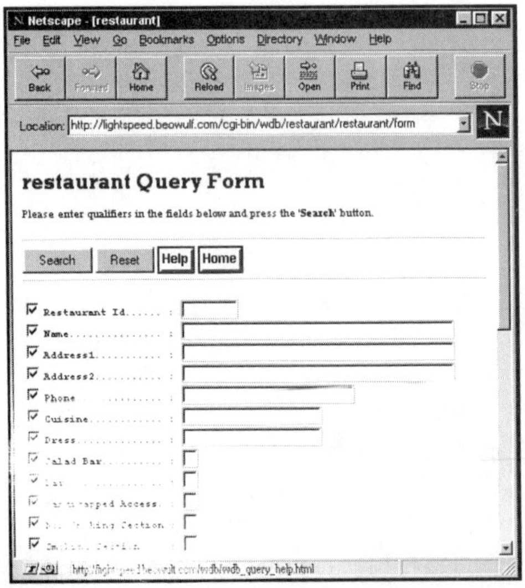

Figure 8.2
A raw WDB query form.

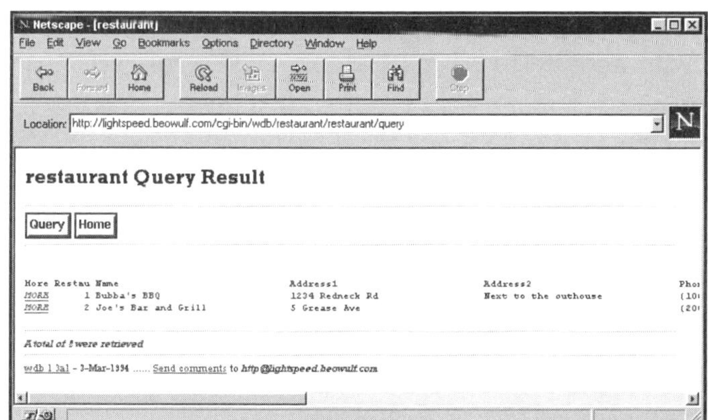

Figure 8.3
A raw WDB result.

Customizing FDF Files

The first thing to do is capitalize some things so they look better in the Web browser. You should change the TITLE, Q_HEADER, and R_HEADER values to "Restaurant." TITLE is the title that appears in the title bar of the Web browser, Q_HEADER is the header of the query form, and R_HEADER is the header of the query results form.

> **Warning**
>
> Do not change the values of NAME, which is the name of the FDF minus the .fdf extension; TABLE, which is the name of the table the FDF represents; or DATABASE, which is the name of the database in which TABLE is located. All of these are case-sensitive and fail if capitalized.
>
> For instance, if you change "NAME = restaurant" to "NAME = Restaurant," WDB will look for a file called Restaurant.fdf. On a Unix system, filenames are case-sensitive. When WDB does not find the file Restaurant.fdf, WDB will fail.

The *label* attribute for each field is the name of the field shown on the Web browser. You can change the label to whatever you want it to say. The *column* attribute is the name of the field in the database and cannot be changed or the database query will fail. You can change the field labels if you prefer the field names to be capitalized or spelled out completely when displayed by WDB.

Although some fields provide good information from the database, the user should not necessarily be allowed to enter search parameters for every field. Using the "no_query" attribute for a field in the FDF allows the user to return the field from a query, but does not allow him to specify values. You might differ with the fields designated as no_query, but the idea here is to show you how they work.

Other changes will be made to the FDF that are too numerous to mention. The polished FDF is shown here with all customizations made for you to use as an example for your own FDF files.

```
NAME         = restaurant
TABLE        = restaurant
DATABASE     = restaurant
TITLE        = Restaurant
Q_HEADER     = Restaurant Query Form
R_HEADER     = Restaurant Query Result
#DOCURL      = # URL to documentation.

#JOIN        = # Join condition ..
#CONSTRAINTS = # Extra query constraints ....
#ORDER       = # ORDER BY columns ...

#RECTOP      = # Record title ....
#PERL        = # Extra perl commands ....
#COMMENTS_TO = # Your e-mail address ....
#-----------------------------------

FIELD   = more
label   = More
from_db = "<i>MORE</i>"
url     = "$WDB/$form{'DATABASE'}/$form{'NAME'}/query/
➥$val{'restaurant_id'}"
length  = 4
computed
forcetab
no_query
no_full

FIELD  = restaurant_id
label  = Restaurant Id
column = restaurant_id
type   = int
length = 6
tablen = 3
key
```

```
FIELD  = name
label  = Name
column = name
type   = char
length = 32
tablen = 20

FIELD  = address1
label  = Address
column = address1
type   = char
length = 32
tablen = 18

FIELD  = address2
label  = Address (cont)
column = address2
type   = char
length = 32
no_query

.
.
.

FIELD  = salad_bar
label  = Salad Bar
column = salad_bar
type   = char
length = 1
no_query
enum   = ""=,Y=Yes,N=No

FIELD  = bar
label  = Bar
column = bar
type   = char
length = 1
no_query
enum   = ""=,Y=Yes,N=No

.
.
.

FIELD  = other_credit_cards
label  = Other Credit Cards
column = other_credit_cards
type   = char
```

```
length = 32
no_query

FIELD  = other_payment_metho
label  = Other Payment Method
column = other_payment_metho
type   = char
length = 32
no_query
```

The Web browser displays the polished FDF much differently. Figure 8.4 shows the query form and figure 8.5 shows the query results.

Figure 8.4
The polished query form.

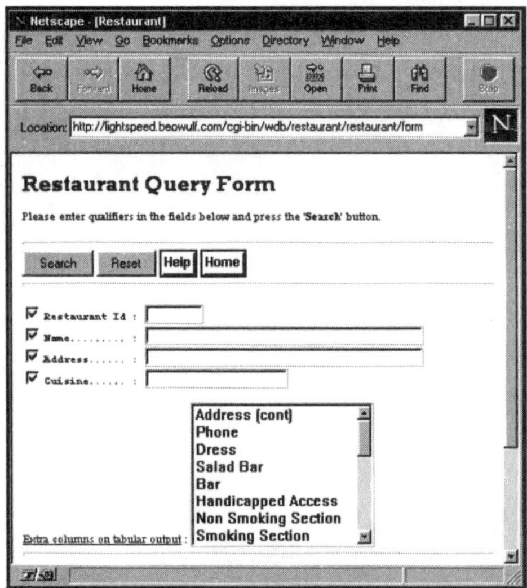

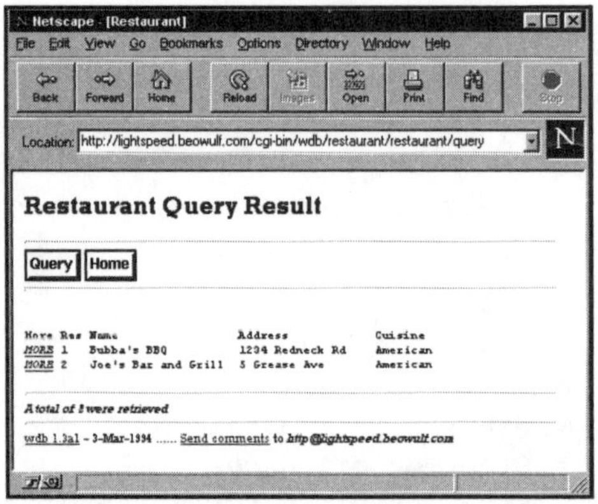

Figure 8.5
The polished query results.

WDB offers many more formatting options than can be shown in one example. You can customize forms in many ways to satisfy the pickiest user.

Creating Web Pages

Now you have a database and FDF forms, but how do you make displaying the forms in a Web browser easy for users? Requiring users to remember and manually enter long URLs is ludicrous and defeats the purpose of using an easy GUI front end such as a Web browser.

The solution to using WDB is as easy as the installation was complicated. All you need is an HTML document with hyperlinks that call wdb and pass the database and form names through the CGI gateway.

The following listing is an HTML document that can call all our FDF forms and display them in a Web browser. You can include anything else on the HTML page, such as instructions or helpful suggestions. All a user has to do is click on a hyperlink and an HTML form appears, ready to query a table in the database.

```
<HTML>
  <HEAD>
    <TITLE> Database Query Links </TITLE>
  </HEAD>
  <BODY>
  <H1> Database Query Links </H1>
  <P>Click on one of the following links to access the corresponding
      table in the database.</P>
  <BR><BR>
  <A HREF="http://lightspeed.beowulf.com/cgi-bin/wdb/restaurant/
    restaurant/form"> Restaurant</A>
  <BR><BR>
  <A HREF="http://lightspeed.beowulf.com/cgi-bin/wdb/restaurant/
    hours/form"> Hours</A>
  <BR><BR>
  <A HREF="http://lightspeed.beowulf.com/cgi-bin/wdb/restaurant/
    menu/form"> Menu</A>
  <BR><BR>
  <A HREF="http://lightspeed.beowulf.com/cgi-bin/wdb/restaurant/
    specials/form"> Specials</A>
  <BR><BR>
  <A HREF="http://lightspeed.beowulf.com/cgi-bin/wdb/restaurant/
    food_reviews/form"> Food Reviews</A>
```

```
    <BR><BR>
    <A HREF="http://lightspeed.beowulf.com/cgi-bin/wdb/restaurant/
      service_reviews/form">
      Service Reviews</A>
    <BR><BR>
    </BODY>
</HTML>
```

Figure 8.6 shows how the preceding HTML code appears displayed in a Web browser.

Figure 8.6
A Web page of WDB hyperlinks.

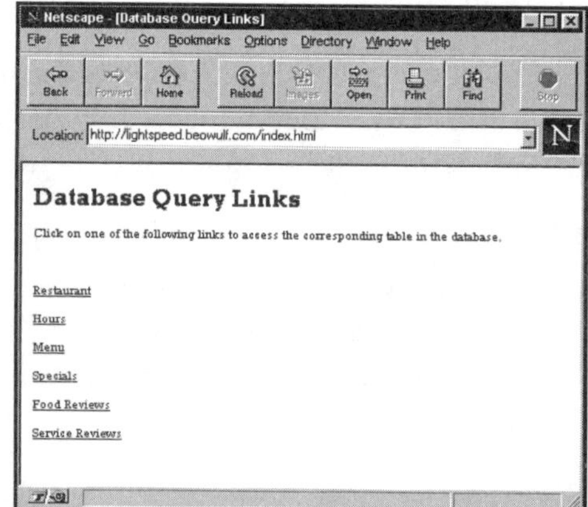

Modifying WDB

WDB is written in Perl, which is not an easy programming language to master. You don't have to be a master of Perl to begin using it with some ease, however, especially if you have a sophisticated example to which to refer, such as WDB.

As an exercise in modifying WDB to meet your needs, you add a feature that follows WDB's original methodology—a good example of using Perl and MsqlPerl to access a Mini SQL database.

Consider the HTML form shown in figure 8.7: a database query form for the hours database table. Requiring users to know the restaurant_id of the restaurant for which they want to find the hours of operation is inconvenient. It forces them to do two queries: first they must query the restaurant table to find out the restaurant_id, then they have to query the hours table using the restaurant_id to find the hours of operation.

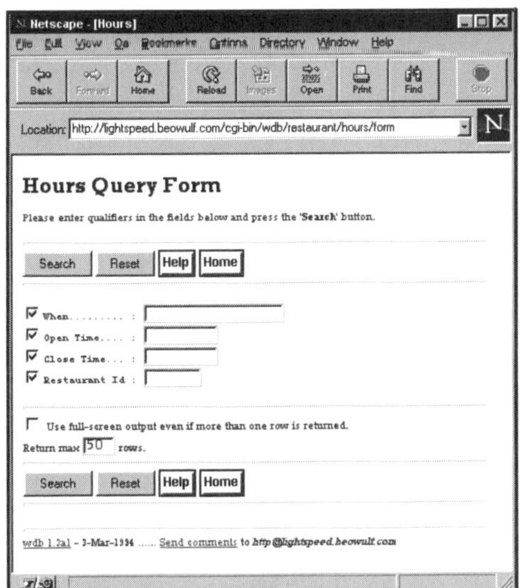

Figure 8.7
The query form for the hours table.

One solution would be to add a field for the restaurant name in the hours table, but the food_reviews and service_reviews tables would need the same thing, and repeating the restaurant name throughout the database wastes space—not to mention, it's also inelegant.

Adding an Attribute to WDB

A better way awaits. Here, you add a *picklist* attribute that can be used in the FDF file like the other field attributes. A picklist provides a way to query the database and get all possible values for a field. The values are put into an HTML SELECT list from which the user can choose, which enables the user to select the name of a restaurant rather than a hard-to-remember id number.

A subtle point of the picklist is that although allowing the user to see a restaurant name is nice, matching database records must be found by using the restaurant id, not the name. This enables WDB to display the restaurant name, but allows searching the database using the matching id.

To accomplish this magic feat, the picklist attribute requires three parameters.

- The name of the table from which to select the values we are looking for.

- The name of the field in the requested table that is the value used to search the database.
- The third parameter is the name of the field that contains the label to present to the user.

If this sounds confusing, an example is in order.

Consider the hours table. Restaurant_id is the foreign key reference to the restaurant table, and is the value that associates hour records with the appropriate restaurant record. If you could select all the restaurant names and ids from the restaurant table and show the user the names, while somehow using the associated id to select matching data from the hours table, users could find their information much more easily.

You want to select restaurant_id and name from the resturant table, show the names to the user, and select the hours data using the restaurant_id of the restaurant the user selects. It might sound hard, but it is surprisingly easy after you figure out how to use HTML to do what you want.

The picklist information uses the following format in the FDF file, where *table_name*, *value_field*, and *label_field* are variables to be replaced by the information in which you're interested:

```
picklist = table_name%value_field,label_field
```

Using this generic format lets you use the picklist attribute wherever you need it, rather than hard coding it so it works only once.

Adding a picklist to the hours.fdf file is the easy part. The restaurant_id field description does not change, except to add one line to the end of the Field listing, like so:

```
FIELD  = restaurant_id
label  = Restaurant Id
column = restaurant_id
type   = int
length = 6
from_db= sprintf("%6d", $val{'restaurant_id'} );
picklist = restaurant%restaurant_id,name
```

The complicated part lies in putting the code to handle the new attribute in just the right place in the WDB program. The right place turns out to be right after the code that processes the "enum" attribute used to limit the user's choices to Yes or No values for some of the fields in the restaurant.fdf file. The picklist attribute works similarly to the enum attribute as well, and here, you borrow some code from the enum attribute processing code.

The pertinent section of the original code is shown from line 290 of the WDB Perl code to line 316.

```
#-----------------------------------------------
# Query field : Selection box or Text input field.
#-----------------------------------------------
if ( $field{$f,'enum'} ) {
    print "<SELECT name=\"$f\">";
    foreach ( split(',',$field{$f,'enum'}) ) {
        ( $value, $title ) = /^\s*(.*)=(.*)$/;
        print "<OPTION value=\"$value\"> $title\n";
    }
    print "</SELECT>";
} else {
    if ( $field{$f,'length'} > (55-$max) ) {
        $length = (55-$max) ;
    } else {
        $length = $field{$f,'length'};
    }
    if ( $field{$f,'default'} ) {
        $default = eval $field{$f,'default'};
        if ( $@ ) {
            print "Error in $f"."'s  'default' attribute :<p>\n $@\n";
            die "Exiting...\n";
        }
    } else {
        $default = "";
    }
    print " <INPUT name=\"$f\" size=$length value=\"$default\" >";
}
```

Your changes begin at line 300, by adding an `elsif` branch to the `if` statement. The elsif branch looks for picklist attributes. The WDB source code is shown with the new code in place. Each line of the new code is numbered and is explained in detail following the source code listing.

```
#-----------------------------------------------
# Query field : Selection box or Text input field.
#-----------------------------------------------
    if ( $field{$f,'enum'} ) {
        print "<SELECT name=\"$f\">";
```

```
        foreach ( split(',',$field{$f,'enum'}) ) {
             ( $value, $title ) = /^\s*(.*)=(.*)$/;
            print "<OPTION value=\"$value\"> $title\n";
        }
        print "</SELECT>";
    } elsif ( $field{$f, 'picklist'} ) {
        if ( -f "$CONFIG_DIR/$DBI_FILE" ) {
            do "$CONFIG_DIR/$DBI_FILE" ||
                die "Error loading database interface file $CONFIG_DIR/
                ➥$DBI_FIL E :\n$@\n";
        } else {
            die "Database interface file '$CONFIG_DIR/$DBI_FILE' not found ?
            ➥\n";
        }
        &dbi_connect( $user, $pswd, $server, $form{'DATABASE'} );
        ( $tablename , $fieldnames ) = split('%',$field{$f,'picklist'});
        ( $value, $title ) = split(',', $fieldnames);
        $sql_query = "select $fieldnames from $tablename order by $title";
        undef @select_fields;
        push( @select_fields, $value );
        push( @select_fields, $title );
        &dbi_fieldnames( @select_fields ) if defined &dbi_fieldnames;
        &dbi_dosql($sql_query);
        if ( %myrow = &dbi_nextrow ) {
            print "<SELECT name=\"$f\">";
            print "<OPTION value=\"\"> <BR>";
            do {
                print "<OPTION value=\"$myrow{$value}\">$myrow{$title}<BR>";
            } while ( %myrow = &dbi_nextrow );
            print "</SELECT>";
        }
        undef @select_fields;
        &dbi_disconnect;
    } else {
        if ( $field{$f,'length'} > (55-$max) ) {
            $length = (55-$max) ;
        } else {
           $length = $field{$f,'length'};
        }
        if ( $field{$f,'default'} ) {
            $default = eval $field{$f,'default'};
            if ( $@ ) {
                print "Error in $f"."'s  'default' attribute :<p>\n $@\n";
                die "Exiting...\n";
            }
        } else {
            $default = "";
        }
```

```
        print " <INPUT name=\"$f\" size=$length value=\"$default\"
        ➥ >";
    }
```

As you can see, if takes only 26 lines of Perl code to add the picklist function. For a true Perl guru, the number would probably be less, but would not be easy for the casual to less-than-casual Perl programmer to read.

Each time WDB is called, it reads the name of the table to access from the $PATH_INFO environment variable. WDB parses the FDF file for the requested table and stores the FDF information in several associative arrays. One of those arrays is the "fields" array, which contains the name of every field in the FDF. WDB processes each field, and the name of the current field is contained in the $f variable.

Line 1 tests the FDF field currently being processed to see if it contains a picklist attribute. If so, the program enters the picklist processing loop.

Lines 2–7 load the database interface file required by the type of database being used. The interface file to use is defined in the wdb.conf file. Any function beginning with "dbi_" is a function defined in the database interface file. The interface file used for Mini SQL is dbi_msql.pl. All the functions in dbi_msql.pl are implemented in MsqlPerl. If Perl wasn't told to load the interface file, Perl would fail because it wouldn't be able to find the database subroutines.

Line 8 uses the dbi_connect( ) function to connect to the database. mSQL doesn't require the username and password. The server is the name of the machine on which the mSQL database server is running. Each FDF contains the name of the database to which it belongs. As WDB starts up, it parses the FDF and the variables at the top of the FDF, such as TITLE and DATABASE, are placed into the associative array named form. Perl finds the name of the database from this array.

Line 9 breaks the picklist information into two parts by using the percent character (%) as the delimiting character. Line 10 gets the two fieldnames by using the comma character (,) as a delimiter. At this point, WDB has the name of the table to query, plus the two fields from which to obtain the values.

Line 11 constructs the SQL SELECT statement; in this case, the following SQL command, which returns the name and id of all the restaurants, sorted in alphabetical order:

```
SELECT restaurant_id, name FROM restaurant ORDER BY name
```

Lines 12–15 tell the database interface the names of the fields to expect from the database query, which lets the interface put the database results into an associative array so the value of a field in each row can be found using the field name.

Line 16 sends the SQL query to the database. Line 17 checks to see if any results were returned from the database by trying to get the first row of results. If a row is returned, WDB enters the processing loop.

Lines 18–24 construct an HTML SELECT list that contains the information returned from the database. The first item in the list is a blank line, inserted at line 19, so the default value for the restuarant name is an empty value. This allows users to return all values from a query, not just values that match a particular restaurant name. The do loop creates options for the select list that display the name of the restaurant, but use the value of the restaurant_id as the value on which to search in the database.

Line 25 cleans up the field names variable so the next query doesn't get confused and line 26 closes the connection to the database. The new code is executed for each field in the FDF that has a picklist attribute, so more than one field can be displayed as a list of options.

Figure 8.8 shows the final result. Having a list of available restaurant names does a much better job of helping users find what they seek.

Do you feel like a Webmaster yet? You have an HTTP server, a database server, and a gateway that connects the two, putting your database on the Web!

Although connecting your database to the World Wide Web might seem like tedious work, this example was a worst-case scenario. Many Unix machines already have Perl installed, and some might already have Mini SQL installed, too. Any piece of the puzzle you already have means that much less work. Plus, after you install all the software, you don't have to limit yourself to using it for accessing a database from the Web. Perl has many uses, and you can use your Mini SQL server to store data that doesn't get served to the Web. All you have done is installed a set of tools. How you use them is up to you.

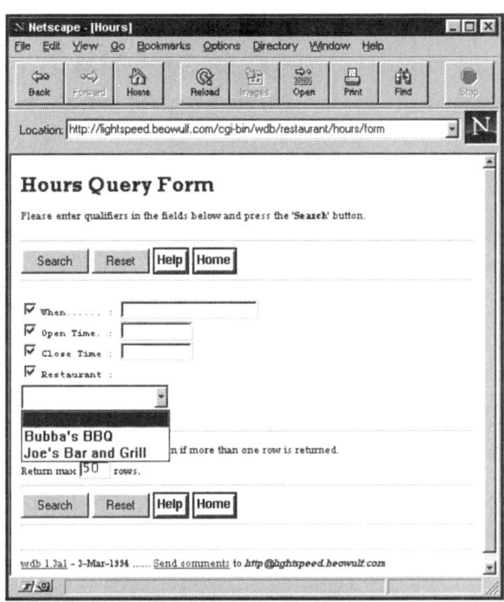

Figure 8.8
Using a picklist to search the hour table.

Case Study 2: Windows NT, SQL Server, dbWeb

The purpose of the second case study is to show you how easy it can be to put a database on the Web for a moderate amount of money. By using Windows NT, the GUI-based setup and administration tools provided by all of the software products involved greatly simplify every aspect of putting a database on the Web.

The following topics are covered in Case Study 2:

- The hardware for Case Study 2
- The software for Case Study 2
- Installing the software
- Constructing the SQL server database
- Using dbWeb

The Hardware for Case Study 2

The computer used for this example is a Micron 133 MHz Pentium with 32 MB of RAM. Although the Pentium CPU is one of the fastest available, 32 MB of RAM is the minimum for a real database server. The RAM suffices for presenting an example, but any databases developed for heavy Web access will require at least 32 MB of RAM, and probably more when you add the overhead of a Web server and associated software.

Windows NT Server is installed on a 350 MB hard drive partition and is dual-booted with Windows 95. This means the computer can run Windows 95 or Windows NT Server, depending on which one you choose when the computer starts up. If you can afford to dedicate a machine to running a Web server, you can remove any other operating system and leave Windows NT Server as the only operating system. If you plan to run the server only part of the time and need another operating system for daily use, NT can coexist with any popular operating system. Just be sure you have enough hard drive space to support multiple systems and the applications for each. Virtually any application written for Windows 95 can run under Windows NT, but the reverse is not true.

The Software for Case Study 2

For this example, all the software packages are commercial products, from the operating system to the gateway program. The software used in this example is:

- Windows NT Server
- Microsoft SQL Server
- dbWeb Gateway
- Alibaba Web Server

The following sections discuss the software listed above.

Windows NT Server

Windows NT comes in two flavors: Windows NT Workstation and Windows NT Server. NT Workstation is designed to run primarily as a single-user desktop operating system. NT Server is designed to handle network and other types of server chores for multiple users.

NT Workstation is optimized to give foreground processes such as word processing or spreadsheet programs the greatest priority. NT Server optimizes background processes, such as network packet transport and electronic mail delivery.

Both versions of NT are more stable and much more robust than other versions of Windows 3.1 or 95. NT is targeted at the business desktop rather than the home computer. Windows NT's security and multithreading support is better suited for corporate deployment than for home multimedia use.

Windows NT is Microsoft's answer to more expensive Unix-based operating systems and simpler, less robust PC operating systems. In many cases the vast array of features and power of Unix are overkill, and the single-user PC does not offer the necessary networking or multiuser support. Windows NT has emerged as a medium-level operating system that contains many of the powerful features of Unix, while offering the user a comfortable GUI.

NT started slowly, but each new version gained more followers. With the latest 3.51 version, Windows NT has established itself as a stable, low-cost alternative to Unix servers that can support powerful multiuser applications. When NT gains the new Windows 95 GUI in 1996, NT truly will have come of age.

Windows NT Server is an ideal operating system for running a powerful database server and a Web server dedicated to serving data to the Web. New applications are being delivered for the NT platform in ever-increasing numbers as vendors realize the power and appeal of Windows NT. Windows NT is the operating system of the future and the platform of choice for serious, low-cost Web development.

Microsoft SQL Server

SQL Server is Microsoft's top-end database management system (DBMS). Originally developed in partnership with Sybase, Inc. from Sybase's database engine, Microsoft has continued to improve the functionality and the administration tools in the newest 6.0 version.

The DBMS is available in two configurations: SQL Server and SQL Workstation. The only difference between the two is that SQL Workstation is intended as a development platform and allows only 15 simultaneous database connections. SQL Server supports hundreds of users, if you have the user licenses for them, and must be installed under Windows NT Server.

SQL Server offers the robustness and features that traditional PC databases lack, which makes it a good choice for serving large amounts of data to the Web. Other vendors, such as Informix and Oracle, have developed NT-based versions of their databases' engines as well, which gives you a good choice of products for putting your database in the Internet.

SQL Server was chosen for this example because it was the first DBMS developed for Windows NT and has had more time to take advantage of the features NT offers. At a list price of $999 for a 10-user license, it's also less expensive than other similar products.

The dbWeb Gateway

dbWeb is a Web-to-database gateway product developed exclusively for Windows NT, and can connect any ODBC-compliant database to the World Wide Web. The graphical administration tools dbWeb provides are far easier to use than the method required to use WDB and Perl in our previous example.

dbWeb has two parts: dbWeb Service and dbWeb Administrator. dbWeb runs as a multithreaded Windows NT service that maintains a constant connection to the database in order to process queries more efficiently. dbWeb Administrator runs under any version of Windows and is the control panel that sets up the data sources and generates the HTML forms that appear in a Web browser to provide access to your data.

As in Case Study 1, most CGI connections require the operating system to load the requested gateway program, connect to the database, submit the query, process the results, and close the database connection. If you have more than one person accessing a database at once, each connection requires the same process. A single instance of dbWeb handles all database interactions and eliminates the overhead of constantly opening and closing database connections.

dbWeb was chosen for this example because the dbWeb developers have chosen to concentrate their efforts entirely on the Windows NT operating system. Other gateway products that run under NT or Windows 3.1 or 95 might be more flexible, but before a product can run under simpler operating systems, it generally must conform to the capabilities of the lowest common denominator and thus cannot take advantage of the high-end features of Windows NT.

The Alibaba Web Server

Like dbWeb, Alibaba runs as a multithreaded service under Windows NT. The Alibaba Web server offers support for DOS-CGI, WINCGI, and 32-bit CGI. Alibaba also supports a DLLCGI feature that preloads the DLLs needed by your CGI scripts and increases Web server performance. The DLLCGI feature still is experimental and can crash the server if it fails, but it is expected to improve in future releases, like any new software.

Many, if not all, familiar Web server functions are supported, such as GET, POST, and HEAD commands, image maps, HTTP access control, server PUSH, and so on. New features designed to keep track of page accesses and other accounting functions are included as well.

dbWeb and Alibaba have formed a strategic product alliance, and though dbWeb works well with other types of Web servers, Alibaba was chosen because of its close relationship with the dbWeb gateway product.

Installing the Software

Unlike in the previous example, you don't need to compile the software used here because it isn't shareware or public domain software and is available only in binary format. All you have to do is install the software and configure it during or immediately after installation.

As with installing the Linux operating system, a tutorial on installing Windows NT extends well beyond the scope of this book. Installing Windows NT is easier than installing Linux owing to fewer configuration options and the fact that Windows NT can automatically detect many elements of your hardware for you and install the appropriate drivers.

Although a complete tutorial is not included here, a brief look at some configuration options that do impact the installation of other software is warranted.

The SQL Server documentation advises you not to install SQL Server on a Windows NT machine that serves as a *Primary Domain Controller* (PDC) or a *Backup Domain Controller* (BDC) because of the processing overhead required to keep track of the network account database and authorize network login requests. This advice assumes, however, that you have another computer available to perform the PDC or BDC functions. If not, and you require a Domain Controller, you have no choice other than to install NT as a Domain Controller. Just be aware of possible performance degradation when using the database.

When you choose a name for the computer during the Windows NT installation, keep in mind the SQL Server software uses the computer name as the name of the database server as well. Be sure to choose a computer name that is a valid SQL identifier. From the SQL Setup Manual:

> The first character must be a letter or an underscore (_). Characters following the first character can be letters, numbers, or the symbols #, $, or _. No embedded spaces are allowed.

Choosing which file system to install should be given serious thought. NT lets you choose between using the DOS *file allocation table* (FAT) file system, the *high-performance file system* (HPFS), or the *Windows NT file system* (NTFS). If you have DOS or another version of Windows on your computer and want them to be able to read files on the hard drive on which Windows NT is installed, choose the FAT option. The NTFS option provides better performance, security, and data security and should be used if possible. The HPFS option is used for compatibility with OS/2.

Another option to note is the selection of the IRQ and I/O address of your network card. Windows NT only recognizes I/O addresses 0x280 and above. If your hardware isn't set up correctly, NT can't use your network card. If you have Windows 95 installed on the target computer, click on the System icon in the Control Panel folder and determine what settings your network card currently uses. If you need to make a change, Windows 95 can tell you if the newly chosen address will conflict with another device.

Installing SQL Server

The GUI-based installation and administration tools provided with the SQL Server database make maintaining the database much easier than issuing commands from a command prompt. The complexity of the database engine and the broad array of features, however, make setting up and using the database harder.

If you are familiar with a big commercial database, SQL Server will be familiar to you as well. If your only DBMS experience is with Mini SQL or Microsoft Access type databases, you will need to do a lot of reading in the SQL Server documentation to understand the power and features of the SQL Sever database engine.

Before installing SQL Server, you should use Windows NT's User Manager in the Administrative Tools folder to create a new user account under which to install the DBMS software. The user account must be a member of the Administrators group, and the password should not be allowed to expire. If the password expires or is changed, the SQL Server no longer works until the password is reset.

For the current example, the user "SQL" is created as the database account. After you create the account, log on to Windows NT as the SQL user to install the DBMS software. Because Windows NT runs on different hardware platforms, choose the directory on the SQL installation CD that matches your machine architecture; for the Pentium machine in this example, the i386 directory.

Configuration Settings During Installation

Installing the SQL Server software is fairly straightforward but certain configuration options deserving of discussion are available during the installation.

One such option is the choice of which character set to use for storing data. The set you choose determines the characters SQL Server allows you to store in a database. The default set is ISO 8859-1, which is the standard ANSI set used on Windows computers. If you need support for different languages, the Code Page 850 character set contains support for most of the special characters required. If you need to store special graphic characters, the Code Page 437 character set supports graphic characters.

Another option is the sort order SQL Server uses to sort the data returned from an SQL statement, which uses ORDER BY or DISTINCT clauses. There are several different dictionary orders to choose from, whether case-sensitive or insensitive. The default is standard dictionary order, case-insensitive.

Be advised that your choice of character set and sort order combine to determine how long SQL Server takes to install. If you choose the default values for both, the installation completes much more quickly than if you choose otherwise.

When choosing what form(s) of network protocol SQL Server will support, TCP/IP Sockets should be included if the target machine is connected to the Internet or a network that contains Unix-based machines. If the database will be available only to a local network, choosing the IPX/SPX protocol supports Novell networks.

Services that run under Windows NT can be started manually from the Server Manager, or NT can start them automatically when the machine is started. You can choose which option you prefer during the installation. If your machine is a dedicated database server machine, SQL Server and SQL Manager should be started automatically.

At this point in the installation process, you are asked what user account will host the database software. From the list of accounts presented, choose the "SQL" user account you created earlier. The account name you use might be different. The database server name matches the computer name on which it is installed. In this case, the server is named BEOWULF.

The last installation option is the licensing mode. Licensing can be confusing, but you have two choices: Per Seat Mode and Per Server Mode. Per Seat Mode requires every machine that accesses SQL Server to have a client license installed. Per Server Mode allows any machine to connect to SQL Server, but only as many connections as you have licenses for. Per Server Mode is the most flexible arrangement, but Per Seat Mode can be used as an additional security factor by allowing only properly configured computers to access the database. Choose the mode that you prefer.

After you configure the database, you install the software. Installation time depends on the character set and sort order. After you install SQL Server, be sure to run the test provided in the setup manual to determine if everything was installed correctly. If so, you are ready to proceed to the next section.

Configuration After Installation

After you install the SQL Server DBMS software, you should perform the following actions immediately:

- Start up the database server and SQL Enterprise Manager
- Register the database server with SQL Enterprise Manager
- Assign a system administrator password
- Set the server configuration options

Starting up the SQL Server applications can be done in many ways. One way is to use the Services program in the NT Control Panel folder. Another way is to use the SQL Service Manager in the Microsoft SQL Server 6.0 folder. Here, the Service Manager is used. To start up the database server and SQLExecutive, do the following:

1. Double-click on the SQL Service Manager icon. Figure 8.9 shows the Service Manager.
2. Double-click on the green light and wait for the database server to start up.

3. When the server starts, choose SQLExecutive from the Services pull-down menu and double-click the green light again. Both services are now started.

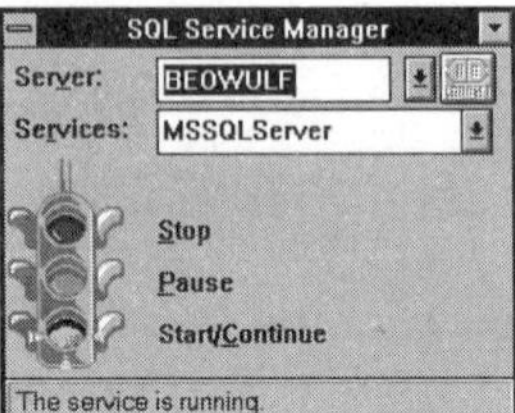

Figure 8.9
Starting up SQL Server services.

You use the SQL Enterprise Manager to register the server. The Enterprise Manager is used to administer all facets of SQL Server and you must register a server before Enterprise Manager can manage it.

When you start up SQL Enterprise Manager for the first time, you automatically see the Register Server form. If you'll be managing multiple servers, you might want to create server groups to categorize the purpose of the servers; for example, you might have a development server group, a group for accounting, one for inventory, and so on. If you need to create server groups, do so before you register the server. In the example, you create a Development group and assign the BEOWULF server to that group. Figure 8.10 shows the SQL Enterprise Manager form used to register a server.

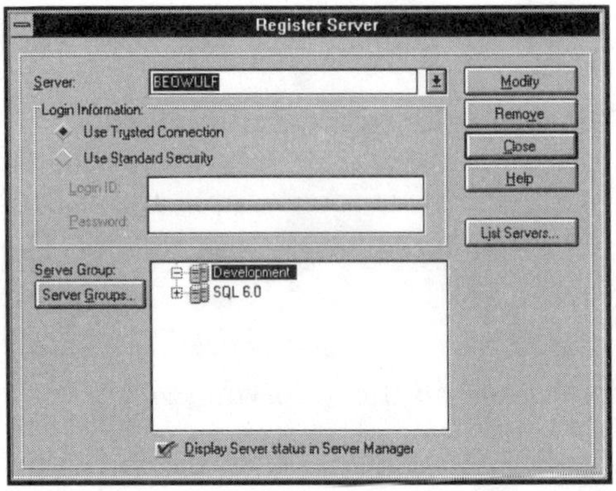

Figure 8.10
Registering a database server.

To register a database server with SQL Enterprise Manager, follow these steps:

1. Choose the server name from the drop-down menu or type it into the field provided.
2. When choosing the type of login, Use Tr**u**sted Connection uses Windows NT security. The Use S**t**andard Security option uses SQL Server's login validation process to check the user's login id and password.
3. Create a new server group by clicking on the Server **G**roups button and enter the name **Development**. Click on the **A**dd Group button to add the new group.
4. Choose the Development group from the list of Server Groups on the Register Server form. The last option, **D**isplay Server status in Server Manager, shows whether the server is running, paused, or stopped in the Server Manager form.
5. Next, assign a password for the server system administrator (sa) login. The sa user account is the one used for server administration, which includes creating a new database, adding and deleting tables, and configuring database parameters. When the database is installed, no password is assigned to the sa account.

Note

If you chose to use Windows NT security to validate database connections, no password is necessary because NT will control user access. If you chose to use standard security, however, the sa user requires a password.

6. Select the BEOWULF server in the Server Manager window and click on the **M**anage menu option.
7. Select **L**ogins, and Enterprise Manager connects to the BEOWULF database server to retrieve login id information. Figure 8.11 shows the Manage Logins form.

8. Select the sa user from the pull-down list of users and enter the new password.

9. Click on the Mo**d**ify button to save the new password.

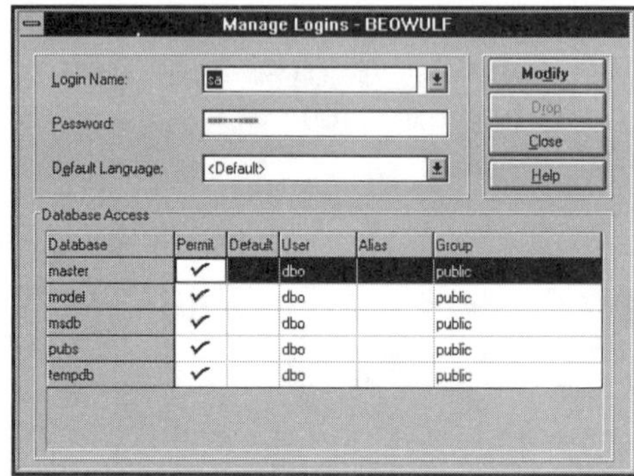

Figure 8.11
Assigning a database user password.

The next thing to do is set the server configuration options. Select the **S**erver menu option and select **C**onfigurations. Figure 8.12 illustrates the Server Configuration form. Click on the Configuration tab to see the SQL Server configuration options.

Server Configuration/Options - BEOWULF

Server Options | Security Options | Configuration | Attributes

Configuration	Minimum	Maximum	Running	Current
max async IO	1	255	8	8
max worker threads	10	1024	255	255
media retention	0	365	0	0
memory	1000	1048576	2048	6144
nested triggers	0	1	1	1
network packet size	512	32767	4096	4096
open databases	5	32767	5	5
open objects	100	2147483647	100	100
procedure cache	1	99	30	30
RA worker threads	0	255	3	3
recovery flags	0	1	0	0

Description:
Maximum size (in 2K units) of system memory available for SQL Server. Takes effect when SQL Server is restarted.

OK | Cancel | Apply Now | Help

Figure 8.12
Configuring server options.

The configuration option with which to be most concerned is the memory option. This number represents the amount of memory dedicated to SQL Server. SQL Server locks memory and doesn't allow any other application to use it, so allotting the appropriate amount of memory to the database server without degrading the performance of Windows NT is important.

The server in this example has 32 MB of RAM, and Windows NT requires about 12 for system overhead, so 20 MB are available for SQL Server if the database engine is the only application running on the machine. The amount of memory dedicated to SQL Server is listed in 2 KB units, so 2,048 represents 4 MB, 4,096 represents 8 MB, and so on.

If all 20 MB of RAM are dedicated to SQL Server, the additional overhead of the Web server and gateway programs will cause plenty of paging as processes are swapped in and out of RAM into virtual memory on the hard drive. To prevent excessive paging, 12 MB are dedicated to SQL Server and the rest are available for other applications. This is a good example of why an NT machine used as a database server on the Internet should contain 32 MB or more of RAM.

This concludes the minimum amount of configuration needed to set up an SQL Server DBMS. As you add new databases and data over time, or new hardware to the server machine, you will need to change the database configuration to keep pace. Tuning the performance of the database server is an important job of the database administrator (DBA). SQL Server gives you the power and flexibility to customize the database server to meet your needs.

Installing Alibaba

The Web server used in this example is a demo version of Alibaba downloaded from the dbWeb page at the following URL:

```
http://www.aspectse.com/Product/dbWeb/dbWeb.html
```

The installation of Alibaba is as easy as it gets. The demo distribution package is in the PKZIP format. Use PKUNZIP to unpack the software in a temporary directory and run the included setup program. The only question the setup program asks is where you want Alibaba installed. In a matter of seconds, Alibaba is installed as a system service and the administration tools are placed in a folder in the Windows NT Program Manager.

You can use the Alibaba Administration Tool to change options such as the directory in which CGI programs are stored, the port to use for HTTP connections, recognized mime types, and so on, but the default values of all of the settings work fine.

To start up Alibaba, open the Windows NT Control Panel and double-click the Services icon. Alibaba should be near the top of the list of available services. Click on Alibaba and click on the **S**tart button. Alibaba starts and begins to listen to the standard HTTP server port 80, assuming you haven't changed the configuration settings.

To test the Web server, start up a Web browser and try to connect to your server. Figure 8.13 shows the Web page that your Web browser should display.

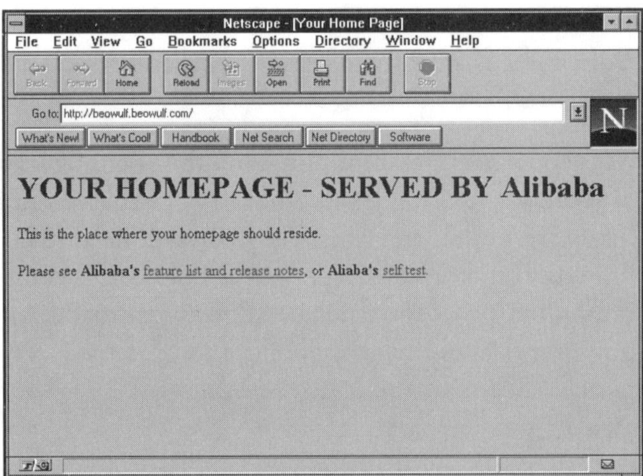

Figure 8.13
The default Web page provided by Alibaba.

Now that you have a database server and a Web server, all you need is a gateway to connect the two. After you install dbWeb, all the pieces will be complete.

Installing dbWeb

Installing dbWeb is only a little more complicated than installing Alibaba. The dbWeb setup program is a setup Wizard that asks you where to install the dbWeb software and which elements of the software to install: dbWeb Server, dbWeb Administrator, Microsoft ODBC 2.5, and Examples.

The Setup Wizard then asks you which Web server is running on your system and offers you a list of several choices. The Setup Wizard knows where the listed Web servers store CGI programs and installs the dbWeb programs in the Web server directory tree. If you reinstall the dbWeb software for some reason, the Setup Wizard asks if you want to overwrite existing database files.

When choosing which ODBC drivers to install, the Microsoft Access driver is required by dbWeb and this example requires the SQL Server ODBC driver. The Install Wizard checks to ensure the version you install is newer than the one that exists on your system. At the end of the installation process, you can view the README file that contains last-minute updates and instructions for the dbWeb software.

One possible problem might arise during the dbWeb installation program, involving the sample databases included with dbWeb to be used in the examples presented in the dbWeb Getting Started manual. An error might state that the sample databases cannot be found. The dbWeb README file presents a solution to this problem. Of the two databases supposedly present, dbWeb's solution works for one but not the other. Reinstalling the dbWeb software subsequently solves the problem and no other problems are encountered.

After you install the dbWeb software, you must do the following three things as detailed in the README file to finish the software configuration and test the software to make sure it was installed correctly:

- Run the ODBC setup program
- Start up the dbWeb service
- Test your configuration

In the dbWeb folder that was just created is an ODBC Setup icon. Double-clicking on the icon runs Microsoft's ODBC setup program. The setup program gives you the option to install any or all of a variety of ODBC drivers for applications such as Access, Excel, FoxPro, dBASE, Paradox, and SQL Server. dbWeb requires the Microsoft Access driver and you also need the SQL Server driver. Choose those and any other ODBC drivers you might need and install them by clicking on the OK button.

Use the Services program in the Windows NT Control Panel to start the dbWeb service. Open the Services program, click on dbWeb in the list of available services, and press the **S**tart button. Windows NT will attempt to start the dbWeb service and will succeed if dbWeb is installed correctly.

To test the dbWeb installation, start up your Web browser and access the following URL:

`http://`*`servername.com`*`/dbweb/dbwtest.htm`

Be sure to replace *`servername.com`* with the name of your machine. Figure 8.14 shows the Web page that your Web browser should display.

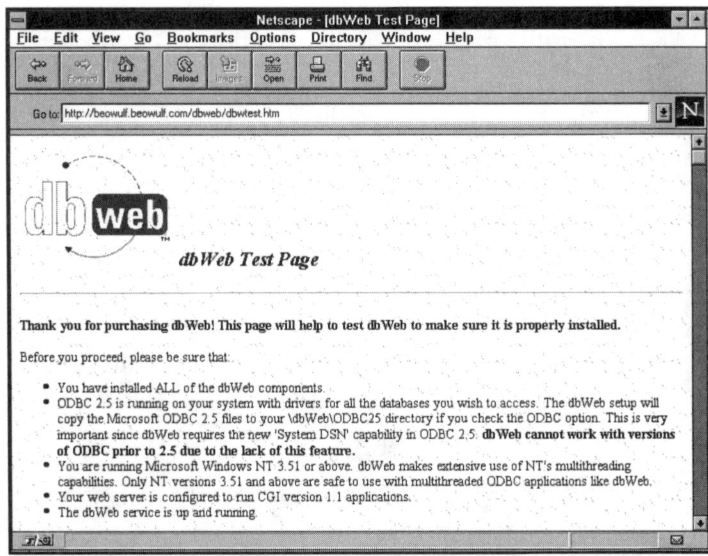

Figure 8.14
The dbWeb test page.

Choose the Alibaba test from the Web servers listed, and click on the Authors link. If dbWeb is working correctly, figure 8.15 shows the Web page that appears.

If all the software is installed and working correctly at this point, you now are ready to use SQL Server's database management tools to create the restaurant databasc and publish it on the Web.

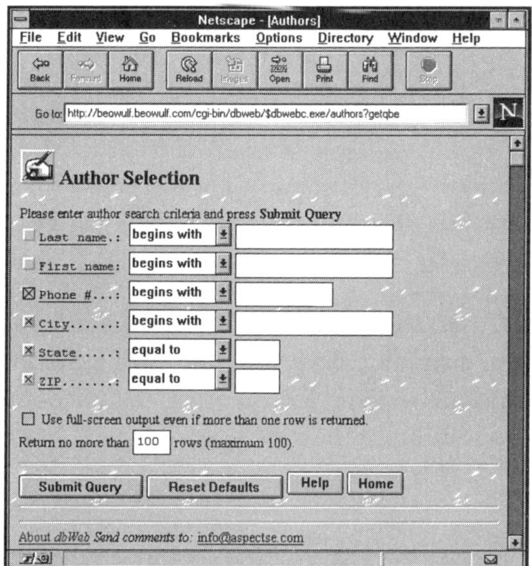

Figure 8.15
Testing dbWeb and Alibaba.

Constructing the SQL Server Database

Although the GUI-based tools provided by SQL Server make setting up and administering the database much easier than using command-line tools, the power and complexity of the database engine require that a DBA do more work to create and maintain databases.

Creating and loading a database using Mini SQL is very simple, because mSQL uses the Unix file system for database files, and the database engine runs like any other process under the Unix operating system, which allows the Unix kernel to handle process scheduling and file access.

Not so with SQL Server. Before a database can be published on the Internet, you must perform several processes to prepare space for the database and allow the SQL Server engine to recognize and manage the new database. Before you try to create a new database, be sure the MSSQLServer and SQLExecutive services are running, by starting them with the SQL Service Manager, or the Windows NT Services tool.

Creating a New Database Device

The first activity that must be performed is the creation of a new *database device.* A database device is a file used by the database engine to store databases and their transaction logs. A *dump device* is used to store database and transaction log backups. One device can contain multiple databases and logs, but if the information stored in a device becomes too large, the device must be *extended* to make it bigger so it can hold more data.

For the restaurant database, a database device dedicated to the restaurant database is created, as well as a separate device to hold the restaurant database transaction logs. Storing the database and logs in separate devices increases performance and enables you to dump the logs separately from the database if necessary.

You use the SQL Enterprise Manager to manage database devices, as follows:

1. Open the Enterprise Manager and select the name of your server. In this case, the name is BEOWULF.

2. Under the Manage menu item, select Devices.

3. On the Manage Database Devices form, press the New Device button. Figure 8.16 shows the New Database Device form.

4. Enter the name of the device.

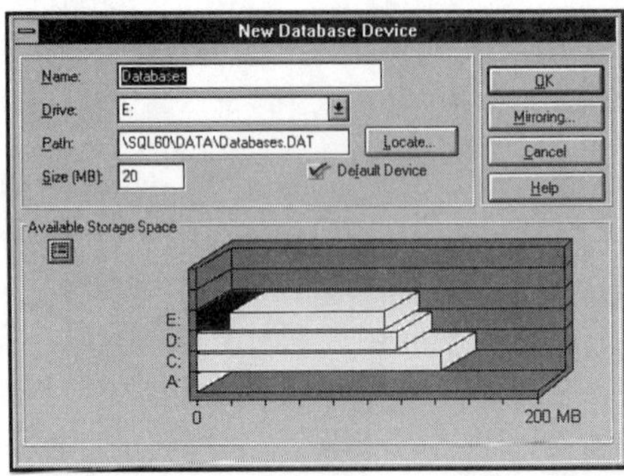

Figure 8.16
Creating a new database device.

Here, you create enough space to hold more than one database and name it Databases. The new device will reside on the E: partition and be 20 MB in size. The new device will be designated as a default device as well. When SQL is installed, the master device is designated as the default device. This means any new database will be created in the master device. After you create a new default device, seriously consider using the Edit Device button on the Manage Database Devices form to remove the master device as a default device so new databases are created in the new device.

5. Press the **O**K button to create the new device.

Follow the same procedure to create a new device for transaction logs. The log device will be 25 percent as large as the database device, which creates enough space to log transactions for heavy database traffic. Figure 8.17 shows the devices available after the Logs device is created.

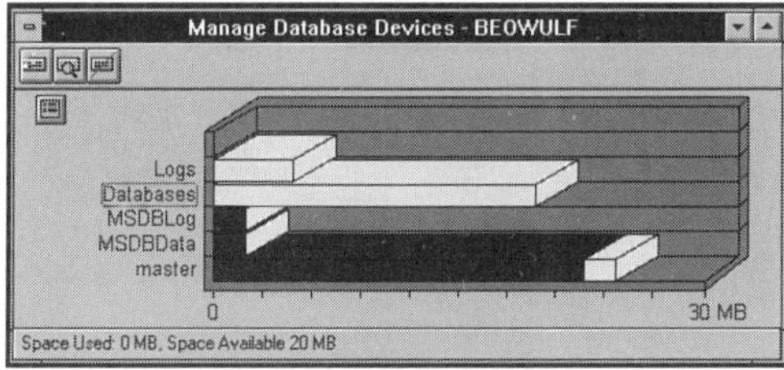

Figure 8.17
All available database devices.

Now that you have created new database devices for the database and transaction logs, you can create the new restaurant database in the Databases device.

Creating a New Database

The SQL Enterprise Manager is used to create a new database. From the **M**anage menu, select **D**atabases. On the Manage Databases form, press the New Database button. Figure 8.18 shows the New Database form.

The database name is restaurant. It resides on the Databases device, and the transaction logs reside on the Logs device. If you have data in a format that is ready to load into the database (usually a | delimited file that contains the data), choose the Create for Load button. The database is created faster, but the database will be unusable until the data is loaded. In our case, command files will be used to load data, so you will not select this option. Press the OK button to create the database. Figure 8.19 shows the databases available after the restaurant database is created.

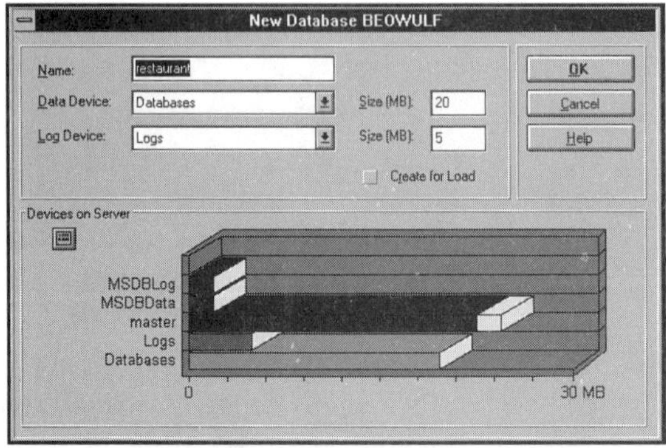

Figure 8.18 *Creating a new database.*

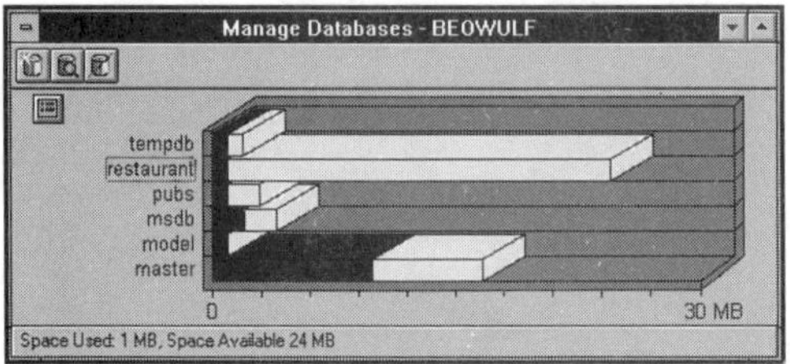

Figure 8.19 *All available databases.*

After you create a new database, you should dump the master database. This provides you with a backup copy of the master database if you must rebuild your server or reconstruct a corrupted database. To dump the master database, do the following:

1. From the **T**ools menu of the SQL Enterprise Manager, select **B**ackup/Restore. Figure 8.20 shows the Database Backup/Restore form.
2. Select the diskdump device from the Dump Devices menu, and press the **A**dd button to add the diskdump device to the list of Backup Devices. The diskdump device was created when the SQL Server software was installed and can be used to back up any database as long as the database is not larger than the dump device.
3. Select master from the list of databases to back up, and select **E**ntire Database as the amount of data to dump.

4. Select Append to Device to add the dump to existing dumps, or deselect it to overwrite all existing dumps.

5. Finally, press the **B**ackup Now button to immediately dump the master database.

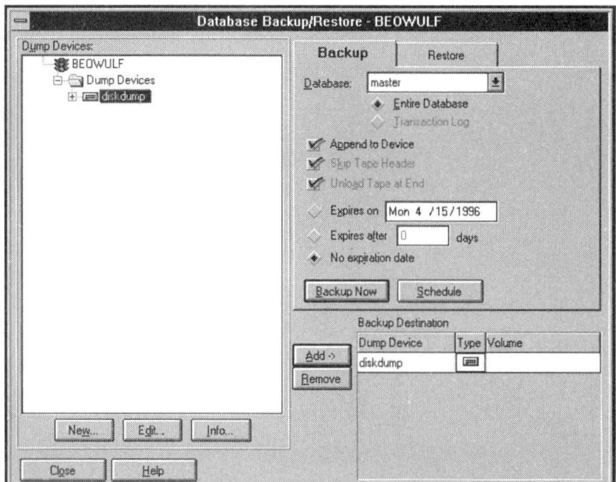

Figure 8.20
Dumping the master database.

Now that you have created the restaurant database and have made a backup copy of the master database, you can construct the individual tables and load the data into the restaurant database.

Constructing the Database

SQL Server provides a feature called isql, which is similar to the msql command-line interface provided by Mini SQL. isql can be used in the same way as msql from a DOS command window, but SQL Server provides a graphical tool called isql/w that makes using the isql command-line interface much easier.

After the database commands are typed into isql/w and executed to see if they are correctly formulated, they are saved into command files that can be loaded and executed if the entire restaurant database or a single table needs to be rebuilt for any reason.

The command files used in this example are virtually identical to those used to build the Mini SQL database used in the previous case study. Only a minor change or two is needed to make use of the extended functionality of SQL Server. The command to create the "restaurant" table is shown in figure 8.21.

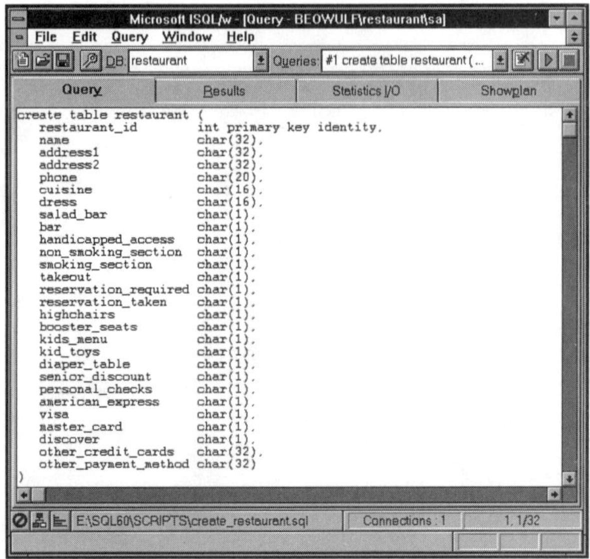

Figure 8.21
The command for creating the restaurant table.

SQL Server has a data type called IDENTITY, which is the same as the serial data type discussed in previous chapters. The IDENTITY data type is a unique key field that the database engine automatically generates. When you insert data into the restaurant_id field, SQL Server fills the field of the new record with the next available value.

The other database tables are created in a similar manner. Figure 8.22 shows the commands to create the hours, food_reviews, and menu tables. All of the identifying fields are of the IDENTITY data type.

The create index commands are used to index the foreign key field restaurant_id for improved performance while joining tables. SQL Server lets you place a FOREIGN KEY constraint on the restaurant_id field in each of these tables. The constraint allows you to insert only restaurant_id values that exist in the restaurant table into a foreign key field.

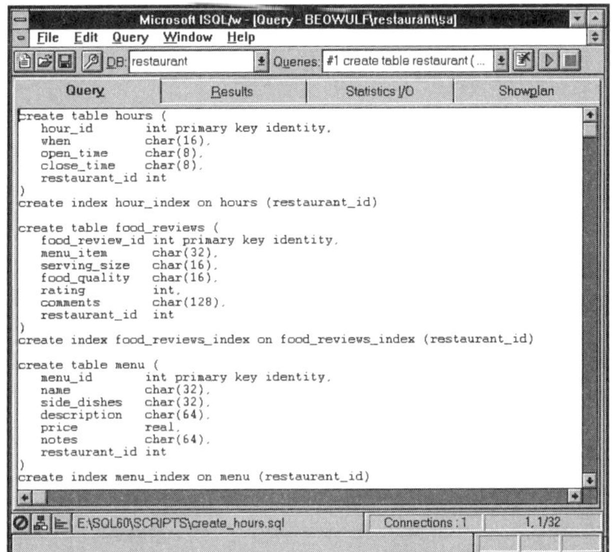

Figure 8.22
Commands for creating the hours, food_reviews, and menu tables.

When you create a primary key field, an index is automatically created on the field. Not so with a foreign key field. Regardless of whether you designate restaurant_id as a foreign key, you need to explicitly create an index on it.

The remaining tables, "service_reviews" and "specials," are created using the command shown in figure 8.23, and receive indexes on the foreign key field as well.

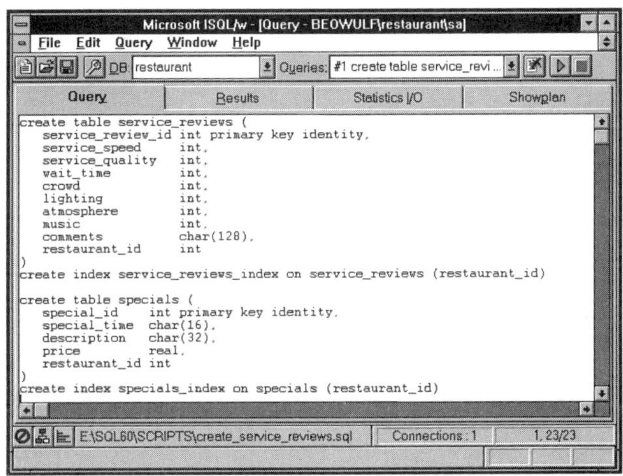

Figure 8.23
Commands for creating the service_reviews and specials tables.

You have now constructed the database tables and they are ready to accept data.

Loading the Database

Because in this example the database engine is used to generate key values for the restaurant_id field in the restaurant table, loading the database is more complex than just selecting values for restaurant_id and propagating the values to the records in the other tables.

The restaurant table is loaded first and restaurant_id key values are generated by the database engine. The generated key values must be used as the foreign key values for corresponding records in the other tables.

As an example, when the first record is inserted into the restaurant table, it receives a restaurant_id value of 1. Data that refers to the newly inserted restaurant record must be inserted into the other tables using the same value of 1. The process would continue for each new row inserted into each table.

Although this might seem obvious and simple, if a database table has existing records in it, the key values generated would not start at 1. In fact, if rows have been deleted from the table, the next key value might not be one larger than the largest existing key value because any existing larger value has been deleted. The key value generated by the database might be several numbers higher than the largest existing key value.

In short, this precludes just looking at the largest key value and expecting the database to generate the next number as the new key value. When you load a database, you must use the key value that the database generates as the foreign key value when inserting data into other tables. If not, the wrong foreign key values could be used and the database becomes corrupted because of incorrect data.

Loading large amounts of data this way by hand is prohibitively tedious and prone to inaccuracy. If you must load data into a database that enforces foreign key constraints, or any other type of constraint, you really ought to write a program to do it correctly for you and use it each time data is loaded.

In this case, few records need to be loaded and the database is new, so key values should start at 1. You don't want to depend on this, however, and for this exercise, you are to load records into the restaurant table first, then retrieve the key values the database generates. The verified key values will be used to load the other tables. Figure 8.24 shows the SQL command used to insert data into the restaurant table, and the SQL query to retrieve the generated key values. Notice that no value is specified for the first field, which is the restaurant_id field.

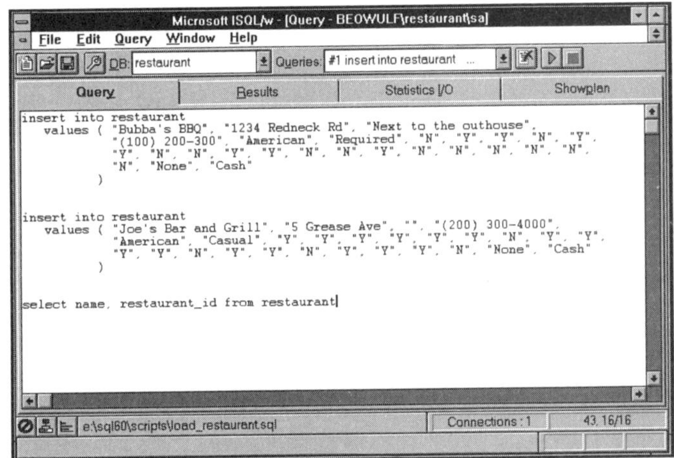

Figure 8.24
Inserting data and verifying the key values.

Executing the query shown in figure 8.24 produces the results shown in figure 8.25. The key values returned are what you might expect, but data integrity is too important to take lightly.

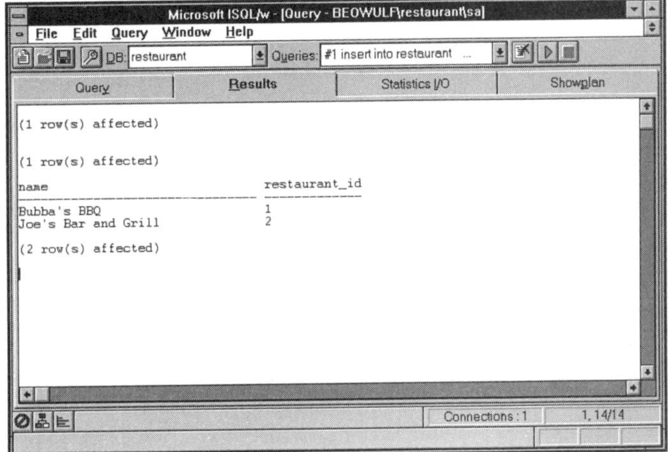

Figure 8.25
The results of the SQL insert and select commands.

The generated key values are used as foreign key values when inserting data into the other tables. Figure 8.25 shows the insert commands used to insert data into the hours and menu tables.

Figure 8.26
Inserting data into the hours and menu tables.

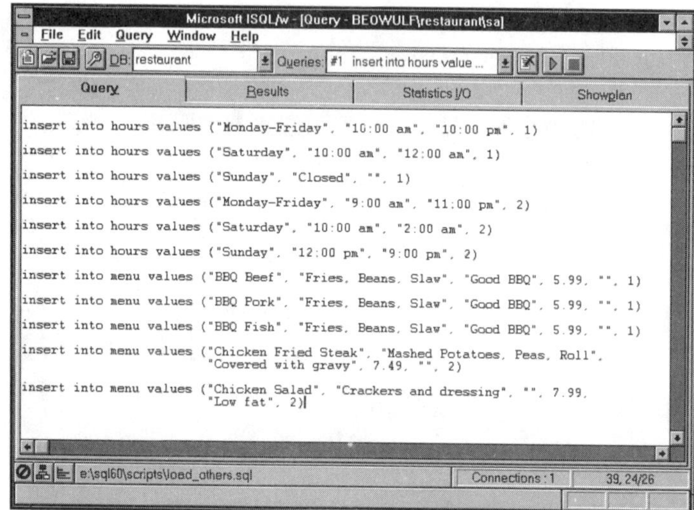


```
insert into hours values ("Monday-Friday", "10:00 am", "10:00 pm", 1)
insert into hours values ("Saturday", "10:00 am", "12:00 am", 1)
insert into hours values ("Sunday", "Closed", "", 1)
insert into hours values ("Monday-Friday", "9:00 am", "11:00 pm", 2)
insert into hours values ("Saturday", "10:00 am", "2:00 am", 2)
insert into hours values ("Sunday", "12:00 pm", "9:00 pm", 2)
insert into menu values ("BBQ Beef", "Fries, Beans, Slaw", "Good BBQ", 5.99, "", 1)
insert into menu values ("BBQ Pork", "Fries, Beans, Slaw", "Good BBQ", 5.99, "", 1)
insert into menu values ("BBQ Fish", "Fries, Beans, Slaw", "Good BBQ", 5.99, "", 1)
insert into menu values ("Chicken Fried Steak", "Mashed Potatoes, Peas, Roll",
                         "Covered with gravy", 7.49, "", 2)
insert into menu values ("Chicken Salad", "Crackers and dressing", "", 7.99,
                         "Low fat", 2)
```

Figure 8.27 shows the SQL command used to finish inserting data into the restaurant database by filling the food_reviews, service_reviews, and specials tables.

Figure 8.27
Inserting data into the food_reviews, service_reviews, and specials tables.

Microsoft ISQL/w - [Query - BEOWULF\restaurant\sa]
File Edit Query Window Help
DB: restaurant Queries: #1 insert into food_reviews ...
Query | Results | Statistics I/O | Showplan

```
insert into food_reviews values ("BBQ Fish", "Huge", "Swallow-able", 6,
                                 "Lots of grease and BBQ sauce.  Yum", 1)
insert into food_reviews values ("Chicken Fried Steak", "Big", "Excellent", 8,
                                 "Juicy and crisp.", 2 )
insert into food_reviews values ("Chicken Salad", "Average", "Adequate", 7,
                                 "Ok for diet food.  I wanted a hamburger.", 2 )
insert into service_reviews values (4, 4, 0, 5, 1, 1, 0,
                                 "Lousy place for a family, great for truck drivers", 1)
insert into service_reviews values (8, 9, 3, 5, 8, 8, 0,
                                 "Good service, good atmosphere.", 2)
insert into service_reviews values (6, 7, 5, 7, 8, 9, 0,
                                 "Slow service, but a big crowd.  Quiet.", 2)
insert into specials values ("Weekdays", "BBQ Whale Deal with fries", 4.99, 1)
insert into specials values ("Thursday 11-1", "Lunch seafood buffet, all you can eat.",
                             5.99, 2)
insert into specials values ("Monday 7-9", "Prime rib dinner", 9.99, 2)
```

E:\SQL60\SCRIPTS\load_others.sql | Connections : 1 | 1, 1/26

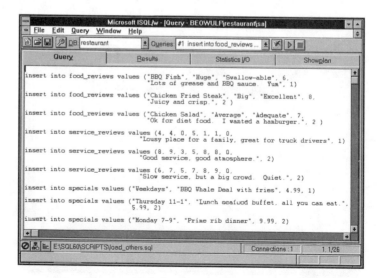

SQL Server has been set up correctly, the restaurant database has been created, and data has been loaded into the database. Only one process remains before the restaurant database is available on the World Wide Web.

Using dbWeb

dbWeb is the program that will be used to serve the database information to the World Wide Web. dbWeb will first present a query form the user can enter specifications into. The specifications are used to build a query statement for finding the requested information. Any results returned from the query statement are displayed in a tabular format.

Creating a New Data Source

dbWeb uses ODBC drivers to access data in a database. Before dbWeb can access the restaurant database using the SQL Server ODBC driver, you must add the database server as a data source with which dbWeb can work. To add a data source, do the following:

1. Open the dbWeb Administrator program and under the **U**tilities menu, choose the **O**DBC Manager item.

2. When the Data Sources dialog box appears, press the **A**dd button.

3. On the Add Data Source dialog box, select SQL Server from the list of Installed ODBC Drivers and press the OK button. Figure 8.28 shows the forms used for this procedure.

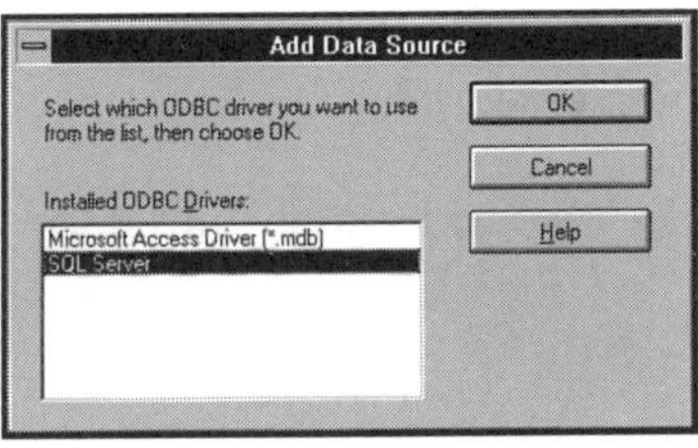

Figure 8.28
Adding SQL Server as a data source.

4. Selecting the SQL Server ODBC driver as a data source brings up the ODBC SQL Server Setup dialog box. Enter a descriptive name and description, and enter the name of the database server in the Server field. In our case the server name is BEOWULF.

5. Press the **O**ptions button and enter **restaurant** in the Database Na**m**e test box. Figure 8.29 shows the ODBC SQL Server Setup dialog box.

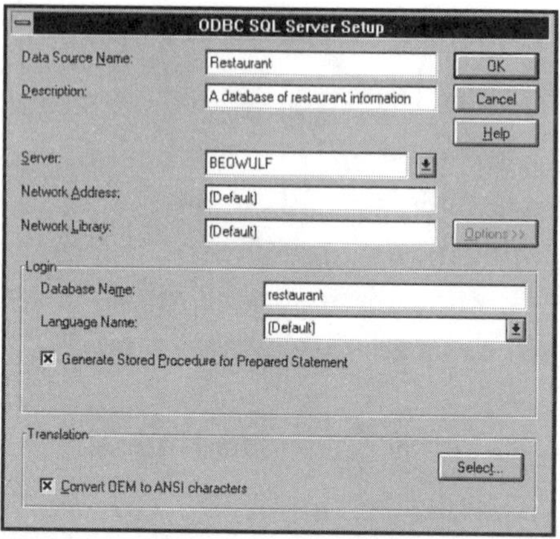

Figure 8.29
Setting up the SQL Server ODBC data source.

6. Press the OK button to add the SQL Server ODBC driver to the list of System Data Sources on the Data Sources dialog box, (see fig. 8.30).

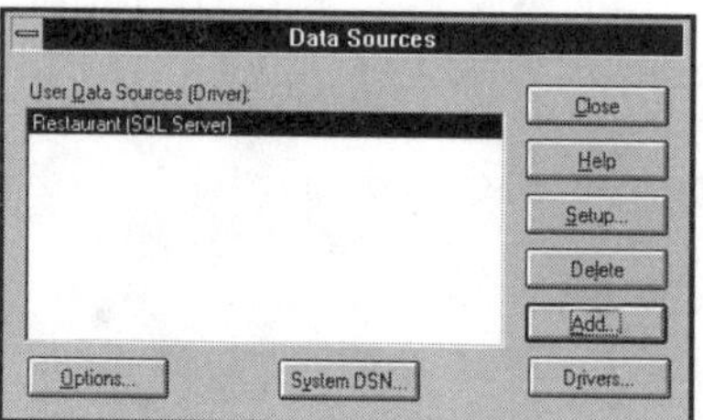

Figure 8.30
The new Restaurant data source.

7. From the Data Sources dialog box, press the S**y**stem DSN button to bring up the System Data Sources form.

8. Press the **A**dd button to open the Add Data Source dialog box. Select SQL Server from the list of Installed ODBC Drivers, and press the OK button. Figure 8.31 shows the forms used in this process.

9. After the ODBC SQL Server Setup dialog box appears, enter the same information as you did when you set up the new data source, which includes pressing the **O**ptions button and entering **restaurant** in the Database Name text box.

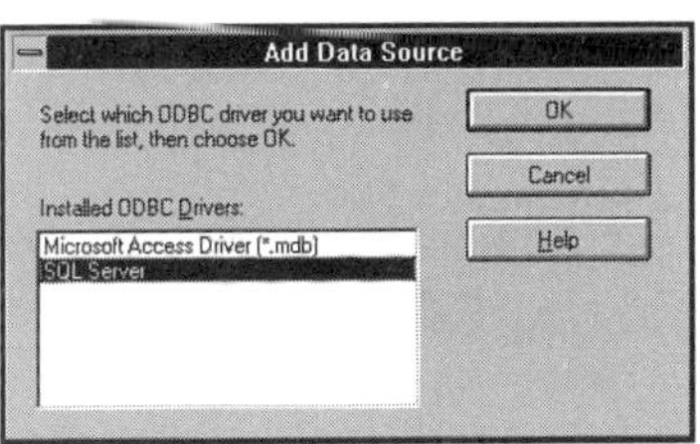

Figure 8.31
Creating a new DSN.

Tip

When defining a SQL Server data source, it is necessary to specify the name of the database in the Database Name text box. Otherwise, the ODBC driver will connect to whatever database is defined as the default database in the SQL Server configuration.

This can be frustrating to figure out.

10. Press the OK button to add the new system data source name to the list of System Data Sources. dbWeb requires a data source to be available system-wide, rather than local to a particular user. If you don't declare a data source as a DSN, you can't access the data from a Web browser.

Creating a New Schema

Now that the database server has been added as a data source, you need to create a new schema for dbWeb to use, as follows:

1. Select Data Sources and Schemas from the dbWeb Administrator form and press the <u>N</u>ew Datasource button. The Data Source dialog box appears.

2. Select Restaurant - SQL Server (32 bit) from the pull-down selection list in the Data Source Name field (see fig. 8.32).

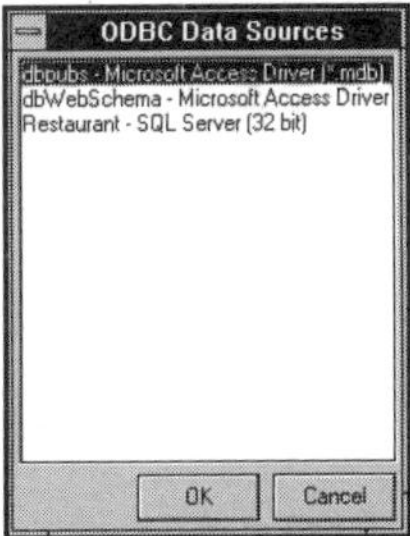

Figure 8.32
Selecting the Restaurant data source.

3. Enter **restaurant** as the Database Name and **sa** as the user ID, unless you created another user id for your database and prefer to use that.

4. Enter the password for the user ID you have decided to use. Figure 8.33 shows the completed Data Source dialog box.

5. Press the OK button to add the new data source to the list of dbWeb data sources.

Figure 8.33
Creating a new data source.

6. Select Restaurant from the list of Data Sources and press the **N**ew Schema button to bring up the New Schema dialog box. As shown in figure 8.34, you have a choice of creating a new schema yourself, or using the Schema Wizard. A *wizard* is a program designed to help you do something in Microsoft Windows by giving you step-by-step instructions. The dbWeb Schema Wizard is designed to make creating a new dbWeb schema as easy as possible. After you create the schema, dbWeb uses it to generate database query forms for a Web browser.

7. Click on the Schema **W**izard button for automated schema creation, or the **N**ew Schema button to do it yourself. For this example, the Schema Wizard will be used. The next few steps will take you through the Schema Wizard process.

8. From the Choose a table dialog box, select the restaurant table (see fig. 8.34).

9. Press the **N**ext button and the "Choose the data columns to query" dialog box appears.

10. For this example, press the >> button to select all fields in the table (see fig. 8.35). The fields selected in this dialog box will be presented to the user as fields to query on.

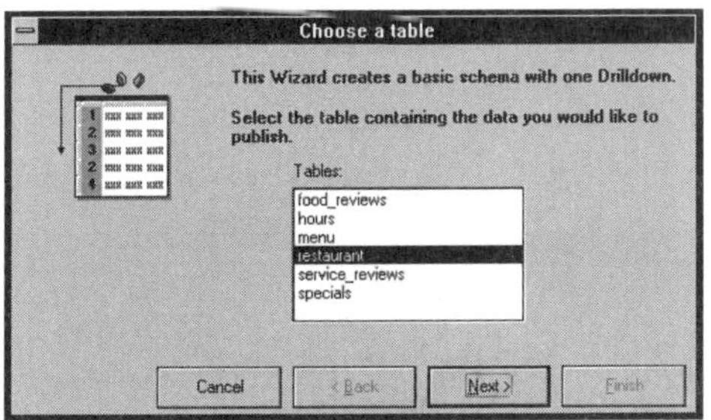

Figure 8.34
Choosing a table to develop a schema for.

11. Press the **N**ext button to open the "Choose tabular form data columns" dialog box.

12. Again, press the >> button to select all fields (see fig. 8.36). The fields selected in this form will be presented to the user as the result of a query. These two Schema Wizard boxes enable you to present a limited number of query fields to the user and still display data from all database fields on the results page.

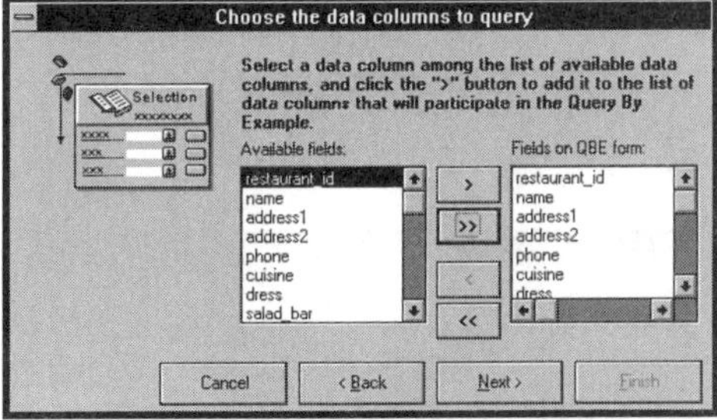

Figure 8.35
Choosing the query fields to display in the Web browser.

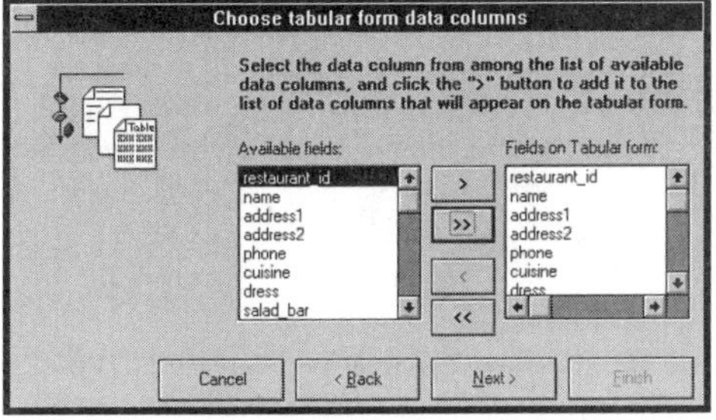

Figure 8.36
Choosing the result fields to display in the Web browser.

13. Press the **N**ext button to open the "Specify a Drilldown SmartLink" dialog box.

14. Choose restaurant_id as the *drilldown smartlink*, which is a hyperlink that enables you to display the data for a single record in the database. Figure 8.37 shows the drilldown smartlink selection.

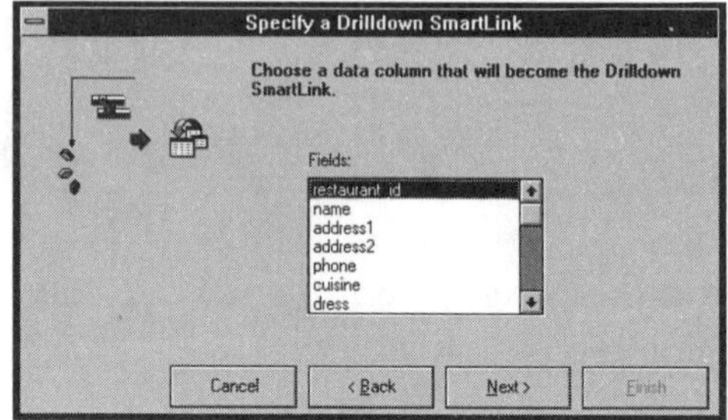

Figure 8.37 *Choosing a drilldown smartlink.*

15. Press the **N**ext button to open the "Enter schema name" dialog box, which is the final Schema Wizard box.

16. Enter a name for the newly created schema, keeping in mind schema names must be unique. If a schema belonging to any data source has the same name you choose, an error message appears, and you must change the name of the new schema. In this example, call the new schema **Restaurants** (see fig. 8.38).

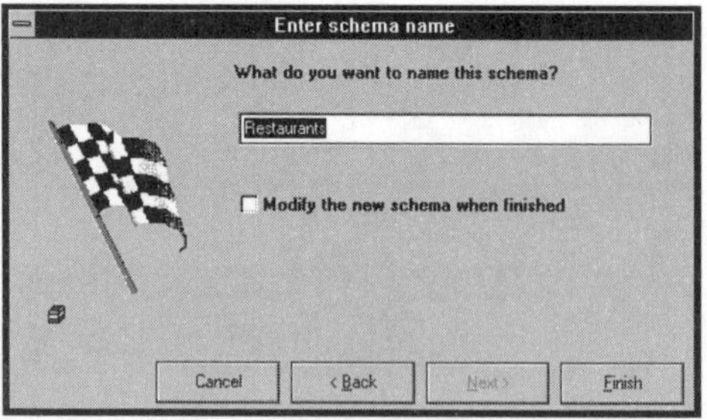

Figure 8.38 *Choosing a schema name.*

17. Press the **F**inish button to generate the new schema and add it to the list of schemas for the Restaurant data source. You can follow the same procedure for every table in the database you want to make available to the Web, as shown in figure 8.39.

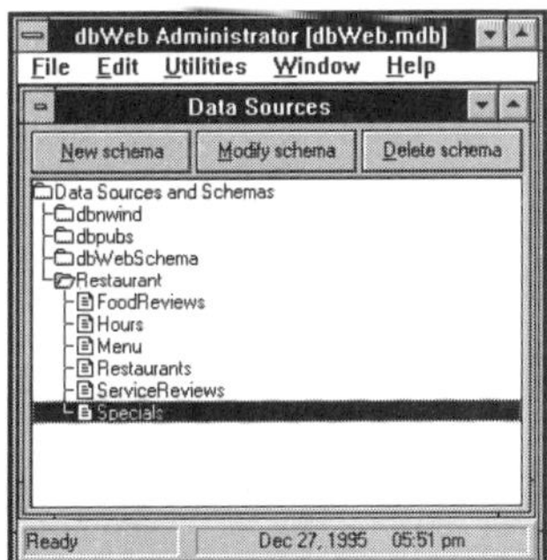

Figure 8.39
Schemas created for the Restaurant data source.

Publishing the Database on the Web

As a final step, you need to create a Web page from which to access the dbWeb schemas. The following HTML code creates the hyperlinks for calling the dbWeb program and displaying the selected query forms to access the restaurant database.

```
HTML>
  <HEAD>
    <TITLE> Database Query Links </TITLE>
  </HEAD>
  <BODY>
  <H1> Database Query Links </H1>
  <P>Click on one of the following links to access the
     ➥corresponding table in the database.</P>
  <BR><BR>
  <A HREF="http://beowulf.beowulf.com/cgi-bin/dbweb/$dbwebc.exe/
     ➥restaurants?getqbe">
    Restaurants</A>
  <BR><BR>
  <A HREF="http://beowulf.beowulf.com/cgi-bin/dbweb/$dbwebc.exe/
     ➥hours?getqbe">
    Hours</A>
  <BR><BR>
  <A HREF="http://beowulf.beowulf.com/cgi-bin/dbweb/$dbwebc.exe/
     ➥menu?getqbe">
    Menu</A>
  <BR><BR>
  <A HREF="http://beowulf.beowulf.com/cgi-bin/dbweb/$dbwebc.exe/
     ➥specials?getqbe">
    Specials</A>
  <BR><BR>
  <A HREF="http://beowulf.beowulf.com/cgi-bin/dbweb/$dbwebc.exe/
     ➥foodreviews?getqbe">
```

```
    Food Reviews</A>
  <BR><BR>
  <A HREF="http://beowulf.beowulf.com/cgi-bin/dbweb/$dbwebc.exe/
  ➥servicereviews?getqbe">
    Service Reviews</A>
  <BR><BR>
  </BODY>
</HTML>
```

When you click on the Restaurants link, your Web browser should display the Web page shown in figure 8.40.

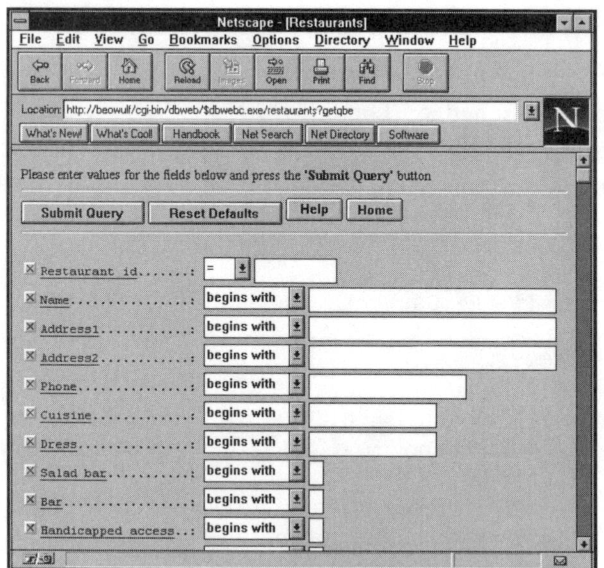

Figure 8.40
The query form generated by dbWeb.

If the user does not enter any query specifications and the Submit Query button is pressed, the Web browser displays the results shown in figure 8.41.

You now have a SQL Server database that is accessible via the World Wide Web! dbWeb enables you to customize your Web pages to suit your own needs and gives you insert, update, and delete functionality from a Web browser.

Whether you choose a hands-on environment in which you can do most of the work yourself, such as Unix, or a GUI-based environment in which most things operate with the click of a mouse, such as Windows NT, you can make your database accessible to the World Wide Web. All it takes is patience and a little guidance. Although this book cannot address the former, hopefully it does address the latter.

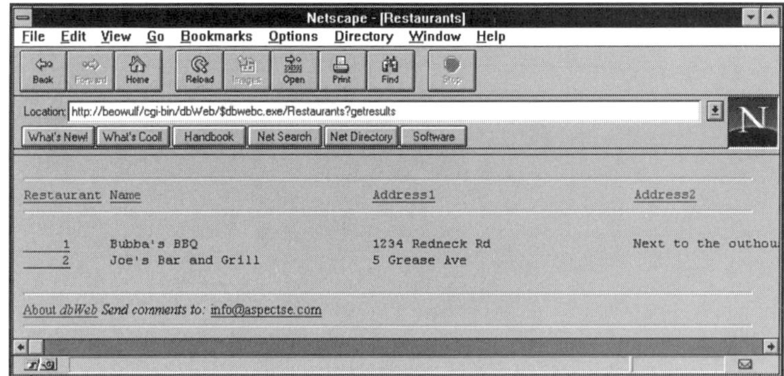

Figure 8.41
The query results from the restaurant database.

Alternatives to Databases

Many people have the misconception that a database requires complex, expensive hardware and software to store information. Hopefully, the preceding chapters have corrected that misconception—databases do not have to be complex or expensive. In fact, they do not even have to be databases!

A common fallacy about databases is that they require some sort of traditional structure for storing the data and a convoluted query language to get meaningful information back out again. Not so. Although the relational database model is the most widely used type of database, there are many others, some of which might not be considered databases at all. This chapter covers the following alternatives to traditional database servers and gives examples of how to use them:

- *Wide Area Information Servers (WAIS)*
- *DBM*
- *HTMLBBS*

Keep in mind that any method of organizing, storing, and retrieving information can be considered a database. Plain text files of information, files used by an electronic mail program to store mail messages, and configuration files used by application software are all databases in various formats.

A traditional database can be used for many things, but is not the best tool for storing all forms of data. You might require a different data storage tool, or a different way of thinking about data. This chapter introduces you to some alternative ways of working with information.

Using Wide Area Information Servers (WAIS)

A traditional database is a powerful tool for storing information in an organized manner and returning portions of it in response to user queries. In many cases, however, information is already in electronic format but would not work well in a relational database. There are millions of documents on computers around the world. Users need a way to search these documents for topics without opening each one and looking through it using a text editor. While these documents could be stored in a database, traditional databases are not built for indexing every word in a set of documents and giving a user the tools to search for key words.

A powerful alternative information storage and retrieval program is the *Wide Area Information Server* (WAIS), which is one of the most widely used search programs used on the Internet. WAIS is a trademark of WAIS Incorporated, which offers the commercial version of WAIS. Because the WAIS engine is based on the ANSI standard Z39.50 protocol, free versions of WAIS-like engines have been developed to the same standard and are available as well.

WAIS is used solely as a way to index and search text files. Every word over two characters long in a set of documents can be indexed and a search for keywords will return a list of documents that contain the keywords.

The WAIS software is composed of four main parts:

- The *indexer*, which performs the following functions:

    1. Scans the files to be indexed.
    2. Creates a sorted list of words found in the files.
    3. Counts the number of times each word occurs in a file.
    4. Creates a WAIS database entry for each word and each document.

- The *database*, which is created by the indexer, and contains several primary parts:

    1. A *filename* list, which contains a list of all filenames present in the database.
    2. A *headline* list, which contains a headline for each file in the database. The headline is shown when a file is returned as a result of a keyword search.
    3. The *document* table, which contains a record for each file in the database, and includes a pointer to the filename and headline lists.
    4. A *dictionary*, which contains a sorted list of all words contained in the database.
    5. An *inverted file*, which is the main portion of the database. It contains a list of words and a reference to each document that uses the word.
    6. The *catalog*, which is a human-readable copy of the document table.

- The *server*, which processes queries to find information in the database. The WAIS server returns one of two types of information: a list of headlines for files that match a query, or a particular file selected from the headline list.

- The *query interface*, or *WAIS client*, which is a program that sends a query to the WAIS server and displays the results.

Refer to figure 9.1 to help you follow the chain of events that occur when a WAIS client sends a request to a WAIS server.

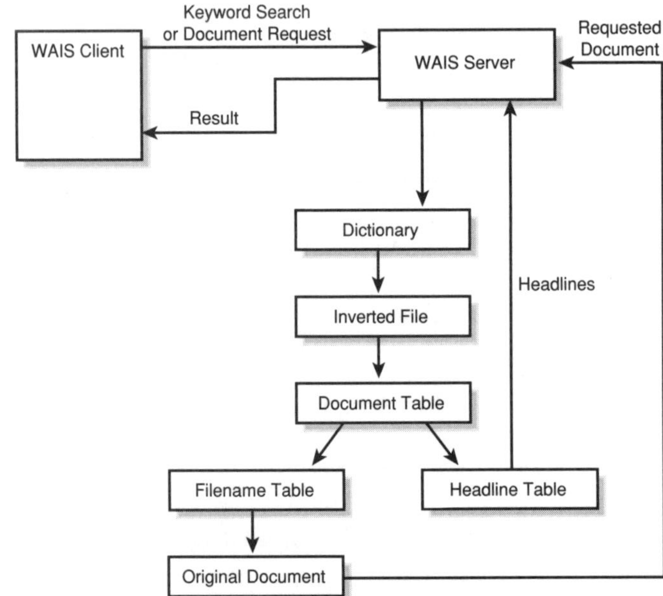

Figure 9.1
How the WAIS server uses the index during a search.

The WAIS server looks up the keywords in the dictionary. Using information from there, the server uses the inverted file to look up documents containing the keywords. This provides a pointer to the document table, which points to the headline table and then to the filename table. The filename table provides the location of the original document, and the results are returned to the client.

Results returned from a WAIS query are *weighted* according to how many times the keywords are found in a particular document. Documents with a higher weight are displayed first in the headline list because they are assumed to be the most relevant to the keyword search.

As you might expect, there are words that are not included in the index, such as "and," "the," and other common words. Most WAIS distributions enable you to add words to the excluded list, or create your own that overrides the default one. You are thus enabled to customize searches based on the specific type of documents you have.

Building an Example WAIS Application

To demonstrate what WAIS can do, you are here shown an example that uses WAIS to enable a user to search HTML files from a Web browser. The HTML files used in previous examples throughout this book will be indexed, and a Web interface will be constructed that uses a freeWAIS product and interface. The WAIS software package is freeWAIS-sf, and the WAIS gateway interface is SFGate.

Indexing HTML files is a good way to enable Web visitors to search for information contained in any of your Web pages. When the information has been located, clicking on a hyperlink loads the requested HTML document into the user's Web browser.

To construct a WAIS database of HTML files and make them available to Web visitors, you will need to know how to do the following:

- Install the freeWAIS-sf Software
- Install the SFGate software
- Build a WAIS database
- Test the WAIS database
- Start up the WAIS server
- Create an HTML query form that uses SFgate
- Use a WAIS format file
- Use the URL document type

Each step will build on the previous steps until you have a complete database of your HTML documents and a Web-based query interface to search your HTML pages for keywords.

The freeWAIS-sf Software

freeWAIS-sf is an enhanced version of freeWAIS, which is the free version of WAIS. That might sound complicated, but that sort of thing happens often on the Internet—a free version of software is developed that mimics a commercial software package, and other programmers grab it and customize it for their own use. The customized version often includes neat features not included in the original, which entices other programmers to use it as well.

freeWAIS-sf was developed by the Clearinghouse for Networked Information Discovery and Retrieval (CNIDR). The "sf" suffix stands for *structured fields*, an indexing and search feature not present in the unenhanced freeWAIS software. More information about freeWAIS can be found at this Web site:

```
http://ls6-www.informatik.uni-dortmund.de/freeWAIS-sf/
freeWAIS-sf.html
```

The freeWAIS-sf software distribution package can be obtained from the following ftp sites:

```
ftp://ftp.maxwell.syr.edu/infosystems/wais/FreeWAIS-sf/

ftp://ftp.egg.com/pub/infosystems/freeWAIS-sf-2.0/

ftp://ftp.germany.eu.net/pub/infosystems/wais/Unido-LS6/
```

This example uses version 20.0.60 of freeWAIS-sf.

Installing freeWAIS-sf

Unpack the freeWAIS-sf distribution package with these commands:

```
gunzip freeWAIS-sf-2.0.60.tar.gz
tar -xf freeWAIS-sf-2.0.60.tar
```

This creates the directory /home/http/freeWAIS-sf-2.0.60 and puts all of the freeWAIS-sf files into it. (Your directory name may be different.) Enter the /home/http/freeWAIS-sf-2.0.60 directory and run the "Configure" program. Configure asks you a few questions and "familiarizes" itself with your system. Of the questions Configure asks, the following questions are reproduced because they will have the most impact on the installation of freeWAIS-sf.

The comments are not part of the configuration program but are provided as additional information for some of the configuration options.

If you do not have root access on your machine, freeWAIS-sf can be installed in your home directory. For this example, /home/http/freewais-sf is used. After you answer this question, any other questions that deal with installation directories will start with the directory you name here.

```
By default, freewais-sf will be installed in /usr/local/bin, manual
pages under /usr/local/man, etc..., i.e. with /usr/local as prefix for
all installation directories. Typically set to /usr/local, but you
may choose /usr if you wish to install freewais-sf among your system
binaries. If you wish to have binaries under /bin but manual pages
under /usr/local/man, that's ok: you will be prompted separately
for each of the installation directories, the prefix being only used
to set the defaults.

Installation prefix to use? (~name ok) [/usr/local] /home/http/
freewais-sf
```

Increased performance is always a good thing, so use the patch unless you find it causes problems under your operating system. As a warning, this patch seems to cause problems with regular expression matching under Linux 1.2.13. No problems seem to occur under SunOS 4.1.3.

```
I added a patch from Alberto Accomazzi for speeding up usage of
synonym files. He writes about his patch:
For those of you who have fairly large synonym files (> 10Kb) and are
running the software on a machine that supports shared memory (your
machine does) enabling this feature will speed up the waisserver
response time by a significant factor.
For those of you who do not have shared memory, I have rewritten the
memory allocation part of synonym.c so that bigger memory chunks are
allocated and used rather than allocating memory for each word and
synonym, so the code should be a little faster for you too.

Do you want to use shm cache? [n] y
```

If you are absolutely sure you will never need special characters (for printing languages not currently recognized by your computer) you can answer yes to this question. If you need the extra characters provided by freeWAIS-sf, keep the default answer as done here.

```
You can compile freeWAIS-sf with its own ctype package. You should do
this, if you want to use special (country specific) chars, which are
not supported by your system's ctype.

Use your system's ctype? [n]

Ok, will use my own ctype.
```

These characters may look strange, but let freeWAIS-sf use the defaults unless you have your own special characters to use.

```
I will now ask for your special letters. If you do not want to give
them now, edit config.h after this Configure run. Input your uppercase
letters in the same order as your lowercase letters. toupper() and
tolower() depend on this order. Input letters that are upper- and
lowercase in both strings.

What are your lowercase letters? [äöüß]
What are your uppercase letters? [ÄÖÜß]
```

It will take a *lot* of files to exceed 16 MB of headlines. This limit is usually not a problem, but if you have massive amounts of data to index, answer yes to this question.

```
Waisindex will generate <database>.hl files which will contain all
headlines of a WAIS database. Normally the offset in the file is
stored as tree byte integer. This confines the size of the file to
16 MB. If you want, you can have four byte offset.

Will you have HEADLINE files greater than 16 MB [n]
```

freeWAIS-sf provides its own text-based WAIS search client. If you will have many local users (people on the same machine as the WAIS database) who will be using the freeWAIS-sf client, the local search capability can eliminate a lot of overhead by searching the WAIS database files directly, bypassing the WAIS server. The size of the client executable code will be larger with the search capability added, but searches will be faster.

```
You can compile and link the clients with the capability to search
index files directly. So you need not install a server, for local
searches. The clients will be greater, but faster with local searches.

Do you want to compile with -DLOCAL_SEARCH? [y]
```

It is usually safe to use the regular expression software included with the freeWAIS-sf distribution. However, if the provided version breaks under your operating system, rerun the Configure program and answer yes to this question.

```
Checking if your system's regexp implementation works ...
Yes, it works

Do you want to use your system's regexp.h? [n]
```

Until this feature is documented better, it is probably a good idea to answer no to this question.

```
This version of freeWAIS-sf supports new proximity operators by Tom
Snee. He also fixed the string search code. You can now enable them
at the cost of dropping the string search capability. There is
currently no description of the proximity operators. Have a look in
ir/query_l.l to learn about them.

Use proximity instead of string search? [n]
```

This is your call. If you are the paranoid type, disable the UDP packet. If you do not care or you feel the author is entitled to this small request, accept the default answer.

```
As distributed, freeWAIS-sf will send a UDP packet to my workstation
every time waisserver reindexes his info database, containing your
(numeric) UID, your operating system, your compiler version, and the
freeWAIS-sf version.

This is JUST because I would like to get an idea of which
systems/compilers "freeWAIS-sf 2.0 PL 60 string" has be ported to
and how many people use it, and keep on using it (rather than "tried
it once" folks). It will NEVER become a licensing scheme or some crazy
thing like that. But, you can disable it by answering "yes" to the
following question. If you do that, please let me know, if you are
running freeWAIS-sf on a system/compiler, which is not mentioned in
the FAQ.

Disable the UDP packet sending? [n]
```

This is a neat feature. By using the modified URL type, you can index “live” copies of your HTML documents where they exist and the WAIS server will return, as hyperlinks, the URLs of HTML documents that match a keyword search. Users can click on the URL and display your Web pages directly.

The Web pages will behave exactly as if they had been accessed through the HTTP server, which means all hyperlinks will be active, all images will appear correctly, and all CGI programs can be called normally. In this example, HTML documents are the targeted document type and we will using SFgate, so this feature will be used.

```
You can modify the URL document type, to put the URL of the indexed
in the document id instead of the headline. If you use this modifica-
tion you can customize the headline (with the -t fields option, for
example). Also it is not required to keep a copy of the documents for
retrieval with the wais server. But currently only SFgate can handle
this modified docids. Normal clients will not correctly interpret the
docids and try to retrieve the document from a wais instead of the
corresponding http server.

Do you want to use the modified URL handling? [y]
```

The default answer provided to any questions other than the ones reproduced here will probably work fine for you. Configure is a pretty intelligent program for figuring out your system. That is why so many software packages use it. If you make a mistake or want to change something later, Configure saves your answers, and you can keep any of your previous settings and change the ones you want.

After you answer all the configuration questions, you will need to compile and install the freeWAIS-sf software. Although you might expect that instruction on how to do so would be in the README file included with the distribution, all the README file contains is the following line:

```
See ./doc/SF/fwsf.*
```

Looking in the /home/http/freeWAIS-sf-2.0.60/doc/SF directory, there are several files in different formats, none of which are plain ASCII test. There are PostScript and LaTex files, and the LaTex file fwsf.texi can be deciphered with a little work if you need more instructions than what is provided here. If you have the LaTex word processing program on your Unix systems, that would work better.

After Configure has finished creating the configuration files, compile and install the software with the following commands:

```
make

make install

make install.man (if you choose to install the man pages)
```

While freeWAIS-sf is compiling, you might look in the /home/http/freeWAIS-sf-2.0.60/doc/SF directory for a copy of the freeWAIS-sf frequently asked questions, which can be very useful if you plan to do more than just basic WAIS database searches. The FAQ contains a lot of handy information about operating system and compiler compatibility with freeWAIS-sf, ftp sites for obtaining necessary software, and how to use the freeWAIS-sf software.

The SFgate Software

SFgate is a CGI program written in Perl and is designed to provide an interface between Web browsers and a WAIS server. SFgate is developed by CNIDR to be used with freeWAIS-sf, but any freeWAIS server can be used.

SFgate's prime function is to provide a Web front end for WAIS database queries. SFgate can connect to any number of WAIS servers, either remotely or on a local machine. SFgate can perform local queries without using a WAIS server by using waisPerl. *WaisPerl* is a Perl extension that uses the freeWAIS programming API to build a version of Perl that can access a WAIS database directly, bypassing the WAIS server and increasing performance for WAIS queries performed on a local machine.

More information about SFgate can be obtained at the following Web site:

```
http://ls6-www.informatik.uni-dortmund.de/SFgate/
```

The SFgate software distribution package can be obtained from the following ftp sites:

```
ftp://ftp.maxwell/syr.edu/infosystems/wais/SFgate-4.0/

ftp://ftp.egg.com/pub/infosystems/SFgate-4.0/

ftp://ftp.germany.eu.net/pub/infosystems/wais/Unido-LS6/
```

This example uses version 4.0.18 of SFgate.

Installing SFgate

Unpack the SFgate distribution package with these commands:

```
gunzip SFgate-4.0.18.tar.gz
```

```
tar -xf SFgate-4.0.18.tar
```

This creates the /home/http/SFgate-4.0.18 directory and puts all of the SFgate files into it. (Your directory name may be different.) Enter the /home/http/SFgate-4.0.18 directory and run the configure program. Note the lowercase *c* on the program name, which is different from the uppercase *C* on the program used to configure freeWAIS-sf. There is no special significance to the different spelling, but you should be aware the program name is different to avoid any momentary confusion when trying to run the configure program.

The configuration of SFgate involves answering questions about your system setup and HTTP server configuration. The following questions are reproduced from the SFGate configure program.

The SFgate configuration program looks for waisPerl extensions that are built into the system version of Perl. WaisPerl is just like other Perl extensions, such as MsqlPerl, in that it adds WAIS functions to Perl and allows Perl programs to access WAIS databases directly. WaisPerl speeds up SFgate by not having to use the freeWAIS-sf client software but by performing searches on the WAIS databases directly. Also, waisPerl increases performance by enabling SFgate to bypass the WAIS server for searches performed locally.

```
checking /usr/bin/perl for wais buildins
Can't locate Wais.pm in @INC at -e line 1.
No perl with wais buildins found! Ok.
Will use plain perl. That will run significantly slower!
```

If you do not have access to the HTTP source directories, you might need to use a path such as /home/*username*/public_html for your documents.

```
Where do your html pages reside
 (/home/robots/www/pages)?
/home/http/httpd/htdocs
```

If you do not have HTTP access, you will need to use a virtual name like /~*username*/SFgate.

```
Virtual name means the name you want to use in URLs,
for example in http://somehost/SFgate/demo.html
the virtual name of the document directory is "/SFgate"
What is the virtual name of /home/http/httpd/htdocs/SFgate
(/SFgate)?
```

With no HTTP directory access, this would look like /home/*username*/public_html/cgi-bin.

```
Where is your real CGI dir
 (/home/http/httpd/htdocs/cgi-bin)?
/home/httpd/httpd/cgi-bin
```

If you do not have HTTP access, this name would be similar to /~*username*/cgi-bin.

```
What is the virtual name of /home/httpd/httpd/cgi-bin
(/htbin)?
/cgi-bin
```

Without HTTP directory access, this would be /home/*username*/public_html/SFgate.

```
In which directory should the application files go
 (/home/robots/www/etc/SFgate)?
/home/http/httpd/htdocs/SFgate
```

Without HTTP directory access, this could be /home/*username*/public_html/SFgate.

```
In which directory should the logfile SFgate.log go
 (/home/robots/www/log)?
/home/http/httpd/SFgate/htdocs/log
Will write logs to /home/http/httpd/htdocs/SFgate/log/SFgate.log
```

After the configuration program is finished, use the following commands to compile, test, and install the SFgate software:

```
make

make check

make install
```

To make sure the software installed correctly, open your Web browser and go to this URL, substituting your own machine name:

`http://machinename/SFgate/`

If the SFgate software is installed, your Web browser should display the Web page shown in figure 9.2.

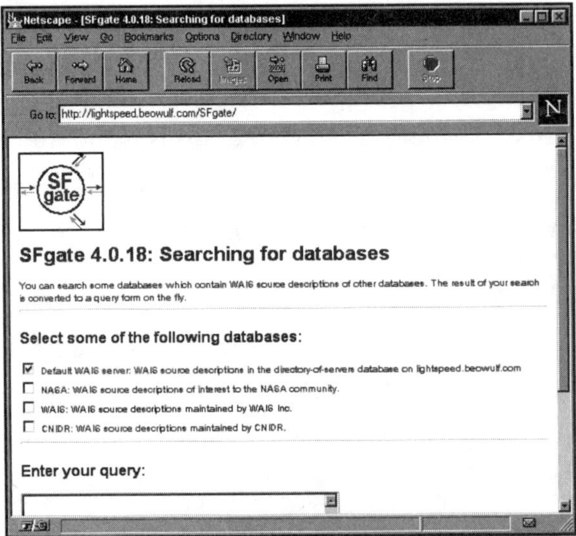

Figure 9.2
The SFgate demonstration page.

When you have freeWAIS-sf and SFgate installed, you are ready to build a WAIS database to search from a Web browser.

Building a WAIS Database

Building a database for any WAIS program can be a time-consuming and frustrating experience if you want to construct anything more than a basic database and you are not familiar with the tools or syntax required to use the WAIS indexing program.

This example looks at indexing a bare-bones database for freeWAIS-sf, and then a slightly more complicated example that uses a WAIS format file. Even the freeWAIS-sf documentation calls format files "the horrible database.fmt file" because of the tinkering required in many cases to get the format file just right.

A Simple WAIS Database Example

For this example, the freeWAIS-sf software is installed into the /home/http/freewais-sf directory. The executable programs are in the /home/http/freewais-sf/bin directory, which includes the waisindex, waisserver, and waissearch program.

Waisindex is used to create the WAIS database. *Waisserver* is the WAIS server, as you would expect. *Waissearch* is the client program used to query the WAIS database and display results. There are other subsidiary programs, but these three are the ones that form the core of the freeWAIS-sf program.

The first thing to do is gather up the HTML files you want to put into the database and put them somewhere. For this example, the directory /home/http/freewais-sf/bin/database will hold the database and HTML files.

After you have collected the HTML files you want to index, the following waisindex command creates a database of HTML documents:

```
/home/http/freewais-sf/bin/waisindex -T HTML -d html *.html
```

The `-T HTML` parameter tells waisindex the document type is `HTML` and to create a database for delivering HTML documents to an HTTP server. The `-d html` parameter indicates the name of the database to create is "html." The `*.html` parameter is the pattern of all files to put into the database. When the waisindex command is issued, it responds with the following output:

```
irbuild: setting type to HTML
236: 0: Jan  3 20:01:49 1996: 6: Starting to build database html
236: 1: Jan  3 20:01:50 1996: -2: Warning: couldn't open
./html.syn - synonym translation disabled
236: 2: Jan  3 20:01:50 1996: 6: Indexing file:
customer_comments.html
236: 3: Jan  3 20:01:50 1996: 6: Indexing file: index.html
236: 4: Jan  3 20:01:50 1996: 6: Indexing file: lookup.html
236: 5: Jan  3 20:01:50 1996: 6: Indexing file: mars_welcome.html
236: 6: Jan  3 20:01:50 1996: 6: Indexing file: template.html
236: 7: Jan  3 20:01:50 1996: 6: Indexing file: w3-msql.html
236: 8: Jan  3 20:01:50 1996: 6: Flushing 783 different words,
1369 total words to disk...
236: 9: Jan  3 20:01:50 1996: 6: Done flushing version 0
236: 10: Jan  3 20:01:50 1996: 6: Merging version 0 into master
```

```
version and generating dictionary.
236: 11: Jan  3 20:01:50 1996: 100: Total word count for
dictionary is: 1369
236: 12: Jan  3 20:01:50 1996: 6: Rewriting source description.
236: 13: Jan  3 20:01:50 1996: 6: New source description should be
exported.
236: 14: Jan  3 20:01:50 1996: 6: Finished build
```

The output tells you which files have been put into the WAIS database and how many words have been indexed. To see if the WAIS database was built correctly, use the *waissearch* command to search for a keyword. Because the client was built with direct-search capabilities when the freeWAIS-sf software was compiled, the WAIS server does not need to be running to execute this local search, which enables you to test your WAIS database before starting the WAIS server and making your database available to the Internet.

Note

You have the choice to limit WAIS searches on your database. You can provide local search capabilities so only WAIS clients on your local machine can access the databases, or you can choose to open the WAIS databases to anyone on the Internet who has a WAIS client.

To make your WAIS databases available to Internet searches, add the parameter *-export* to the waisindex command line when creating WAIS databases. This parameter adds the hostname and machine port to the database description for use by the remote clients.

Enter the following command to search the html database you just created for the keyword "html":

```
/home/http/freewais-sf/bin/waissearch -d html html
```

Waissearch responds with the following results:

```
Search Response:
  NumberOfRecordsReturned: 6
   1: Score:   75, lines:  10 'template.html'
   2: Score:   53, lines:   9 'index.html
   3: Score:   33, lines:  20 'mars_welcome.html'
   4: Score:   26, lines:  26 'lookup.html'
   5: Score:   23, lines:  38 'customer_comments.html'
   6: Score:    9, lines: 326 'w3-msql.html'
```

```
View document number [type 0 or q to quit]:
```

As you would expect, all of the HTML documents contain the word "html."

> **Note**
>
> WAIS keyword searches are case-insensitive. Thus, searching for the keyword "html" will find all occurrences of the words "html," "HTML," "Html," and so on.

If you tell waissearch to display document number 3, the mars_welcome.html document is displayed as follows:

```
View document number [type 0 or q to quit]: 3
Headline: mars_welcome.html
<HTML>
  <HEAD>
    <TITLE>
      Mars Web Server
    </TITLE>
  </HEAD>
  <BODY>
    <H1>
      Mars Web Server
    </H1>
    <HR><BR><BR>
    Welcome to the very first Web server on the planet Mars!
    <BR>
    Before taking a virtual tour of all our tourist attractions,
    please sign our guest book.  Enter your name and planet of
    origin.  Rest assured, no salesmen will call on you.
  </BODY>
</HTML>

View document number [type 0 or q to quit]:
```

It might not be particularly useful to view raw HTML output, but this was merely a test to see if the WAIS database was built correctly, and it was. Now that you know the database is built correctly, you can start the freeWAIS-sf server.

Running the freeWAIS-sf Server

The standard machine port used for a WAIS server is port 210. Only the root user has access to ports below number 1024 on a Unix-based operating system, so if you do not have the proper access, you will need to pick another port for the WAIS server to run on. For this example, you will use port 2100.

The waisserver program resides in the /home/http/freewasis-sf/bin directory, so enter this directory before starting the server. When starting the freeWAIS-sf server, the waisserver program recognizes several command-line parameters. For this example, the command line looks like the following:

```
waisserver -p 2100 -d database
```

The `-p` parameter is used to dictate the port for the server to run on, and the `-d` parameter tells waisserver the name of the directory that contains the databases that should be served to the Internet. Executing the preceding command starts the WAIS server on port 2100. Now that the WAIS server is running, and a WAIS database has been indexed, you will see how to use SFgate to display the HTML file using a Web browser.

Creating an HTML Query Form that Uses SFgate

SFgate uses information passed from HTML forms to formulate WAIS database queries. This requires HTML form elements to be named the same as fields in your WAIS database. The example database does not use fields, so the only HTML tag that is required is one named "database." When SFgate is installed, it creates several HTML files to use as examples. For this example, the files are installed in /home/http/httpd/htdocs/SFgate. Using the /home/http/httpd/htdocs/SFgate/index.html file as a basis, the following HTML file is created to access the WAIS database:

```
<HTML>
  <HEAD>
    <TITLE>SFgate 4.0.18: Searching for databases</TITLE>
  </HEAD>
  <BODY>
    <A HREF="/SFgate/SFgate.html">
      <IMG ALIGN=TOP SRC="/SFgate/SFgate.gif"></A>
```

```
    <H1>SFgate 4.0.18: Searching for databases</H1>

    Use this page to search all HTML files on this server.

    <HR>

    <FORM METHOD=GET ACTION="http:/cgi-bin/SFgate">

      <H2>Select from the following databases:</H2>

      <INPUT NAME="database"
        TYPE="checkbox"
        VALUE="lightspeed.beowulf.com/html"
        CHECKED>
      HTML database on lightspeed.beowulf.com<BR>

      <HR>

      <H2>Enter your keywords to search for:</H2>

      <INPUT NAME="text" SIZE=50><BR>

      <P>

        <INPUT TYPE="submit" VALUE="Start Search">
        <INPUT TYPE="reset"  VALUE="Reset Query">

    </FORM>
    <HR>
  </BODY>
</HTML>
```

When displayed in a Web browser, the preceding HTML file looks like the screen shown in figure 9.3.

If a search for the word "html" is submitted, the results are returned by SFgate as shown in figure 9.4.

The name of the file is displayed as the headline, and each headline is a hyperlink. If the link for "customer_comments.html" is selected, a form you first saw in Chapter 3 is returned, as shown in figure 9.5.

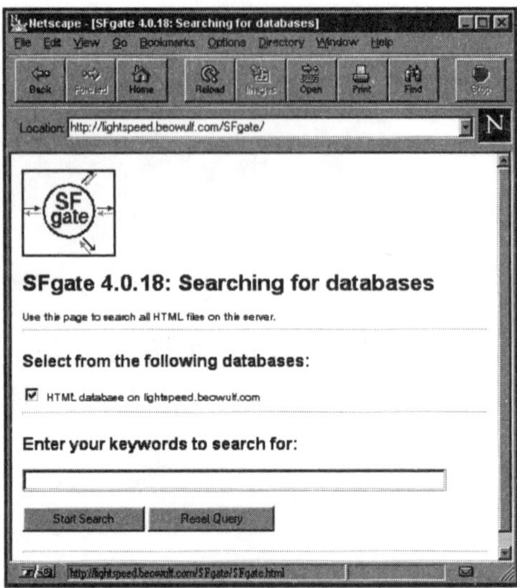

Figure 9.3
The WAIS query form.

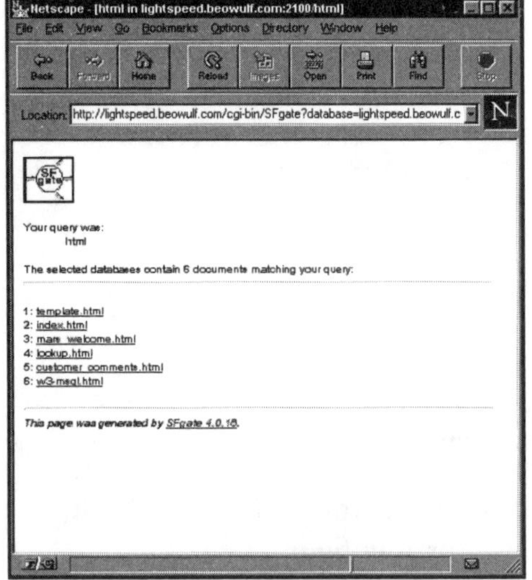

Figure 9.4
The WAIS query results.

Displaying HTML files in a Web browser is much more useful than using the waissearch client program to see the HTML source code returned from a WAIS query. However, if your HTML files change often or the name of the html file is not descriptive enough to use as a headline returned from a WAIS query, there are a couple of useful enhancements that freeWAIS-sf and SFgate provide to solve these problems.

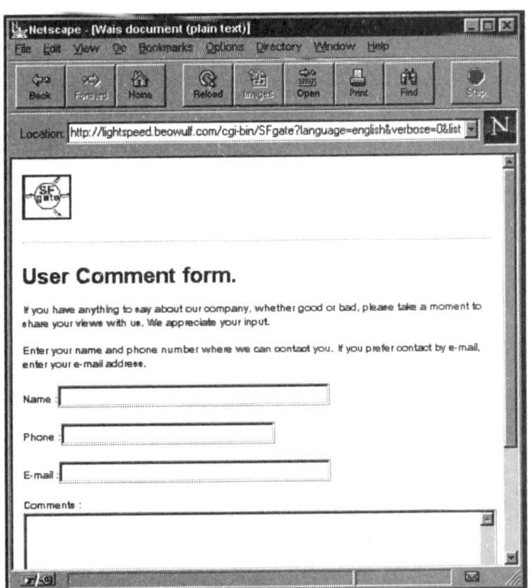

Figure 9.5
The user comments form returned by SFgate.

Using a freeWAIS-sf Format File

The study of WAIS format files could occupy a chapter all by itself and is beyond the scope of this book. The freeWAIS-sf FAQ, however, contains a very simple format file that can be used to capture the HTML title of an HTML document and use it as the headline for a document in the WAIS database. The "html.fmt" file is as follows:

```
record-sep: /\n\n/ # never matches

layout:
headline: /<[Tt][Ii][Tt][Ll][Ee]>/ /<\/[Tt][Ii][Tt][Ll][Ee]>/ 80
   /<[Tt][Ii][Tt][Ll][Ee]> */
end:

region: /<[Hh][Tt][Mm][Ll]>/
stemming TEXT GLOBAL
end: /<.[Bb][Oo][Dd][Yy]>/
```

Note

WAIS format files are used to process documents one line at a time, which means any pattern in the format file must match a single line of an HTML file, or it will not match at all. This might require editing your HTML files to get them to work with the html.fmt file, as will be shown in a moment.

The first line of the html.fmt file defines a record separator. Your HTML documents are each a single document so the separator of two newline characters is used because it will never match a line in an HTML file. A WAIS format file requires you to provide a record separator in case there are multiple records in a document that is being indexed. In this example, each HTML file is a single record, so the standard separator in this case is two newline characters. The waisindex program never finds two newlines together in an HTML file, so each file is treated as a separate record when creating WAIS database entries.

The layout section looks for the <title> </title> pair of HTML tags, using any mixture of upper- and lowercase characters. The format file instructs waisindex to use as the document headline whatever is between the two <title> tags. If waisindex does not find the starting and ending tags on the same line, it skips the starting tag and uses the next 80 characters as the headline. This has undesirable results, as will be shown shortly, because some of the HTML files have to be reformatted to match the pattern.

The third section tells waisindex to index every word between the beginning <HTML> tag and the ending </BODY> tag in every HTML document that is put into the WAIS database.

The following command tells waisindex to use the html.fmt file when creating headline entries in the database.

```
waisindex -T HTML -d html -t fields *.html
```

The only additional parameter needed is `-t fields`, which tells waisindex to look for a filename that matches the name of the database and has the extension .fmt. That file should be used as a pattern to index files.

After the HTML files are indexed using the format file, a query for the word "mars" returns the results shown in figure 9.6.

As you can see, the headline is not formatted correctly. A quick look at the HTML file shows why:

```
<TITLE>
   Mars Web Server
</TITLE>
```

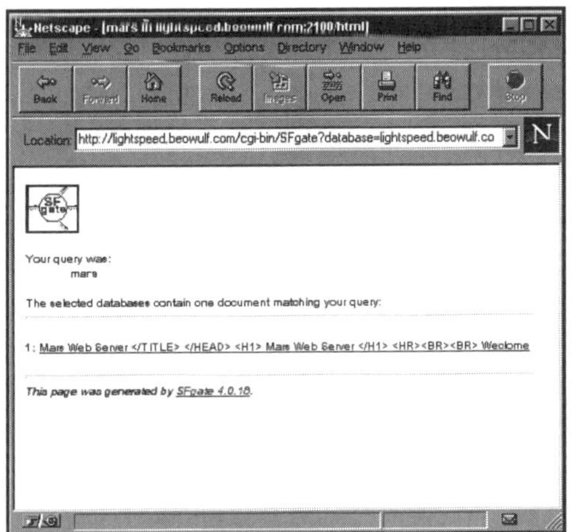

Figure 9.6
A WAIS headline using a format file.

The title tags and text are not on the same line. As mentioned before, waisindex processes files one line at a time. The beginning and ending <TITLE> tags are not on the same line, so the headline pattern is not matched. Because the first tag is found by the indexer, however, the next 80 characters are used as the headline. To fix the problem, all of the HTML source files should be reformatted like so:

```
<TITLE> Mars Web Server </TITLE>
```

Regenerating the database and running the same query again produces the results shown in figure 9.7.

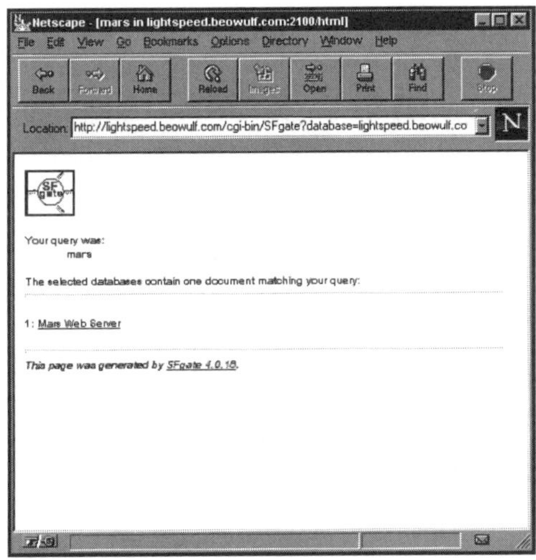

Figure 9.7
A correctly formatted WAIS headline as the hyperlink.

Using the URL Document Type

As a final step, if you prefer not to make copies of your HTML files, or you want all of the inline images and CGI programs to work correctly, you can use the URL document type to index your HTML files "in place" and return the URL of the document as a result of keyword searches.

This method does not make copies of your documents, but refers to them in place. If the user sends a query to the WAIS database that returns an URL to one of your HTML pages, the URL of the HTML page is displayed as an active hyperlink. Clicking on the hyperlink will send the user to the actual HTML page, not to a copy stored in the WAIS database. Because the HTML document is in its proper place when accessed by the Web browser, all images and links will work correctly.

Indexing your HTML files using the URL of each document is not hard but it does require a little more organization on your part. If you keep all your HTML documents in a single directory, you will need to ensure there are no files in the directory that you do not want published on the Web, such as test files or backup copies. If you have several directories with HTML files, the same applies to each directory, plus you should decide which directories of files will be indexed and which will not.

The waisindex parameter that creates the URL headline for the WAIS database is described in the freeWAIS-sf FAQ as this:

```
'-t URL what-to-trim what-to-add'
```

This tells the indexer which part of the path to replace with the HTTP prefix. For example, if your HTML files are located in the /home/http/httpd/htdocs directory, and the name of your HTTP server machine is "lightspeed.beowulf.com," the parameter becomes

```
'-t URL /home/http/httpd/htdocs http://lightspeed.beowulf.com'.
```

If you have your own directory for HTML files that are not part of the HTTP server system directories, the parameter might look something like this:

```
'-t URL /home/username/public_html http://lightspeed.beowulf.com/
~username
```

The real path information is replaced by the virtual path information needed by the HTTP server and stored in the database as a URL instead of a path to the HTML files.

So, assuming you are in the /home/http/freewais-sf/bin/database directory, the complete waisindex command to build a WAIS database using all of the features described here would look like the following (the backslash character (\) at the end of the first line tells the Unix shell this is all a single command):

```
../waisindex -t URL /home/http/httpd/htdocs http://
lightspeed.beowulf.com \
     -T HTML -d html -t fields /home/http/httpd/htdocs/*.html
```

This command would index all HTML files in the /home/http/httpd/htdocs directory. If you have HTML files in other directories that you want included in the WAIS database, there are two ways to tell the waisindex program where to find them.

The first method is to create a test file that is a list of all the files to index, including the complete directory path to the file, and to redirect this file list into the waisindex program. If you have HTML files in the /home/http/httpd/htdocs and /home/http/httpd/htdocs/SFgate directories, for example, a listing of those files could look something like the following and is put into the file file_name.txt in the /home/http/freewais-sf/bin/database directory:

```
/home/http/httpd/htdocs/customer_comments.html
/home/http/httpd/htdocs/index.html
/home/http/httpd/htdocs/lookup.html
/home/http/httpd/htdocs/mars_welcome.html
/home/http/httpd/htdocs/template.html
/home/http/httpd/htdocs/SFgate/SFgate.html
/home/http/httpd/htdocs/SFgate/SFproxy.html
/home/http/httpd/htdocs/SFgate/author.html
/home/http/httpd/htdocs/SFgate/bibdb-html.html
/home/http/httpd/htdocs/SFgate/demo.html
/home/http/httpd/htdocs/SFgate/index.html
```

To give this file list to the waisindex program, use the following command (as before, this command is all a single line):

```
../waisindex -t URL /home/http/httpd/htdocs http://
lightspeed.beowulf.com \
     -T HTML -d html -t fields 'cat file_list.txt'
```

This is a good way to specify exactly which files you want included in the database, but the major drawback to this method is that you are required to keep the file list up to date. If you create new HTML files or move existing ones, you have to update file_list.txt to reflect the changes in order for the new files to be included the next time you use the waisindex program to create a new WAIS database.

A more flexible way is to use the Unix *find* command to locate all HTML files in a directory and all subdirectories. The command to print out all HTML files in the HTTP server directories is as follows:

```
find /home/http/httpd/ -type f -name "*.html" -print
```

Adding this command to the waisindex command produces the following:

```
../waisindex -t URL /home/http/httpd/htdocs http://
lightspeed.beowulf.com \
     -T HTML -d html -t fields \
     'find /home/http/httpd/ -type f -name "*.html" -print'
```

This command finds every HTML file in the /home/http/httpd directory and in every subdirectory below it. This is a great command to run daily, perhaps using the Unix *crontab* command, which directs the operating system to run a command at specified intervals. Running the waisindex command daily would capture any changes made to any HTML files that day, as well as adding newly created files to the WAIS database.

By following this example, you now have an indexed database of all your HTML files, and they are available to any Web visitor via an HTML form you provide. Other types of documents can be indexed as well, giving you multiple WAIS databases that can be searched for keywords.

Note

By running a freeWAIS-sf server on your machine, anyone who has access to your machine, a WAIS client program, and knows the port number on which the WAIS server is running can access your databases, without using the Web or being limited to the searches provided by your HTML forms. Keep this in mind when you set up your WAIS server.

Do not put information into a freeWAIS-sf database that depends on HTTP server security, or any other Web-based security, to keep unauthorized users out of the database. freeWAIS-sf databases are designed to make information freely available, without data security in mind. Commercial WAIS databases often provide access control, but freeWAIS-sf does not.

Using the Unix DBM Program

DBM stands for *database management*, and the DBM program has been a part of the Unix operating system for a long time. DBM is a simple database program that has been improved over the years as new versions increased the capabilities of the program. If you take a look on your Unix system, there is a good chance you will find some version of DBM. If you need a minimal database to store simple data in, DBM is what you need.

Programs that make use of DBM functions can be written in C, using the API provided by the version of DBM used. C programs can create databases and store, fetch, update, and delete data based on the key values entered with the data. DBM is free and can handle modest amounts of data.

Although writing C programs is a good way to use DBM, there is an easier way. The Perl language comes with built-in support for several versions of DBM, and if there is no version of DBM on your system, Perl provides one of its own, called *SDBM*.

Note

The DBM support for versions of Perl prior to the 5.002 beta does not work for Linux 1.2.13 (non-ELF). If you want to use any form of DBM under this version of the Linux operating system, you will have to get version 5.002 of Perl.

To help you keep track of the DBM versions available and some of the good and bad points of each, the following table is taken from the AnyDBM_File.pm file in perl's "lib" directory:

Table 9.1
DBM Versions: Old DBM, New DBM, Standard DBM, gnu DBM, and Berkeley Standard DBM

	odbm	ndbm	sdbm	gdbm	bsd-db
Linkage comes w/ Perl	yes	yes	yes	yes	yes
Src comes w/ Perl	no	no	yes	no	no
Comes w/ many Unix OS	yes	yes[1]	no	no	no
Builds ok on Unix	?	?	yes	yes	?
Code Size	?	?	small	big	big
Database Size	?	?	small	big?	ok[2]
Speed	?	?	slow	ok	fast
FTPable	no	no	yes	yes	yes
Easy to build	n/a	n/a	yes	yes	ok[3]
Size limits	1 KB	4 KB	1 KB[4]	none	none
Byte-order independent	no	no	no	no	yes
Licensing restrictions	?	?	no	yes	no

1 On mixed universe machines, may be in the bsd compat library, which is often shunned.
2 Can be trimmed if you compile for one access method.
3 See DB_File. Requires symbolic links.
4 By default, but can be redefined.

Using the GDBM Version of DBM

For this example application, GDBM version 1.7.3 is used to create and maintain a database of employee phone numbers that will be available from a Web browser. One of the features that makes GDBM a good choice is that it gives you is the capability to have more than one user reading the database at one time.

When a user accessed a database using the original DBM (ODBM), the entire database file was locked until the database application released it. GDBM locks the file when inserts or updates are performed, but queries allow multiple accesses at the same time.

As a description of what GDBM is and how it works, the following explanation comes from the GDBM man page.

> GNU DBM is a library of routines that manages data files that contain key/data pairs. The access provided is that of storing, retrieval, and deletion by key and a non-sorted traversal of all keys. A process is allowed to use multiple data files at the same time. A process that opens a GDBM file is designated as a *reader* or a *writer*. Only one writer may open a GDBM file, and many readers may open the file. Readers and writers cannot open the GDBM file at the same time.

Another good reason for using GDBM is the source code is readily available for download on the Internet. GDBM can be downloaded from the following places:

```
http://www.nectec.or.th/pub/mirrors/gnu

http://sunsite.doc.ic.ac.uk:81/public/gnu/

http://www.lbl.gov/%7Esls/woa/distrib/

http://gatekeeper.dec.com/pub/GNU/

http://www.astro.nwu.edu/lentz/mac/unix/home-mac-unix.html
```

Compiling and installing GDBM is very easy. The following commands unpack the GDBM source code into the /home/http/gdbm-1.7.3 directory:

```
gunzip gdbm-1.7.3.tar.gz

tar -xf gdbm-1.7.3.tar
```

Enter that directory and run the Configure program. Unlike for other programs, Configure does not ask you any questions but ascertains everything it needs to know unaided. After Configure is completed, running *make* compiles the program, and the **make install** command installs GDBM. That is all there is to it.

Creating Database Management Programs for GDBM

For this example, searching the phone number database is the only function that is available from a Web browser. Adding and deleting phone numbers is done on the local machine by trusted personnel using Perl scripts.

The phone number database will consist of two fields: a person's name (which is the key value for a record) and a text string that contains the telephone number and any other important information, such as the extension number. Each person can be listed more than once, enabling users to search by first name, last name, login id, and so on. The database and Perl scripts to add, search, and delete data will reside in the /home/http/httpd/cgi-bin/gdbm directory.

Adding Phone Number Information

The first thing needed for our database of phone numbers is a way to add new phone numbers to the database. The Perl script for adding phone numbers to a GDBM database requires two command-line arguments. A third arugment is optional. The command-line arguments recognized by add_pn are:

- -N name(s), a comma-delimited list of names to associate with a telephone number
- -P string, a message to associate with each name
- -D database, the name of the database to add data to (optional; the default database name is "pndb")

If a name already exists in the selected database, add_pn replaces the existing data with the new data. The Perl program "add_pn" is listed here:

```
#!/usr/bin/perl

use GDBM_File;
$num_args = 0; $database = ""; $names = "", $number = "";

# Pick up the command line arguments
while ($ARGV[0] && $ARGV[0] =~ /^-/) {
  $_ = shift;
```

```
  if (/^-[dD]/) { # database name

    $database = ($1 ? $1 : shift);

  } elsif (/^-[nN]/) { # list of names

    # It's possible there are spaces when full names are listed.
    # This gets everything up to the next parameter or the end of
    # line.
    while ($ARGV[0] && $ARGV[0] !~ /^-/) {
      $names = $names." ".($1 ? $1 : shift);
    }
    $num_args++;

  } elsif (/^-[pP]/) { # phone numbers and other messages

    while ($ARGV[0] && $ARGV[0] !~ /^-/) {
      $number = $number." ".($1 ? $1 : shift);
    }
    $number =~ s/^\s*//; $number =~ s/\s*$//;
    $num_args++;

  } else {
    die "Unrecognized switch: $_\n";
  }
}

if ($num_args < 2) {
  print "\nUsage: add_pn -N name[,name,...] -P number [-D
  ➥database]\n\n";
  print " -N names  : comma separated list of names to add to
  ➥database\n";
  print " -P number : the phone number to attach the names to\n";
  die " [-D database] : optional name of database to use (default
  ➥= pndb)\n\n";
}

if ( !$database ) { $database = "pndb"; }

@namelist = split(',', $names);

#dbmopen(%PNDB, $database, 0666) || die "No such database\n";
tie(%PNDB, GDBM_File, $database, GDBM_WRCREAT, 0666)
    || die "Can't open database: $database\n";
print "Opened database file: $database\n";
```

```
foreach $n (@namelist) {

  # Force the names to lowercase and remove leading and trailing
  # spaces for easier searching.
  $n =~ tr/A-Z/a-z/;
  $n =~ s/^\s*//; $n =~ s/\s*$//;

  # Assign the phone number information to the name, which is the
  key value.
  $PNDB{$n} = $number;
  print "$n = $number added.\n";
}

#dbmclose(%PNDB);
untie(%PNDB);
```

Note

You may notice the function calls dbmopen() and dbmclose() are commented out. In versions of Perl prior to version 5, the DBM commands were the only ones available. Version 5 and later introduced the *tie* command, which is the preferred method because it makes the multi-user capabilities possible with GDBM.

If you have Perl on your system prior to version 5, uncomment the DBM commands, comment out the "use GDBM_File" line and the tie commands, and add pn will work on your system.

Searching for Phone Number Information

The next thing needed is a way to find data in the database. Although the find function is available from the Web, it would also be nice if those responsible for maintaining the database could see what it contains. The Perl script to find phone numbers in a GDBM database requires one command-line argument and one that is optional. The command-line arguments recognized by find_pn are the following:

- -N name(s), a comma-delimited list of names to search for
- -D database, the name of the database to search (optional; the default database name is "pndb")

If the name given is "all," all of the data in the database will be returned. The Perl program "find_pn" is listed here:

```
#!/usr/bin/perl

use GDBM_File;
$num_args = 0; $database = ""; $names = "";

# If the user asks for help, give it.
while ($ARGV[0] =~ /^-/) {
  $_ = shift;

  if (/^-[dD]/) { # database name

    $database = ($1 ? $1 : shift);
    $num_args++;

  } elsif (/^-[nN]/) { # list of names

    # It's possible there are spaces when full names are listed.
    # This gets everything up to the next parameter or the end of
    line.
    while ($ARGV[0] && $ARGV[0] !~ /^-/) {
      $names = $names." ".($1 ? $1 : shift);
    }
    $num_args++;

  } else {
    die "Unrecognized switch: $_\n";
  }
}

if ($num_args < 1) {
  print "\nUsage: find_pn -N name[,name,...] -D database\n";
  print "  -N names        : list of names to delete from
  ➥database\n";
  die "  [-D database]  : optional name of database (defaults to
  ➥pndb)\n\n";
}

if ( !$database ) { $database = "pndb"; }

# Open the database.  If it doesn't exist, bail out.
# dbmopen(%PNDB, $database, 0) || die "No such phone number
database\n";
tie(%PNDB, GDBM_File, $database, GDBM_READER, undef)
    || die "No such database: $database\n";
```

```
print "Opened database file: $database.\n";

@namelist = split(',', $names);

for each $n (@namelist) {

  # Force the names to lowercase and remove leading and trailing
  # spaces for easier searching.
  $n =~ tr/A-Z/a-z/;
  $n =~ s/^\s*//; $n =~ s/\s*$//;
  print "Searching for: <$n>\n";

  # If all names are wanted, print them and exit.
  if ($n eq "all") {
    $count = 0;
    foreach $name (%PNDB) {
      $count++;
      if ($count % 2 == 0) { next; }
      printf "%24s: %s \n", $name, $PNDB{$name};
    }
    exit;
  }

  # If a name is in the database, print it.
  if ($PNDB{$n}) { printf "%24s: %s \n", $n, $PNDB{$n}; }
}

#dbmclose(%PNDB);
untie(%PNDB);
```

Deleting Phone Number Information

The final program needed to manage a GDBM database is the ability to remove information from the database. The Perl script to delete phone numbers from a GDBM database requires one command-line argument and one that is optional. The command-line arguments recognized by del_pn are as follows:

- -N name(s), a comma-delimited list of names to search for
- -D database, the name of the database to search (optional; the default database name is "pndb")

If the name given is "all," all of the data in the database is deleted. The Perl program "del_pn" is listed on the following page:

```
#!/usr/bin/perl

use GDBM_File;
$num_args = 0; $database = ""; $names = "";

# Pick up the command line arguments
while ($ARGV[0] =~ /^-/) {
  $_ = shift;

  if (/^-[dD]/) { # database name

    $database = ($1 ? $1 : shift);
    $num_args++;

  } elsif (/^-[nN]/) { # list of names

    # It's possible there are spaces when full names are listed.
    # This gets everything up to the next parameter or the end of
    # line.
    while ($ARGV[0] && $ARGV[0] !~ /^-/) {
      $names = $names." ".($1 ? $1 : shift);
    }
    $num_args++;

  } else {
    die "Unrecognized switch: $_\n";
  }
}

if ($num_args < 1) {
  print "\nUsage: find_pn -N name[,name,...] -D database\n";
  print "   -N names        : list of names to delete from
  ➥database\n";
  die "   [-D database]   : optional name of database (defaults to
  ➥pndb)\n\n";
}

if ( !$database ) { $database = "pndb"; }

@namelist = split(',', $names);
w
#dbmopen(%PNDB, $database, undef) || die "No such database\n";
tie(%PNDB, GDBM_File, $database, GDBM_WRITER, 0666)
    || die "No such database: $database\n";
print "Opened database file: $database\n";
```

```
foreach $n (@namelist) {

  # Force the names to lowercase and remove leading and trailing
  # spaces for easier searching.
  $n =~ tr/A-Z/a-z/;
  $n =~ s/^\s*//;
  $n =~ s/\s*$//;
  print "Searching for: <$n>\n";

  # If the name is "all", delete all data.  If a name is in the
  # database, delete it.
  if ($n eq "all") {
    print "   Deleting all data in the database\n";
    $count = 0;
    foreach $name (%PNDB) {
      delete $PNDB{$name};
    }
    exit;
  } elsif ($PNDB{$n}) {
    delete $PNDB{$n};
    print "   $n deleted.\n";
  }
}

#dbmclose(%PNDB);
untie(%PNDB);
```

Using the GDBM Database

Now that the database management programs are written, the database should have data in it. The following commands add several names and phone numbers to the "officers" database.

```
add_pn -N jeff rowe,jeff,rowe,jrowe -P "(123) 456-7890, ext.
➥13" -D officers
add_pn -N john davis,john,jdavis -P \
       "(098) 765-4321 before 5:00 pm, (102) 938-4756 after"
       ➥-D officers
```

The add_pn program adds the names jeff rowe, jeff, rowe, and jrowe to the database with the same telephone number. This is fine for a small company with only one person named Jeff working there. If a new record is entered in a similar manner for Jeff Smith, however, the first record for jeff is overwritten.

To see if the information was entered correctly, the following command returns the information in the database for jeff, john, and jrowe:

```
find_pn -N jeff,john,jrowe -D officers
```

When executed, the preceding command returns the following results:

```
Searching for: <jeff>
               jeff: (123) 456-7890, ext. 13
Searching for: <john>
               john: (098) 765-4321 before 5:00 pm, (102)
               938-4756 after
               Searching for: <jrowe>
               jrowe: (123) 456-7890, ext. 13
```

To print all the records in the database, use the following command:

```
find_pn -N all -D officers
```

which elicits the following results:

```
 jeff rowe: (123) 456-7890, ext. 13
    jdavis: (098) 765-4321 before 5:00 pm, (102) 938-4756 after
      jeff: (123) 456-7890, ext. 13
     jrowe: (123) 456-7890, ext. 13
      rowe: (123) 456-7890, ext. 13
john davis: (098) 765-4321 before 5:00 pm, (102) 938-4756 after
      john: (098) 765-4321 before 5:00 pm, (102) 938-4756 after
```

To delete the record for jeff, john, and rowe from the database, use the following command:

```
del_pn -N jeff,john,rowe -D officers
```

which gives the following results:

```
Opened database file: officers
Searching for: <jeff>
   jeff deleted.
Searching for: <john>
   john deleted.
Searching for: <rowe>
   rowe deleted.
```

As verification that the delete worked, issuing the "find_pn -N all -D officers" command once more returns the following results:

```
 jeff rowe: (123) 456-7890, ext. 13
    jdavis: (098) 765-4321 before 5:00 pm, (102) 938-4756 after
     jrowe: (123) 456-7890, ext. 13
john davis: (098) 765-4321 before 5:00 pm, (102) 938-4756 after
```

As you can see, the correct database entries were deleted.

Searching for Phone Number Information from the Web

Now that you have established a database and verified that the database management programs work correctly, you need to do the following two things:

- Construct a Web page to access the information.
- Construct a CGI program that duplicates the functionality of find_pn, but returns information readable by an HTTP server.

The following HTML file, phone_book.html, displays a search form for users to enter names and submit them for database searches:

```
<HTML>
  <HEAD>
    <TITLE>Beowulf Enterprises Phone Book</TITLE>
  </HEAD>
  <BODY>
    <H1>Beowulf Enterprises Phone Book</H1>

    <FORM ACTION="http://lightspeed.beowulf.com/cgi-bin/
    ➥phone_book.cgi"
     METHOD="POST">

    <INPUT NAME="action" TYPE="hidden" VALUE="find">
    Choose the telephone database to search:
    <BR>
    <BR>
    <INPUT NAME="database" TYPE="radio" VALUE="officers">Corporate
    ➥Officers
    <BR>
    <INPUT NAME="database" TYPE="radio" VALUE="service"
    ➥CHECKED>Customer Service
    <BR>
    <INPUT NAME="database" TYPE="radio" VALUE="shipping">Shipping
    ➥Department
    <BR>
    <BR>
    <HR>
```

```
    Enter the name or names to look up in the phone book.
    <BR>
    Separate multiple names with commas.
    <BR>
    (Ex: frank smith, george, bjones)
    <BR>
    <BR>
    To find all names, enter the name 'all'.
    <BR>
    <BR>
    <INPUT NAME="names" TYPE="text" SIZE=40>
    <BR>
    <BR>
    <INPUT NAME="submit" TYPE="submit" VALUE="Start Search">
    <INPUT NAME="reset" TYPE="reset" VALUE="Reset Form">
    <FORM>
  </BODY>
</HTML>
```

When displayed in a Web browser, phone_book.html appears like the search form in figure 9.8.

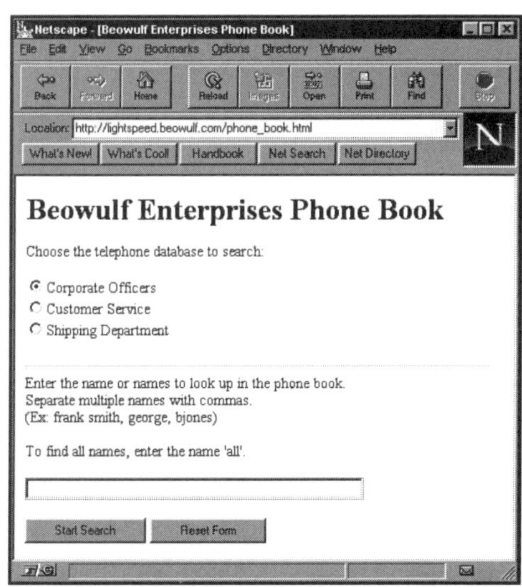

Figure 9.8
An HTML search form used to search GDBM databases.

All that is left to complete the project is a CGI program to search the databases. The following CGI program, phone_book.cgi, mimics the find_pn program, with a few changes so it can be used with an HTTP server. The phone_book.cgi program is purposely designed so the functions to insert or delete phone numbers can be added easily if you would like to include them for Web visitors:

```
#!/usr/bin/perl

#----------------------
# Include perl libraries
#----------------------
use GDBM_File;
require "cgi-lib.pl";

print &PrintHeader;

&ReadParse;


#-----------------------
# Add other functions here
#-----------------------
if ( $in{'action'} eq "find" ) {
   &Find_Phone_Number;
} else {
   print "Unrecognized action.\n";
   exit;
}

sub Find_Phone_Number {

   print "<head><title>Phone Book Search Results</title></
   ➥head>\n";
   print "<body><h1>Phone Book Search Results</h1>\n";

   if ( ($in{'names'} && $in{'names'} eq "" )
        || ($in{'database'} && $in{'database'} eq "") ) {
      print "You must enter at least one name and choose a
      ➥database ".
         "to search.\n";
      exit;
   }

   $database = "/home/http/httpd/cgi-bin/gdbm/"."$in{'database'}";
   $names = $in{'names'};

   $db_dir = 1;
   chdir "/home/http/httpd/cgi-bin/gdbm" || $db_dir--;
if ($db_dir == 0) {
      print "Error: cannot find database directory";
      exit;
   }
```

```
    # Open the database.  If it doesn't exist, bail out.
    if ( !tie(%PNDB, GDBM_File, $database, GDBM_READER, undef) ) {
       print "No such database: $in{'database'}\n";
       exit;
    }
    print "Opened database file: $in{'database'}.<BR><BR>\n";

    @namelist = split(',', $names);

    foreach $n (@namelist) {

       # Force the names to lowercase and remove leading and
       # trailing spaces for easier searching.
       $n =~ tr/A-Z/a-z/;
       $n =~ s/^\s*//; $n =~ s/\s*$//;
       print "Searching for: $n<BR><BR>\n";

       # If all names are wanted, print them and exit.
       if ($n eq "all") {
          $count = 0;
          foreach $name (%PNDB) {
             $count++;
             if ($count % 2 == 0) { next; }
             printf "%24s: %s <BR>\n", $name, $PNDB{$name};
          }
          exit;
       }

       # If a name is in the database, print it.
       if ($PNDB{$n}) { print "$n: $PNDB{$n}<BR>\n"; }
    }

    untie(%PNDB);
    print "</body>\n";
}
```

If the phone_book.html form is used to search for all phone numbers in the "officers" database, the results shown in figure 9.9 are displayed.

GDBM and the other versions of DBM can be used for storing just about anything. It is free, easy to use, and does not require any knowledge of the SQL language to use it. Writing Perl programs to use GDBM makes database programming even easier. GDBM is ideal for small projects that don't need a full-blown database but still need a way to store and retrieve data by key values. Using the sample programs presented here, you can adapt them to your own projects and access your own GDBM databases from the Web.

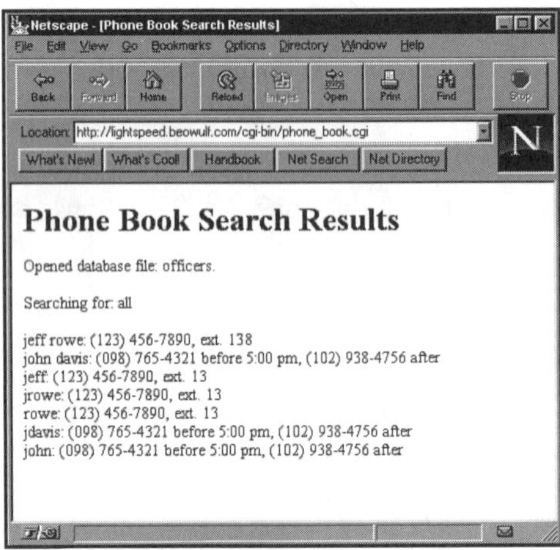

Figure 9.9
Searching a GDBM database using phone_book.cgi.

Using HTMLBBS

As mentioned at the beginning of this chapter, many people have the mistaken idea that a database is some arcane piece of software that is big and complicated and does magical things with your data so you can store and retrieve it. Some databases are that way, but you don't need a traditional database if all you want to do is store and retrieve text strings that are written by one person and read by many others, like a message board on the Web.

All you need is a program that will accept a message entered by a user and display it to anyone who visits the Web site later. The messages don't need to be stored in any special format because they are just plain text, and no special search engine is needed because all messages are displayed on a browsable page. This is exactly how HTMLBBS works.

HTMLBBS is a bulletin board system (BBS) that uses version 4 or later of Perl to manage database files written in HTML. HTMLBBS was authored by Eric Murray (`ericm@lne.com`) and can be downloaded from the following site:

`http://www.lne.com/ericm/htmlbbs`

One of the nice features of HTMLBBS is that the messages posted using the program are stored in HTML files and can be edited with any text editor. There is no binary or proprietary file format to deal with. Each posted message is given an ID number that is stored in an HTML comment block. The HTMLBBS programs use the message id to manage the messages as database records.

HTMLBBS gives users the capability to create their own topics to post messages to, if the existing topics do not cover the subject. After a topic is created, messages can be posted on the HTML page dedicated to that topic. The main page contains a list of topics that are hyperlinks to the individual topic pages. A form at the bottom of the main page enables users to create new topics. Each topic page also has a form at the bottom for users to post messages.

Installing HTMLBBS

The HTMLBBS program comes packed into a "shar" file, which stands for *shell archive.* A *shar* file is a self-extracting Bourne shell script that creates the following files in the current directory:

Copyright	bbsedit	htmlbbs.pl	newtopic.cgi
Future	findold	htmlbbs.shar	rmmsg
Makefile	htmlbbs-conf.pl	mkindex	
README	htmlbbs.cgi	mktopic	

Create a directory to hold the HTMLBBS files. For this example, the files are put into the /home/http/htmlbbs directory. Enter this directory and edit the htmlbbs.shar file, removing the top few lines as the instructions at the top of the shar file tell you, then enter the following command:

```
sh htmlbbs.shar
```

This runs htmlbbs.shar as a shell script. Htmlbbs.shar unpacks several files into the /home/http/htmlbbs directory. Consult the README file for instructions on how to install the HTMLBBS programs.

Note

The HTMLBBS programs assume you have access to the HTTP server system directories and the Perl system library directories. If you do not, it is possible to get HTMLBBS to work, but it requires a bit of tinkering with the HTMLBBS configuration files and requires you to have a version of Perl to which you can add files to the library directory.

If your Perl program is somewhere other than /usr/local/bin/perl, edit the following HTMLBBS files and change the first line that says #!/usr/local/bin/perl to reflect the path to your Perl program.

htmlbbs.cgi

newtopic.cgi

bbsedit

findold

mkindex

mktopic

rmmsg

Next, edit the file htmlbbs-conf.pl and set the values of the following variables to reflect the setup of your system files. The values used here are specific to the system used for the example and may differ from the values you use.

Note

The HTMLBBS configuration program does not recognize symbolic links when installing the BBS software. If your HTTP server is really in the /home/http/httpd_1.5a directory, for example, and you have a symbolic link to that directory so you can use the path /home/http/httpd, you will have to use the *real* path name, not the link name, for HTMLBBS to install correctly.

```
# set server root.  THIS MUST BE SET!
$server_root="/home/http/httpd";

# set the cgi directory (without server root, i.e. ifserver root is
# /home/www and the cgi directory is /home/www/cgi-bin then
# $cgi_dir is "cgi-bin".  THIS MUST BE SET!
$cgi_dir = "/cgi-bin";

# where is the start (under $server_root) of the HTMLBBS tree?
$htmlbbs_root = "$server_root/htdocs/bbs";

# set the bin directory where you will be installing the scripts.
$usrlocal = "/home/http/bin";
```

There are also options to enable users to put HTML tags in posted messages and to limit the length of messages. Set these options as you wish.

The next step is to edit the Makefile and set the values of the following variables:

```
CGIBIN = /home/http/httpd/cgi-bin

# name of cgi bin relative to server root:
HTTPCGIBIN = /cgi-bin

BINDIR = /usr/http/bin

LIBDIR = /usr/lib/perl5
```

The HTMLBBS installation program attempts to copy the files htmlbbs-conf.pl and htmlbbs.pl to the Perl library directory you specified with the variable LIBDIR. In most cases, this requires you to have root access unless you have your own copy of Perl installed.

If you are installing into the system Perl directories, first become the root user, then enter the command **make install**. This copies the HTMLBBS files to where they need to go, based on the values you entered in the htmlbbs-conf.pl file.

Creating HTMLBBS Topics

The bulletin board files for this example are created in the /home/http/httpd/htdocs/bbs directory. From that directory, use the "mkindex" program to create the top-level HTML page for your topics. Enter the following command to create the HTML file index.html with the title `Connecting a Database to the WWW`:

```
/home/http/bin/mkindex index.html "Connecting a Database to the
WWW"
```

Figure 9.10 shows the file that is created.

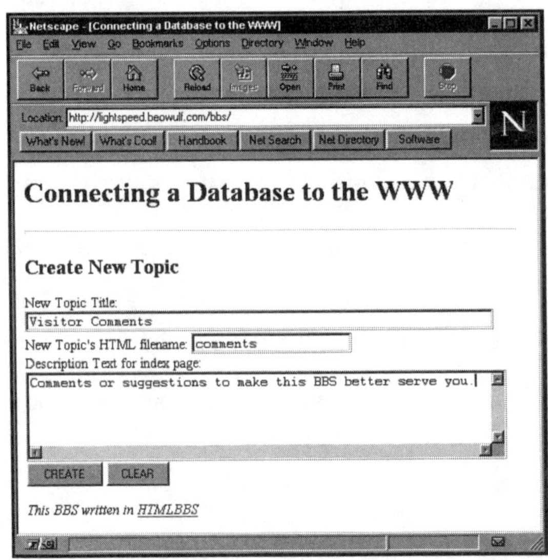

Figure 9.10
The main Web page created by mkindex.

Use the Create New Topic portion of the form to create the following topics: `Visitor Comments`, `Been there, done that`, and `Tips and Hints`. After the topics have been created, they are shown in figure 9.11.

Click on the `Visitor Comments` hyperlink and post a message using the provided form. The message appears as shown in figure 9.12.

Your BBS is up and running! Now you can share information and experience with the people who visit your Web site. All of the files created by HTMLBBS are written in standard HTML, so you can edit the files and add headers, images, or whatever you want to customize the BBS to suit yourself.

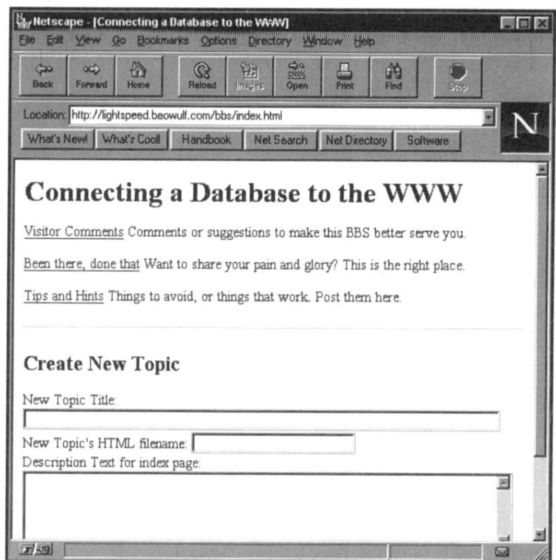

Figure 9.11
New topics for your BBS.

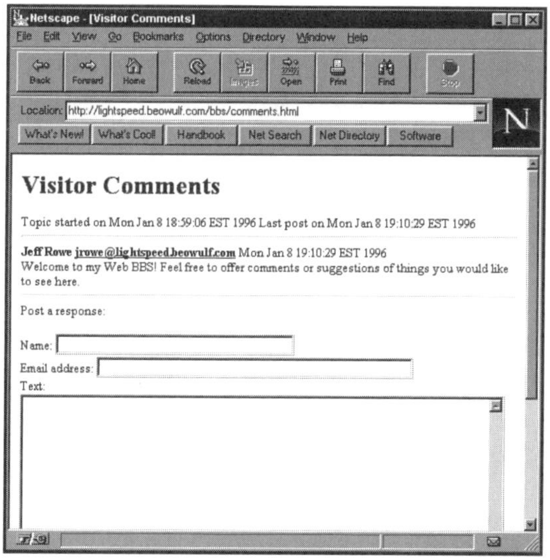

Figure 9.12
Your first BBS message.

The HTMLBBS package also includes some administration tools to help you manage your BBS. The tools included are these:

- **bbsedit.** A program to edit your BBS message files. Use bbsedit to edit messages while the BBS is running. Bbsedit locks the message file to prevent users from posting messages while you edit and then saving your changes over the new messages.

- **findold.** A program to list the message IDs of messages in a topic file that are older than the number of days you give as the parameter.
- **rmmsg.** A program to remove messages from topic files based on a list of message IDs you provide.

You can use these tools to clean out old messages, edit posted messages if needed, and keep your BBS tidy. No one likes visiting a Web site that is never changed or updated. A dead or untidy Web site is a depressing site.

Hopefully, these alternatives to traditional databases have given you ideas on how to make your information available to the Internet community and to the World Wide Web without having to be a database expert.

With a little time and the examples provided in this book, you can publish virtually any kind of information on the Web. The Internet is all about making information freely available, and the Web makes it easy to do exactly that.

mSQL—Manual

Mini SQL

A Lightweight Database Server Version 1.1

mSQL has been developed as part of the Minerva Network Management Environment.

HTML version of the manual produced by Thomas R. Kimpton

tom@selene.utval.net

Table of Contents

Introduction and History

Mini SQL, or mSQL, is a lightweight database engine designed to provide fast access to stored data with low memory requirements. As its name implies, mSQL offers a subset of SQL as its query interface. Although it only supports a subset of SQL (no views, sub-queries, etc.), everything it supports is in accordance with the ANSI SQL specification. The mSQL package includes the database engine, a terminal "monitor" program, a database administration program, a schema viewer, and a C language API. The API and the database engine have been designed to work in a client/server environment over a TCP/IP network.

The decision to write yet another database package was made due to the hole in the range of "free" or "freely available" databases. At the time of writing, there are no other database packages available that support SQL as the query language. The most notable database package for research work, Postgres from the University of California at Berkeley, offers a superset of the original Ingres QUEL known as PostQUEL as its query language.

mSQL has been developed as the database backend for the Minerva Network Management Environment. Originally, Minerva utilized Postgres as its database and generated PostQUEL queries to access it. During initial alpha testing of Minerva, a comment was made that if Minerva generated SQL queries, sites with an existing database installation, such as Ingres or Oracle, could use their commercial databases rather than have to support Postgres as well. To accommodate that wish, mSQL was written initially as an SQL to PostQUEL translator so that sites without commercial database could still use Postgres (seeing as there were no "free" SQL engines available).

As time passed, and Minerva developed further, it became apparent that Postgres was too resource hungry to support the evolving mechanisms provided by Minerva. To gain speed, Minerva was extended to perform monitoring and data acquisition in parallel. Unfortunately, each process that communicated with the database forced another copy of the Postgres backend to be spawned. The fact that each Postgres backend consumes close to 1.5 megabytes of memory soon put a stop to the parallel data acquisition operations.

Although Postgres is a very large and capable package, it is supported on only a handful of platforms. This proved to be a problem as a couple of the original Minerva alpha testers wished to run Minerva on Silicon Graphics machines. Unfortunately, Postgres did not support the SGI machines so they could not participate in the testing. The fact that Minerva itself utilized only a fraction of the features of Postgres and needed to be portable to most platforms proved that tying Minerva to Postgres was not the best option. From that decision Mini SQL was developed.

It should be noted that Postgres is an excellent database package offering a vast array of powerful features and that the above comments in no way try to detract from its success. The fact that Minerva utilizes very few database features (it doesn't even need a relational join) showed that a database as capable and advanced as Postgres was overkill.

Mini SQL Specification

The mSQL language offers a significant subset of the features provided by ANSI SQL. It enables a program or user to store, manipulate, and retrieve data in table structures. It does not support relational capabilities such as table joins, views, or nested queries. Although it does not support all the relational operations defined in the ANSI specification, it does provide the capability of "joins" between multiple tables.

Although the definitions and examples below depict mSQL key words in uppercase, no such restriction is placed on the actual queries.

The Create Clause

The create clause as supported by mSQL can only be used to create a table. It cannot be used to create other definitions such as views. It should also be noted that there can only be one primary key field defined for a table. Defining a field as a key generates an implicit "not null" attribute for the field.

```
CREATE TABLE table_name (
        col_name    col_type    [ not null | primary key ]
    [ , col_name    col_type    [ not null | primary key ] ]**
)
```

For example

```
CREATE TABLE emp_details(
     first_name    char(15) not null,
     last_name     char(15) not null,
     dept          char(20),
     emp_id          int primary key,
     salary          int
)
```

The available types are the following:

char (len)

int

real

The Drop Clause

Drop is used to remove a table definition from the database:

```
DROP TABLE table_name
```

For example

```
DROP TABLE emp_details
```

The Insert Clause

Unlike ANSI SQL, you cannot nest a select within an insert (that is, you cannot insert the data returned by a select). Currently, you must also specify the names of the fields into which the data is to be inserted. You cannot specify the values without the field name and expect the server to insert the data into the correct fields by default.

```
INSERT INTO table_name ( column [ , column ]** )
VALUES (value [, value]** )
```

For example

```
INSERT INTO emp_details ( first_name, last_name, dept, salary)
VALUES ('David', 'Hughes', 'I.T.S.','12345')
```

The number of values supplied must match the number of columns.

The Delete Clause

The syntax for mSQL's delete clause is

```
DELETE FROM table_name
WHERE column OPERATOR value
[ AND | OR column OPERATOR value ]**
```

```
OPERATOR can be &lt;, &gt;, =, &lt;=, &gt;=, &lt;&gt;, or like
```

For example

```
DELETE FROM emp_details WHERE emp_id = 12345
```

The Select Clause

The select offered by mSQL lacks some of the features provided by the SQL spec:

No nested selects

No implicit functions (e.g. count( ), avg( ))

It does however support:

Joins

DISTINCT row selection

ORDER BY clauses

Regular expression matching

Column to Column comparisons in WHERE clauses

So, the formal syntax for mSQL's select is:

```
SELECT [table.]column [ , [table.]column ]**
FROM table [ , table]**
[ WHERE [table.] column OPERATOR VALUE
     [ AND | OR [table.]column OPERATOR VALUE]** ]
[ ORDER BY [table.]column [DESC] [, [table.]column [DESC] ]

OPERATOR can be &lt;, &gt;, =, &lt;=, &gt;=, &lt;&gt;, or like
VALUE can be a literal value or a column name
```

A simple select may be

```
SELECT first_name, last_name FROM emp_details
WHERE dept = 'finance'
```

To sort the returned data in ascending order by last_name and descending order by first_name the query would look like this:

```
SELECT first name, last_name FROM emp_details
WHERE dept = 'finance'
ORDER BY last_name, first_name DESC
```

And to remove any duplicate rows, the DISTINCT operator could be used:

```
SELECT DISTINCT first_name, last_name FROM emp_details
WHERE dept = 'finance'
ORDER BY last_name, first_name DESC
```

The regular expression syntax supported by LIKE clauses is that of standard SQL:

> '_' matches any single character
>
> '%' matches 0 or more characters of any value
>
> '\' escapes special characters (for example, '\%' matches % and '\\' matches \ )

All other characters match themselves.

So, to search for anyone in finance whose last name consists of a letter followed by 'ughes', such as Hughes, the query could look like this:

```
SELECT first_name, last_name FROM emp_details
WHERE dept = 'finance' and last_name like '_ughes'
```

The power of a relational query language starts to become apparent when you start joining tables together during a select. Let's say you had two tables defined, one containing staff details and another listing the projects being worked on by each staff member, and each staff member has been assigned an employee number that is unique to that person. You could generate a sorted list of who was working on what project with a query like

```
SELECT      emp_details.first_name, emp_details.last_name,
          project_details.project
FROM emp_details, project_details
WHERE emp_details.emp_id = project_details.emp_id
ORDER BY emp_details.last_name, emp_details.first_name
```

mSQL places no restriction on the number of tables "joined" during a query, so if there were 15 tables all containing information related to an employee ID in some manner, data from each of those tables could be extracted, albeit slowly, by a single query. One key point to note regarding joins is that you must qualify all column names with a table name. mSQL does not support the concept of uniquely named columns spanning multiple tables, so you are forced to qualify every column name as soon as you access more than one table in a single select.

The Update Clause

The mSQL update clause cannot use a column name as a value. Only literal values may by used as an update value.

```
UPDATE table_name SET column=value [ , column=value ]**
WHERE column OPERATOR value
       [ AND | OR column OPERATOR value ]**

OPERATOR can be &lt;, &gt;, =, &lt;=, &gt;=, &lt;&gt;, or like
```

For example

```
UPDATE emp_details SET salary=30000 WHERE emp_id = 1234
```

The Database Engine

The mSQL daemon, msqld, is a standalone application that listens for connections on a well-known TCP socket. It is a single process engine that will accept multiple connections and serialize the queries received. It utilizes memory mapped I/O and cache techniques to offer rapid access to the data stored in a database. It also utilizes a stack-based mechanism that ensures that INSERT operations are performed at the same speed regardless of the size of the table being accessed. Preliminary testing performed by a regular user of mSQL has shown that for simple queries, the performance of mSQL is comparable to or better than other freely available database packages. For example, on a set of sample queries including simple inserts, updates, and selects, mSQL performed roughly 4 times faster than University Ingres and over 20 times faster than Postgres on an Intel 486 class machine running Linux.

The server may be accessed either via a well-known TCP socket or via a Unix domain socket with the file system (/dev/msqld). The availability of the TCP socket allows client software to access data stored on a machine over the network. Use of the TCP socket should be limited to client software on remote machines because communicating with the server via a TCP socket rather than the Unix socket will result in a substantial drop in performance. See the details on the programming API and also the command-line options to standard programs for details on selecting the server machine.

The engine includes debugging code so that its progress can be monitored. There are currently eight debugging modules available in the engine. Debugging for any of the available modules can be enabled at runtime by setting the contents of the MINERVA_DEBUG environment variable to a colon-separated list of debug module names. A list of available debug modules is given below:

cache	Display the workings of the table cache
query	Display each query before it is executed
error	Display error message as well as send them to the client
key	Display details of key-based data lookups
malloc	Display details of memory allocation
trace	Display a function call trace as the program executes
mmap	Display details of memory mapped regions
general	Anything that didn't fit into a category above

For example, to make the server display the queries before they are processed and also show details of the memory allocation that takes place during the query execution, the following value would be set:

```
setenv MINERVA_DEBUG query:malloc
```

By default, the software is installed into /usr/local/Minerva and the server will use space within that directory for the storage of the databases and also temporary result tables during operations such as joins and ordering.

C Programming API

Included in the distribution is the mSQL API library, libmsql.a. The API enables any C program to communicate with the database engine. The API functions are accessed by including the msql.h header file into your program and by linking against the mSQL library (using -lmsql as an argument to your C compiler). The library and header file will be installed by default into /usr/local/Minerva/lib and /usr/local/Minerva/include respectively.

Like the mSQL engine, the API supports debugging via the MINERVA_DEBUG environment variable. Three debugging modules are currently supported by the API: query, api, and malloc. Enabling "query" debugging will cause the API to print the contents of queries as they are sent to the server. The "api" debug modules cause internal information, such as connection details, to be printed. Details about the memory used by the API library can be obtained via the "malloc" debug module. Information such as the location and size of malloced blocks and the addresses passed to free( ) will be generated. Multiple debug modules can be enabled by setting MINERVA_DEBUG to a colon separated list of module names.

For example

```
setenv MINERVA_DEBUG api:query
```

msqlConnect()

```
int msqlConnect(char * host)
```

msqlConnect( ) forms an interconnection with the mSQL engine. It takes as its only argument the name or IP address of the host running the mSQL server. If NULL is specified as the host argument, a connection is made to a server running on the localhost using the Unix domain socket /dev/msqld. If an error occurs, a value of -1 is returned and the external variable msqlErrMsg will contain an appropriate text message. This variable is defined in "msql.h".

If the connection is made to the server, an integer identifier is returned to the calling function. This value is used as a handle for all other calls to the mSQL

API. The value returned is in fact the socket descriptor for the connection. By calling msqlConnect( ) more than once and assigning the returned values to separate variables, connections to multiple database servers can be maintained simultaneously.

In previous versions of mSQL, the MSQL_HOST environment variable could be used to specify a target machine if the host parameter was NULL. This is no longer the case.

msqlSelectDB()

```
int msqlSelectDB(sock,dbName)
      int    sock;
      char   *dbName;
```

Prior to submitting any queries, a database must be selected. msqlSelectDB( ) instructs the engine which database is to be accessed. msqlSelectDB( ) is called with the socket descriptor returned by msqlConnect( ) and the name of the desired database. A return value of -1 indicates an error with msqlErrMsg set to a text string representing the error. msqlSelectDB( ) may be called multiple times during a program's execution. Each time it is called, the server will use the specified database for future accesses. By calling msqlSelectDB( ) multiple times, a program can switch between different databases during its execution.

msqlQuery()

```
int msqlQuery(sock, query)
      int   sock;
      char  *query;
```

Queries are sent to the engine over the connection associated with sock as plain text strings using msqlQuery( ). As usual, a returned value of -1 indicates an error and msqlErrMsg will be updated. If the query generates output from the engine, such as a SELECT statement, the data is buffered in the API waiting for the application to retrieve it. If the application submits another query before it retrieves the data using msqlStoreResult( ), the buffer will be overwritten by any data generated by the new query.

msqlStoreResult()

```
m_result *msqlStoreResult()
```

Data returned by a SELECT query must be stored before another query is submitted or it will be removed from the internal API buffers. Data is stored using the msqlStoreResult() function which returns a result handle to the calling routines. The result handle is a pointer to a m_result structure and is passed to other API routines when access to the data is required. Once the result handle is allocated, other queries may be submitted. A program may have many result handles active simultaneously.

msqlFreeResult()

```
void msqlFreeResult(result)
      m_result            *result;
```

When a program no longer requires the data associated with a particular query result, the data must be freed using msqlFreeResult(). The result handle associated with the data, as returned by msqlStoreResult() is passed to msqlFreeResult() to identify the data set to be freed.

msqlFetchRow()

```
m_row msqlFetchRow(result)
      m_result          *result;
```

The individual database rows returned by a select are accessed via the msqlFetchRow() function. The data is returned in a variable of type m_row which contains a char pointer for each field in the row. For example, if a select statement selected 3 fields from each row returned, the value of the 3 fields would be assigned to elements [0], [1], and [2] of the variable returned by msqlFetchRow(). A value of NULL is returned when the end of the data has been reached. See the example at the end of this section for further details.

msqlDataSeek()

```
void msqlDataSeek(result, pos)
     m_result            *result;
     in                  pos;
```

The m_result structure contains a client side "cursor" that holds information about the next row of data to be returned to the calling program. msqlDataSeek( ) can be used to move the position of the data cursor. If it is called with a position of 0, the next call to msqlFetchRow( ) will return the first row of data returned by the server. The value of pos can be anywhere from 0 (the first row) to the number of rows in the table. If a seek is made past the end of the table, the next call to msqlFetchRow( ) will return a NULL.

msqlNumRows( )

```
int msqlNumRows(result)
      m_result           *result;
```

The number of rows returned by a query can be found by calling msqlNumRows( ) and passing it the result handle returned by msqlStoreResult( ). The number of rows of data sent as a result of the query is returned as an integer value. If a select query didn't match any data, msqlNumRows( ) will indicate that the result table has 0 rows (Note: earlier versions of mSQL returned a NULL result handle if no data was found. This has been simplified and made more intuitive by returning a result handle with 0 rows of result data.)

msqlFetchField( )

```
m_field *msqlFetchField(result)
      m_result           *result;
```

Along with the actual data rows, the server returns information about the data fields selected. This information is made available to the calling program via the msqlFetchField( ) function. Like msqlFetchRow( ), this function returns one element of information at a time and returns NULL when no further information is available. The data is returned in a m_field structure which contains the following information:

```
typedef struct {
     char     *name,          /* name of field */
              *table;         /* name of table */
     int       type,          /* data type of field */
               length,        /* length in bytes of field */
               flags;         /* attribute flags */
} m_field;
```

Possible values for the type field are defined in msql.h as INT_TYPE, CHAR_TYPE and REAL_TYPE. The individual attribute flags can be accessed, using the following macros:

```
IS_PRI_KEY(flags)       /* Field is the primary key */
IS_NOT_NULL(flags)      /* Field may not contain a NULL value */
```

msqlFieldSeek()

```
void msqlFieldSeek(result, pos)
     m_result      *result;
     int           pos;
```

The result structure includes a "cursor" for the field data. Its position can be moved using the msqlFieldSeek() function. See msqlDataSeek() for further details.

msqlNumFields()

```
int msqlNumFields(result)
     m_result                 *result;
```

The number of fields returned by a query can be ascertained by calling msqlNumFields() and passing it the result handle. The value returned by msqlNumFields() indicates the number of elements in the data vector returned by msqlFetchRow(). It is wise to check the number of fields returned before; as with all arrays, accessing an element that is beyond the end of the data vector can result in a segmentation fault.

msqlListDBs()

```
m_result *msqlListDBs(sock)
     int           sock;;
```

A list of the databases known to the mSQL engine can be obtained via the msqlListDBs() function. A result handle is returned to the calling program that can be used to access the actual database names. The individual names are accessed by calling msqlFetchRow() passing it the result handle. The m_row data structure returned by each call will contain one field with the name of one of the available databases. As with all functions that return a result handle, the data associated with the result must be freed when it is no longer required using msqlFreeResult( ).

msqlListTables()

```
m_result *msqlListTables(sock)
     int     sock;;
```

Once a database has been selected using msqlInitDB( ), a list of the tables defined in that database can be retrieved using msqlListTables( ). As with msqlListDBs( ), a result handle is returned to the calling program and the names of the tables are contained in data rows where element [0] of the row is the name of one table in the current database. The result handle must be freed when it is no longer needed by calling msqlFreeResult( ).

msqlListFields()

```
m_result *msqlListFields(sock,tableName);
     int     sock;
     char    *tableName
```

Information about the fields in a particular table can be obtained using msqlListFields( ). The function is called with the name of a table in the current database as selected using msqlSelectDB( ) and a result handle is returned to the caller. Unlike msqlListDBs( ) and msqlListTables( ), the field information is contained in field structures rather than data rows. It is accessed using msqlFetchField( ). The result handle must be freed when it is no longer needed by calling msqlFreeResult( ).

msqlClose()

```
int msqlClose(sock)
     int     sock;
```

The connection to the mSQL engine can be closed using msqlClose( ). The function must be called with the connection socket returned by msqlConnect( ) when the initial connection was made.

The mSQL Terminal Monitor

Like all database applications, mSQL provides a program that allows a user to interactively submit queries to the database engine. In the case of mSQL, it is a program simply called 'msql'. It requires one command-line argument, being the name of the database to access. Once started, there is no way to swap databases without restarting the program.

The monitor also accepts two command-line flags as outlined below:

```
-h Host  Connect to the mSQL server on Host.
-q       Process one query and quit returning an exit code.
```

The monitor has been modelled after the original Ingres (and the subsequent Postgres) monitor program. Commands are distinguished from queries due to their being prefixed with a backlashes. To obtain help from the monitor prompt, the \h command is used. To exit from the program, the \q command or an EOF (^D) must be entered.

To send a query to the engine, the query is entered followed by the \g command. \g tells the monitor to "Go" and send the query to the engine. If you want to edit your last query, \e will place you inside vi so that you can modify your query. If you wish to use an editor other than vi to perform query editing, msql will honor the convention of using the contents of the VISUAL environment variable as an alternate editor. When you have completed your editing, exiting the editor in the usual manner will return you to msql with the edited query placed in the buffer. The query can then be submitted to the server by using the \g "Go" command as usual.

The query buffer is maintained between queries not only to enable query editing, but also to allow a query to be submitted multiple times. If \g is entered without entering a new query, the last query to be submitted will be resubmitted. The contents of the query buffer can also be displayed by using the \p "Print" command of the monitor.

To cnable convenient access to database servers running on remote hosts, the mSQL terminal monitor supports the use of an environment variable to indicate the machine running the server (rather than having to specify "-h some.host.name" every time you execute mSQL). Note that this is a function provided by the mSQL terminal monitor *not* the mSQL API library and as such is not available for use with other programs. To use this feature set the environment variable MSQL_HOST to the name or address of the desired machine.

mSQL Database Administration

mSQL databases are administered using the msqladmin command. Several administrative tasks, such as creating new databases and forcing a server shutdown, are performed using msqladmin. Like all mSQL programs, msqladmin accepts the "-h Host" command-line flag to specify the desired machine. The commands available via msqladmin are

`create DataBase`	`Create a new database called DataBase`
`drop DataBase`	`Delete the entire database called DataBase`
`shutdown`	`Tell the server to shut itself down`
`reload`	`Tell the server to reload its access control information`
`version`	`Display various version information from the server`

It should be noted that the server will only accept create, drop, shutdown, and reload commands if they are sent by the root user (as defined at installation time) and are sent from the machine running the server. An attempt to perform any of these commands from a remote client or as a non-root user will result in a "permission denied" error. The only command you can execute over the network or as a non-root user is version.

mSQL Schema Viewer

mSQL provides the relshow command for displaying the structure of a database. If executed with no arguments, relshow will list the available database. If it is executed with the name of a database, relshow will list the tables that have been defined for that database. If given both a database and table name, relshow will display the structure of the table including the field names, types, and sizes. Like all mSQL programs, relshow honors the '-h Host' command-line flag to specify a remote machine as the database server.

mSQL Database Dumper

A program is provided that will dump the contents and structure of a table or entire database in an ASCII form. The program, msqldump, produces output that is suitable to be read by the mSQL terminal monitor as a script file. Using this tool, the contents of a database can be backed up or moved to a new database. By virtue of the '-h Host' option, the contents of a remote database may be sucked over the Net. This can be used as a mechanism for mirroring the contents of an mSQL database onto multiple machines.

msqldump started life as a user-contributed program called msqlsave written by Igor Romanenko (`igor@frog.kiev.ua`). Thanks, Igor.

mSQL Access from Script Languages

ESL

Another development that has arisen from the development of Minerva has been the Extensible Scripting Language, ESL (pronounced Easel). ESL is a C styled scripting language that offers automatic memory allocation, strict typing, associative arrays (both in-core and bound ndbm files), full SNMP support and much, much more. ESL resembles C so closely that any C programmer will be able to code in ESL within a minute or two of scanning the manual. Because both ESL and mSQL have been developed as part of the Minerva project (well, both were developed in the spare bedroom I call an office as part of my Ph.D.), ESL provides full support for the mSQL API. This includes every aspect of the C API as well as the client-server mode of operation.

Access to mSQL from other scripting languages is available using user-contributed extensions to the respective languages. Currently, the following languages are supported:

Perl 5

Andreas Koenig <k@franz.ww.TU-Berlin.DE> has developed MsqlPerl, a Perl 5 adapter for mSQL. It was written against the mSQL 2.0 Patch 1 API but should still work with the 1.0 release because the API hasn't changed (although a couple of semantics have). MsqlPerl is available via ftp from Bond.edu.au in

```
/pub/Minerva/msql/contrib/MsqlPerl-a1.tgz
```

Python

Anthony Baxter <anthony.baxter@aaii.oz.au> has developed PymSQL, a Python module for mSQL. It was written using the msql 0.2 Patch 2 API but should still work well. PymSQL can be found on Bond.edu.au in

```
/pub/Minerva/msql/contrib/PymSQL.tar.gz
```

Tcl

Brad Pepers <pepersb@cuug.ab.ca> has developed tcl_msql, a Tcl interface to mSQL. I can't recall which version of the API Brad was using when he wrote tcl_msql (Brad's been hacking on mSQL since the early days). I'm pretty sure that it will work against release 1.0 and am even more sure that Brad will fix it if it doesn't (that's because he's *such* a nice guy and Tcl/Tk users can be quite persuasive when they need to be).

Access Control

Access control is managed by the msql.acl file in the installation directory. This file is split into entries for each database to be controlled. If the file doesn't exist or details for a particular database aren't configured, access reverts to global read/write. An example ACL entry is included below:

```
# Sample access control for mSQL
database=test
read=bambi,paulp
write=root
host=*.Bond.edu.au,-student.it.Bond.edu.au
access=local,remote
```

Using this definition, database 'test' can be accessed by both local and remote connections from any host in the Bond.edu.au domain except for the machine student.it.Bond.edu.au. Read access is only granted to bambi and paulp. Nobody else is allowed to perform selects on the database. Write access is only available to root.

Control is based on the first match found for a given item. So, a line such as "read=-*,bambi" would not do the desired thing (that is, deny access to everyone other than bambi) because -* will also match bambi. In this case the line would have to be "read=bambi,-*" although the -* is superfluous because that is the default action.

Note that if an entry isn't found for a particular configuration line (such as read) it defaults to a global denial. For example, if there is no "read" line (that is, there are no read tokens after the data is loaded) nobody will be granted read access. This is in contrast to the action taken if the entire database definition is missing in which case access to everything is granted.

Another thing to note is that a database's entry _must_ be followed by a blank line to signify the end of the entry. There may also be multiple config lines in one entry (such as "read=bambi,paulp" "read=root"). The data will be loaded as though it was concatenated onto the same "read" line (that is, "read=bambi,paulp,root").

Wildcards can be used in any configuration entry. A wildcard by itself will match anything whereas a wildcard followed by some text will cause only a partial wildcard (e.g. *.Bond.edu.au matches anything that ends in Bond.edu.au). A wildcard can also be set for the database name. A good practice is to install an entry with database=* as the last entry in the file so that if the database being accessed wasn't covered by any of the other rules, a default site policy can be enforced.

The ACL information can be reloaded at runtime using "msqladmin reload". This will parse the file before it sends the reload command to the engine. Only if the file is parsed cleanly is it reloaded. Like most msqladmin commands, it will only be accepted if generated by the root user (or whoever the database was installed as) on the localhost.

Author's Details

Mini SQL was written by

David J. Hughes
Senior Network Programmer (and Ph.D. lunatic)
Bond University
Australia

E-Mail: `bambi@Bond.edu.au`

HTTP:`//Bond.edu.au/People/bambi`

Fax: `+61 75 951456`

Archive Location

The mSQL software is available for the following:

Current version of mSQL:

`ftp://Bond.edu.au/pub/Minerva/msql/`

User contributed code:

`ftp://Bond.edu.au/pub/Minerva/msql/Contrib/`

Monthly archive of the mailing list:

`ftp://Bond.edu.au/pub/Minerva/msql/Mail-Archive/`

Mailing List

I have set up a mailing list for discussing mSQL. To subscribe, send a message to

`mailto:msql-list-request@Bond.edu.au`

To send a message to the entire list, address it to

`msql-list-request@Bond.edu.au`

`mailto:msql-list@Bond.edu.au`

INDEX

Symbols

A

B

C

D

E

F

G

H

I

J-L

M

N

O

P

Q

R

S

T

U

V

W-Z

GET CONNECTED
to the ultimate source of computer information!

The MCP Forum on CompuServe

Go online with the world's leading computer book publisher! Macmillan Computer Publishing offers everything you need for computer success!

Find the books that are right for you!

A complete online catalog, plus sample chapters and tables of contents give you an in-depth look at all our books. The best way to shop or browse!

- Get fast answers and technical support for MCP books and software
- Join discussion groups on major computer subjects
- Interact with our expert authors via e-mail and conferences
- Download software from our immense library:
  - Source code from books
  - Demos of hot software
  - The best shareware and freeware
  - Graphics files

Join now and get a free CompuServe Starter Kit!

To receive your free CompuServe Introductory Membership, call **1-800-848-8199** and ask for representative #597.

The Starter Kit includes:

- Personal ID number and password
- $15 credit on the system
- Subscription to *CompuServe Magazine*

Once on the CompuServe System, type:

GO MACMILLAN

for the most computer information anywhere!

CompuServe

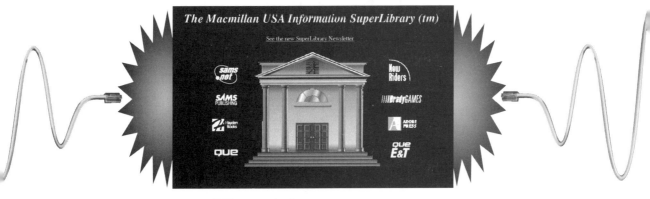

REGISTRATION CARD

Building Internet Database Servers with CGI

Name ______________________________ Title ______________________

Company ______________________________ Type of business ______________________

Address ____

City/State/ZIP ____

Have you used these types of books before? ☐ yes ☐ no

If yes, which ones? ____

____

How many computer books do you purchase each year? ☐ 1–5 ☐ 6 or more

How did you learn about this book? ____

Where did you purchase this book? ____

Which applications do you currently use? ____

____

Which computer magazines do you subscribe to? ____

____

What trade shows do you attend? ____

____

Comments: ____

____

____

Would you like to be placed on our preferred mailing list? ☐ yes ☐ no

☐ **I would like to see my name in print!** You may use my name and quote me in future New Riders products and promotions. My daytime phone number is: ______________________

New Riders Publishing 201 West 103rd Street ◆ Indianapolis, Indiana 46290 USA

Fax to **317-581-4670**

Fold Here

NO POSTAG
NECESSAR
IF MAILED
IN THE
UNITED STAT

BUSINESS REPLY MAIL

FIRST-CLASS MAIL PERMIT NO. 9918 INDIANAPOLIS IN

POSTAGE WILL BE PAID BY THE ADDRESSEE

NEW RIDERS PUBLISHING
201 W 103RD ST
INDIANAPOLIS IN 46290-9058

Installing the CD-ROM

The attached CD contains the following files in either the Unix, Microsoft Windows NT, or Apple Macintosh platform. Please see the contents of this book and the readme files on the CD for installation information. Also note that because of the diversity in operating environments, limited information is available for any specific system installation.

cgi-lib.pl	Steven E. Brenner dbCGI	CorVu Pty Ltd.
dbWeb	Buzz Sterns	Aspect Software Engineering Interperl
Isqlperl	CLI Connect Ltd.	
MiniSQL	Andreas Koenig	Hughes Technologies MsqlPerl
NetLink 4D	Foresight Technology	
OrayWWW	Larry Wall	Department of Natural Resources Canada Perl
Pgperl	Andrew K. Yu	Glue Software Engineering POSTGRES95
Sybperl	Michael Peppler	
WDB	B.F. Rasmussen	
WebDBC 2.0	Nomad Development Corp RWeb	Microrim
Wdb-p95	Doug Dunlop	

Additional information on the availability of the latest releases of the above products is provided in Chapter 7 of the book. Please refer to that information for the Web location of the many products listed in this book.

Also, please see Jeff Rowe's home page on the topic of Web databases at the following URL:

`http://cscun1.larc.nasa.gov/~beowulf/db/existing_products.html`